MW00823795

ACCLAIM FOR SHANE READ

Shane Read has tried over 100 trials to verdict and is a trial consultant who also provides in-house training for law firms throughout the United States.

Winning at Deposition

Winner of the Association of Continuing Legal Education's highest honor for a legal textbook.

"The book is a triumph…. [I]t makes for gripping reading, made all the better by Read's focus on the missteps of the famous lawyers and litigants he studies."

— *The Vermont Bar Journal*

"In every respect, D. Shane Read's book skillfully summarizes the art and science of taking depositions. [It] is an excellent resource for attorneys of all experience levels and areas of practice. *Winning at Deposition* is arranged in cogent chapters addressing everything…. Given the book's almost encyclopedic treatment of deposition topics, it is difficult to imagine that anything significant is omitted."

— *The Colorado Lawyer*

Winning at Cross-Examination: A Modern Approach for Depositions and Trials

"This book is a wealth of well-presented information, accessible and intriguing to those with limited legal knowledge as well as more experienced litigators."

—*Kirkus Reviews*

"Winning at Cross-Examination is so full of so many wonderful things that it is almost impossible to do justice to it with simple descriptions. The scholarship and analysis of the many legal writings and articles on the subject of cross-examination are very insightful and are presented in a very well organized and thoughtful way. No matter whether an attorney practices civil or criminal law, this book is a tremendous and indispensable resource."

—Lewis Sifford, Past President, American Board of Trial Advocates

Turning Points at Trial: Great Lawyers Share Secrets, Strategies and Skill

"Shane Read deserves much credit for expertly curating a project of this magnitude. . . . Read is a master of organization and elucidation, guiding readers point by point through the testimony (with crucial phrases highlighted in boldface), along with practice tips and notable quotes from the profiled attorney set off in the margins and revisited at the end of each chapter.

Required reading for trial lawyers, but also exceptionally informative for anyone interested in legal proceedings."

—*Kirkus Reviews*

Winning at Persuasion for Lawyers

"An exceptional, comprehensive resource for any presenter."

—*Kirkus Reviews* (a starred review)

TESTIMONIALS FOR SHANE READ'S TRIAL CONSULTING AND TRAINING COURSES

"If you follow Shane's advice, he can turn you into a great trial lawyer."

—Lisa Blue, Past President, The National Trial Lawyers and Amercian Association of Justice

"Shane Read is an immensely skilled teacher and storyteller. This is one of the best CLE programs of all time."

—Stacey Thomas, Program Manager, Pennsylvania Bar Institute

"Shane brings a career of studious dissection of what works in trial and what doesn't. Learn from Shane and kick your game way up!"

—Mark Lanier

WINNING
at DEPOSITION

WINNING
at DEPOSITION

D. SHANE READ

© 2013 Westway Publishing.
  All rights reserved.
Printed in the United States of America.

Cover design by George Foster
Interior design by Sherry Williams, Oxygen Design

Publisher Cataloging-in-Publication

Read, D. Shane.
  Winning at deposition / D. Shane Read.
    p. cm.
    ISBN: 978-0-9850271-7-9

    1. Depositions—United States. I. Title.

KF8900.R43 2013

Discounts are available for bulk orders.
    Westway Publishing
    4516 Lovers Lane, Suite 182
    Dallas, TX 75225
    support@westwaypublishing.com
    (888) 992-9782

For Gloria and Dick Pennell

ENHANCE YOUR JOURNEY AS YOU READ THIS BOOK

You can enhance your learning experience in two important ways as you read this book. First, watch the videos that are referenced in the book. You will find them immensely helpful in learning the principles discussed in the text. Second, sign up for Shane Read's free bi-monthly newsletter which contains Shane's latest ideas, tips from other thought leaders, and bonus material not contained in this book.

Access the videos and newsletter at: www.shaneread.com/newsletter.

SHANE READ'S TRIAL CONSULTING AND IN-HOUSE BOOT CAMPS

Shane Read is a nationally recognized expert who has helped thousands of attorneys throughout the USA and Europe transform their deposition, trial, and oral advocacy skills through his consultations, in-house training programs, and keynote speeches. For more information, go to www.shaneread.com.

CONTENTS

CHAPTER THREE

CHAPTER FOUR

CHAPTER FIVE

INTRODUCTION

⎯⎯⎯⎯ ❦ ⎯⎯⎯⎯

> It depends on what the meaning of the word "is"
> is.
>
> *—President Clinton explains to a grand jury*
> *an answer he gave in his deposition.*

It was a deposition that led to one of the most famous statements ever made by a president. It also led to his impeachment by the House of Representatives. Clinton and the lawyers on both sides made so many critical mistakes that it is the perfect starting point to begin our journey to learn how to take winning depositions and successfully defend them. Unlike other books, this book will teach these skills not through hypothetical situations but by examining videos (see chapters nine and ten) and transcripts of actual depositions.

I believe strongly that it is only in the trenches that you can determine if techniques really work. You will see that many failures occurred because lawyers were following conventional wisdom's theories rather than proven strategies.

How would you take the deposition of a president of the United States, a genius, or a famous acquitted murderer? Sound intimidating? You won't feel that way at the end of this book. We will mainly analyze three famous depositions, those of 1) President Bill Clinton, 2) Bill Gates and 3) O.J. Simpson.[1] These witnesses are the smartest and most difficult you will ever find.

Let's take a close look at Clinton's statement above. More details about the case will be given later but, for now, all you need to know is that Clinton gave a deposition in a sexual harassment lawsuit filed by Paula Jones. Before Monica Lewinsky (a White House intern) became famous, Paula Jones' lawyer, James Fisher, asked Clinton about Lewinsky at his deposition. Fisher asked Clinton if he had ever been alone with Lewinsky in the private kitchen at the White House. Clinton's lawyer, Robert Bennett, objected to the innuendo, since Fisher had Lewinsky's affidavit.

Although Lewinsky later recanted, she swore in the affidavit that she had never had a sexual relationship with Clinton. Bennett reminded Fisher that it stated "there *is* absolutely no sex of any kind in any manner, shape or form,

---

[1] Summaries of all three trials can be found in the Appendix.

with President Clinton."

Now, fast forward to the impeachment proceedings against Clinton. The federal grand jury was investigating whether Clinton had committed perjury in his deposition regarding several statements he made about his relationship with Lewinsky. Let's look at Clinton's famous explanation to the grand jury about the verb "is." Even if you did not know the context of the answer (discussed below), it is disingenuous on its face. First, Clinton's answer needlessly splits hairs. Moreover, it is obnoxiously clever. Does he really think people from Main Street (i.e. the grand jurors) believe there can be more than one definition of the simple verb "is"?

If your client is giving a deposition, it is your responsibility to get him prepared for every possible important question. This takes persistence because many witnesses do not feel the need to prepare thoroughly. With proper preparation, Clinton could have been taught to give a truthful answer that would not become ridiculed throughout the media.

What Clinton tried to tell the grand jury was that his lawyer was technically telling the truth because Bennett was speaking in the present tense when he said, "there is absolutely no sex . . . with President Clinton." However, this explanation did not help Clinton because it just showed that he thought it was acceptable for his lawyer to make a technically true statement that was misleading—since people hearing the statement would assume he had misspoken and meant to say that Lewinsky claimed in her affidavit that she had never had sex with Clinton.

Moreover, the truth—and the better answer—was what Clinton tried to say to the grand jury but which was lost against the backdrop of his grammar lesson answer. That is, Clinton told the grand jury that "I don't know what Mr. Bennett had in his mind. I don't know. I didn't pay attention to this colloquy that went on. I was waiting for my instructions as a witness to go forward. I was worried about my own testimony."

In witness preparation for the grand jury, Clinton's legal team should have emphasized the importance of staying on message: you weren't paying attention to what Bennett said at the deposition because you were focusing on your answers. If Clinton had stayed on message, there would have been no way for him to give an implausible answer that Bennett's statement could be true, depending on what the definition of "is" is. No matter how many times the prosecutor asked him about Bennett's statement, all Clinton had to do was to repeat that he did not know what Bennett was thinking because he was focused on his answers. In reality, the only person who could answer that question would be Bennett.

Bill Gates' deposition also provides a tremendous amount of insight. The

Department of Justice (DOJ) and several states sued Microsoft for violating federal antitrust laws. In particular, DOJ claimed that Microsoft used its dominance of the Windows operating system to prevent competition. DOJ also alleged that Microsoft made business arrangements with Internet service providers that restricted those providers from promoting Internet browsers not owned by Microsoft.

With this brief background, let's look at one of the most important rules in taking a deposition: gain the witness' respect. At the outset it is critical to show the witness that you are in control. One way to do that is to show a mastery of the subject matter the witness will be testifying about. If the witness senses that he knows more than you do, he can confidently testify inaccurately, knowing that you do not have the power to prove him wrong. On the other hand, if the witness respects you, he is more likely to answer a difficult question because he knows if he doesn't, you will prove him wrong.

This principle is particularly true when you are taking the deposition of an intelligent person who can outwit you. It is even truer when the witness is Bill Gates.

Unfortunately, at the very beginning of Gates' deposition, the attorney from the New York Attorney General's office failed to garner Gates' respect. As you can imagine, in this lawsuit, it was paramount to be well versed in computer terminology. See what happened.

Q. *I'd like you to look at Exhibit 1, Mr. Gates, right here in front of you. This is a memorandum that purports to be from you to your executive staff dated May 22, 1996, and it attaches, for want of a better word, an essay entitled "The Internet PC" dated April 10, 1996. Do you recall writing that essay?*
A. It looks like this is an e-mail, not a memorandum.

Q. *Do you recall receiving this memorandum or e-mail?*
A. E-mail, no.

Q. *All right. I apologize for using my old-fashioned terminology.*

Gates' tone of voice was incredulous. He was shocked that counsel could not recognize an e-mail. The exchange was one of many memorable ones posted on YouTube.[2] Such a bad question puts the lawyer on the defensive and gives the witness confidence that he, not the lawyer, can control the deposition.

Finally, we will examine O.J. Simpson's deposition in the civil lawsuit filed on behalf of the murdered victims after his acquittal. Fred Goldman's attorney, Dan Petrocelli, was thorough and organized. He explained his

---

[2] See "Gates Deposition Greatest Hits" at www.youtube.com. The question is asked at the two minute seven second mark of the clip.

mindset as follows:

> If a lawyer starts objecting and pushing you around, and you let him, he will continue the manhandling to his benefit. Early on, I wanted both Baker [Simpson's attorney] and Simpson to realize that no amount of objecting, arguing, or evading would deter me from plugging away, that Simpson would have to answer all my questions, that I wasn't going to let him off the hook until I got my answers . . . .[3]

Let's look at one example where Petrocelli's persistence paid off. Petrocelli was asking Simpson about his illegal drug use. Many people had told Petrocelli that Simpson had used drugs, so much so that he had been given the nickname "Hoover" because he snorted so much cocaine.[4] It was important for Petrocelli to get Simpson to deny this so that he could prove through other witnesses that Simpson had lied under oath at his deposition. After Simpson denied smoking marijuana, the following took place.

Q. Were you a cocaine user in June of 1994?
A. [Baker (Simpson's lawyer)] Don't answer that.

A. [Simpson] No.
Q. The answer is you were not?
A. No.

Q. In May of 1994?
A. No.
[Baker] That's enough. Don't answer any more questions about that.

Q. Did you take cocaine at any time in the period January 1994 through June 12, 1994? **[Petrocelli is not deterred by Baker's objections and continues to ask the questions he needs answers to until Simpson stops giving answers.]**
A. No.
[Baker] I am instructing you not to—

Q. Did you take—
[Baker] Am I a potted plant?

Q. Did you take any kind of amphetamines during that period? **[Petrocelli again ignores Simpson's attorney]**
A. No.

Q. Did you use cocaine in the year 1993?
[Baker] Don't answer that!

A. No.

---

[3] Daniel Petrocelli, *Triumph of Justice* 119 (Crown 1998).
[4] *Id.* at 139.

From these depositions, we have learned our first three lessons. The Clinton deposition demonstrated that an answer that is too clever won't be believed, the Gates deposition revealed an attorney must be well prepared to keep control of the deposition, and the Simpson deposition showed us how to keep our cool and continue asking needed questions despite an attorney's objections.

Remember

1. Getting a disingenuous answer is a success since it won't be believed.
2. To get information from a witness, you must gain his respect by being well-prepared.
3. You must stay calm and focused no matter what opposing counsel does.

In the following chapters we will look at the conventional wisdom and see if it makes any sense in light of the realities of human nature and actual depositions. What might sound good in theory often has little value in battle. Just one example comes from the American Bar Association's leading publication on depositions.[5] In the chapter on witness preparation, a witness is advised to follow 130 rules. Common sense tells us that it would be impossible for a witness to remember ten of these rules, let alone 130. Yet, many lawyers continue to inundate their witnesses with rules that simply overwhelm them. Witnesses become ineffective advocates because they are more worried about following a rule than defending their position during questioning.

Get ready to learn new techniques and strategies that will improve your deposition skills dramatically. If the court reporter will swear in the witness, we are ready to begin . . . .

---

[5] Priscilla Schwab and Lawrence Vilardo editors, *Depositions* 65 (ABA 2006).

~⁓~

CHAPTER ONE

The Basics

> Understanding can overcome any situation, however
> mysterious or insurmountable it may appear to be.
> —*Norman Vincent Peale*

M any commentators and lawyers portray depositions as being complicated legal proceedings that can take years to master. For example, at most large law firms, a young associate won't be trusted to take an important deposition for several years. But depositions are not as mysterious or insurmountable as they have been made out to be. The truth is that by learning the techniques in this book, you will become extremely successful in a deposition. And, it won't take you years to become an expert. You will be ready as soon as you've finished the book.

This chapter answers basic questions new attorneys have about depositions and gives an overview of the rules governing them. Since many state rules are modeled after the Federal Rules of Civil Procedure, this book will use those Rules as a starting point.[1] If you have already been in several depositions, go to Chapter Two and use this chapter as a reference tool to brush up on particular procedural issues that interest you.

1.1 DEPOSITION DEFINED

A deposition is the formal questioning by an attorney of a witness (known as the deponent) in a lawsuit. The testimony is under oath and transcribed by a court reporter. No judge is present and, at first glance, the process can seem very informal compared to courtroom testimony. For example, it is the attorneys who make rulings, not a judge.

Also, rules of evidence are not enforced as they would be in court. To illustrate, you may ask the witness questions that allow hearsay answers

---

[1] Throughout this book, "Rule" refers to the Federal Rules of Civil Procedure (2012).

(statements that have been heard by the witness that are offered for their truth) that would not usually be admissible at trial.

Not only are the rules of evidence not enforced, but you may ask the witness about seemingly irrelevant matters that may be inadmissible at trial, as long as the questioning "appears reasonably calculated to lead to the discovery of admissible evidence." (Rule 26(b)(1).) This practice gives great latitude to the examiner.

Although no judge is present, the testimony is serious business. The oath the witness takes is the same as the one taken in court. In addition, any substantial inconsistency given at the deposition can be used by the opposing lawyer at trial to undermine the witness' trial testimony. If the witness is unavailable for trial, the deposition can often be substituted for trial testimony.

A deposition is also a very efficient and powerful discovery tool. It differs markedly from other discovery such as interrogatories. Interrogatories are written questions which are sent to an opposing party. There are several limitations with interrogatories that depositions don't have. First, a party has thirty days to think about the answer to an interrogatory. Second, the party can consult with his attorney before each answer. Third, there can be no spontaneous follow-up questions by the attorney who sent the interrogatories. Fourth, interrogatories can only be sent to a party in the lawsuit and not to a witness.

For all these reasons, depositions are superior to interrogatories. The main disadvantages to a deposition are the costs in money and time. Paying a court reporter for a four hour deposition can cost about $1000. A video deposition may add $100/hour or more. In addition, an attorney must consider the time it takes to prepare for a deposition, to travel to the deposition, to take the deposition, and then to analyze the transcript (For every hour, about forty pages of transcript are produced with approximately 200-250 words per page).

> If the opposing witness is a key player, his deposition needs to be taken.

1.2 WHEN

After the Rule 26 conference (the discovery conference between attorneys at the lawsuit's beginning when they discuss the issues in dispute and agree to a discovery plan), the attorneys are free to begin discovery, including depositions. (Rule 26(d)(1).)   Rule 30 is the primary rule that governs depositions.

1.3 CONTENTS OF THE NOTICE AND WHO GETS IT

You formally schedule a deposition by sending the opposing party a "Notice of Deposition." This notice states the name and address of the witness being deposed, where, how (i.e., oral or video) and when. The notice is very simple. If the witness is not a party, Rule 45 requires that a subpoena be issued by the court, giving the court jurisdiction to command the appearance of a non-party witness.

If the notice is for a business under Rule 30(b)(6) (where a business must designate a witness to testify about particular topics), the notice is different in two respects. It must describe the topics for the examination, and it does not need to identify a witness, since that burden is on the entity receiving the notice. (See discussion below at Deposition of Organizations.)

The notice must be sent to all parties in the lawsuit and is sent to their attorney's address. If the witness is a non-party, a subpoena is used. The subpoena is sent to the witness, and a copy is sent to opposing counsel. Some courts require personal service of a subpoena, so check with your jurisdiction if you have concerns that the non-party witness may fail to attend.

1.4 HOW MUCH NOTICE TO GIVE

You must give "reasonable" notice to the deponent and the parties to the case. Under the Rules, this is at least fourteen days.[2] Local rules may alter this time, and attorneys can agree to a shorter time frame.

1.5 WHO TAKES THE FIRST DEPOSITION AND SCHEDULING

Suppose you and the opposing attorney both want to take the deposition of the other's client before your own client is deposed. Who goes first?

The advantage to going first is that you can lock in the witness' testimony before it can be changed due to facts discovered later. But, the disadvantage is that you may not have learned enough facts in the beginning to ask the right questions. Since each case will be different, keep this strategy in mind as you begin to decide how to schedule depositions.

If both attorneys want to take the first deposition, the rules are silent as to who goes first because it is expected that the attorneys can work this out. If you want to go first, you will have more leverage with opposing counsel if you call him first. Don't expect an immediate answer, as opposing counsel will need to check with his client before committing to a date. To be safe, confirm your phone call in a letter that sets out several suggested dates for the deposition.

---

[2] Rule 32(a)(5) states that "a deposition must not be used against a party who, having received less than fourteen days' notice of the deposition moves for a protective order."

> Unlike overly aggressive attorneys, be reasonable. Call opposing counsel to set a time and place for the deposition rather than sending out a Notice that is good for you but probably inconvenient for him.

A more aggressive way—but not recommended—is to send out a notice with a date you have arbitrarily picked for the deposition. Then, you can call opposing counsel and offer to change the date to a mutually agreeable one. Unlike the phone call and letter, the notice is a legal document which has the force of the Rules behind it. In this scenario, opposing counsel will have to move quickly and decide on a mutually agreeable date or be forced to file a motion with the court to quash (or cancel) the active deposition notice. Although this technique shows opposing counsel that you are in control, turnabout is fair play, and you should expect similar treatment in return.

Remember that any disagreement between attorneys that cannot be resolved will have to be decided by the court through a motion, and the busy judge will be understandably upset with such a petty motion.

1.6 HOW MANY

A party may not take more than ten depositions in a case without seeking the court's permission. (Rule 30(a)(2)(A).) Taking too many depositions is one of the biggest mistakes attorneys make. For the majority of cases, you will never need ten depositions. Unfortunately, many lawyers are not focused and wind up seeking the court's permission to take more than ten.

Notice that the number of depositions are divided by side not by party. Thus, a plaintiff may take ten depositions while two codefendants would have to split ten between themselves.

1.7 HOW LONG

A deposition cannot last longer than seven hours (excluding reasonable breaks and lunch) and no more than one day. (Rule 30(d)(1).) If you are taking the deposition, ask yourself why you ever would want to approach that limit. Remember, you are going to have to review the deposition that you have taken. In a typical deposition, the court reporter will produce about forty pages every hour. Do you really have the time to take a seven hour deposition and then read, analyze and summarize 280 pages at a later date?

Practice Tip

Less is more. If you take a short deposition that is focused and to the point, you not only save time but you will need less time to review it prior to trial when time is precious.

1.8 WHERE

The Rules do not explain where a plaintiff or defendant's deposition should be taken. In general, courts presume that a plaintiff may be deposed in the judicial district where the lawsuit was filed. The reason is that since the plaintiff chose where to file his lawsuit, he is obligated to appear at that location if the defendant chooses. On the other hand, the location of the deposition for a non-resident defendant is presumed to be near the defendant's place of residence. A defendant corporation's deposition is usually taken at the corporation's principal place of business. The location for other witnesses is where they live.[3]

Nonetheless, common sense dictates that what is convenient for the witness and both attorneys governs the day. Remember, any disagreement you cannot work out will have to be brought to the judge pursuant to a motion under Rule 26. That rule requires that attorneys use good faith to resolve issues without the court's help. In the end, the court has wide discretion and will consider many factors including hardship on the witness and counsel, litigation efficiency, and the likelihood of discovery disputes arising.

Another issue that arises is which attorney's office should be used. An unduly confrontational attorney will often designate his office through the notice of deposition or subpoena no matter who the witness is. But wouldn't it be more convenient for the opposing party to have his deposition taken at his own attorney's office? Wouldn't the aggressive attorney want the same courtesy extended for his client? Moreover, if you represent the plaintiff and the witness is not a party but is aligned with the defendant, ask defense counsel where a convenient location would be (i.e. defense counsel's office or witness' workplace), and notice the deposition for that location.

---

[3] See 8A Charles Alan Wright, Arthur R. Miller, Mary Kay Kane & Richard L.Marcus, Federal Practice & Procedure § 2112 (citing cases regarding location for plaintiff, defendant, and other witnesses) and *In re Outsidewall Tire Litigation*, 267 F.R.D. 466, 470-471 (E.D. VA 2010).

1.9 WHOSE DEPOSITION MAY BE TAKEN

Rule 30(a)(1) provides that you may take the deposition of "any person, including a party, without leave of court." So, you are given wide latitude to take the deposition of any individual who may have relevant information to your lawsuit.

1.10 DEPOSITION OF ORGANIZATIONS

Rule 30(b)(6) provides that an attorney may take the deposition of an organization such as a partnership or other type of business entity. The attorney noticing the deposition must state in the notice that it is a "Rule 30(b)(6)" deposition and list the areas the deponent will need to discuss. The responding party must then designate a person or persons who can provide the information that is reasonably available to the organization.

For example, in a medical malpractice case, a plaintiff's attorney may request the deposition of someone at the hospital who can testify to the hospital's procedures for keeping medical records if the destruction of records has become an issue in the case.

1.11 FORCING THE WITNESS TO ATTEND

A party to a lawsuit only needs to be sent a Notice of Deposition by mail to the party's attorney. For other witnesses, a subpoena is required unless an agreement is reached with the witness to appear voluntarily. You can get a blank subpoena from the clerk's office. Rule 45 requires that a subpoena must be personally served on the witness along with an attendance fee ($40/day) and mileage reimbursement (currently $0.50/mile) as set by the General Service Administration (see 18 U.S.C.A. § 1821(c)(2)).

Although Rule 45 requires that the witness fee and mileage reimbursement accompany the subpoena, often an agreement is reached with the witness to pay the witness once he attends and to reimburse him for mileage at that time also. But if you are concerned the witness may not attend, tender the witness fee and mileage cost with the subpoena.

1.12 WHERE TO SIT

The court reporter will arrive early to set up. She knows that your time is valuable and won't want to cause any delay. Where does everyone sit? The answer is that you can sit anywhere. But the following scenario is how it usually plays out. The court reporter sits at the head of the table so she can easily hear everyone, and the witness sits in the chair closest to her on either side of the table. The attorney representing the witness sits in the chair next to the witness (which is two seats away from the court reporter), and the attorney taking the deposition sits across from the witness. If you forget, just ask the court reporter (preferably when opposing counsel isn't around to avoid revealing your lack of experience).

If the deposition is being videoed, the witness—instead of the court reporter—is at the head of the table. The witness is often the only one in the camera's view finder. The videographer (the person taking the video) is at the opposite end from the witness. The court reporter is seated closest to the witness and on one side of the table out of the camera's view. The attorneys sit across from each other with the attorney representing the witness sitting closest to the witness.

Practice Tip

Check with the videographer to see if only the witness is being filmed or also the attorneys. If you are being filmed, be aware that your mannerisms may one day be seen by a jury.

1.13 THE "USUAL AGREEMENTS"

Just before the deposition begins, the court reporter usually asks the attorneys if there are any agreements governing the deposition. It is quite common for an attorney to say casually, "the usual agreements." Although this is common place, it makes no sense and has no effect. What are the usual agreements or rules? There has to be a meeting of the minds in order for there to be an agreement as to what the "usual agreements" are.

Nonetheless, you need to be prepared for it. Simply say, "Let's just agree that the deposition is being taken pursuant to the federal [or state] rules of procedure." That way, you have not waived any rights given to you by the rules. There will also be much less confusion should there be a dispute during the deposition or at trial about which agreements govern a particular question and answer.

On the other hand, opposing counsel may suggest that you agree that all objections will be reserved until trial except for objections to form. There is nothing wrong with agreeing to this proposal since it basically summarizes the federal rules and minimizes the need for objections at the deposition.

1.14 OVERVIEW OF THE DEPOSITION

The deposition begins by the court reporter giving an oath to the witness. Next, the attorney who requested the deposition asks questions. After he conducts the examination, opposing counsel has an opportunity to ask questions.

The Rules provide that any objection to evidence, to a party's conduct, or to any other aspect must be concisely stated in a non-argumentative and non-suggestive manner. However, even if there is an objection, the witness must answer the question. The reason the witness must answer is that the objection preserves the issue for trial but is not supposed to impede the lawyer from getting information from the witness. Consequently, Rule 30(c)(2) provides that "a person may instruct a deponent not to answer only when necessary to preserve a privilege, to enforce a limitation ordered by the court, or to present a motion under Rule 30(d)(3) [i.e. a motion to terminate deposition for bad faith or harassment]."

After the deposition concludes, the court reporter will prepare the transcript, send it—if requested—to the witness for review, and the witness has thirty days to review the transcript and make changes if necessary. Once the review period is over, all counsel will be given a copy of the transcript if it has been ordered from the court reporter.

ANY DOCUMENTS THAT WERE USED AS EXHIBITS AT THE DEPOSITION WILL BE ATTACHED TO THE DEPOSITION TRANSCRIPT. 1.15 WHO MAY ATTEND

The Rules state that the examination proceeds as it would at trial except that the trial rule (Federal Rule of Evidence 615) which allows a party to exclude potential witnesses at trial does not apply. (Rule 30(c)(1).) The Rule does not automatically exclude other witnesses but exclusion can be ordered under Rule 26(c)(5). Some local rules specifically allow attendance by other witnesses.[4] The federal rule does not address attendance by the public or press. Nonetheless, the custom of many attorneys is that attorneys of record and the parties may attend, but no one else is usually expected.[5]

If you want other people to attend, mention your desire to opposing counsel prior to the deposition so that you can work out an agreement and avoid surprise. For example, sometimes the attorney taking the deposition will have an expert at the deposition in order to help formulate questions or lines of inquiry that develop during a deposition. In addition, a family member of the deponent may attend, particularly in a personal injury case. These are normal requests which attorneys usually agree to.

---

[4] "A witness or potential witness in the action may attend the deposition of a party or witness unless otherwise ordered by the court." E.D.N.Y. Local Rule 30.4 (2011).

[5] The Advisory note to Rule 30 states that courts have disagreed as to whether potential deponents may attend a deposition. The rule was revised in 1993 so that there was not an automatic exclusion of witnesses. Courts have disagreed on this issue. If you get into a dispute, you may file a motion under Rule 26 (c) (1) (E) seeking an order from the court which designates who may attend the deposition.

1.16 RE-DEPOSING THE SAME WITNESS

You only get one bite at the apple. Rule 30(a)(2)(A)(ii) requires that an attorney seek the court's permission to take the deposition of someone who has already been deposed. Generally, you will need to show good cause why you need to subject the witness to a second deposition, so make sure you are thorough in your questioning the first time around. Circumstances where you might be granted permission to ask more questions would arise if the witness changes the substance of his testimony when reviewing the transcript, or opposing counsel belatedly turns over important documents after the witness' deposition.

1.17 EXHIBITS

When taking a deposition, bring three copies of every document (i.e. exhibit) you intend to use. One copy is for the court reporter to mark with an exhibit sticker which will be shown to the witness, one copy is for opposing counsel, and one copy is for you. If you have many documents, have them marked before the deposition starts.

A bad—but unfortunately very common—way that exhibits are numbered is sequentially, starting with exhibit one for each deposition. To illustrate, in a contract dispute, after three depositions, exhibit one in the first deposition may refer to the contract; exhibit one in the second deposition may refer to a letter; and exhibit one in the third deposition may refer to a witness' resume. This causes problems when your write a motion for summary judgment, and you have several different documents that have the same label (i.e. exhibit one).

Practice Tip

Mark the exhibits sequentially, starting at the first deposition. For example, if your first deposition ends with exhibit 10, start the next deposition with exhibit 11. This will help avoid confusion when you need to refer to exhibits in your summary judgment motion.

1.18 SCOPE

You may ask the witness any question that is relevant to any party's claims or defenses. (Rule 26(b)(1).) Relevant information does not need to be admissible at trial as long as it "appears reasonably calculated to lead to the discovery of admissible evidence." (Rule 26(b)(1).) Consequently, a deposition's scope is very broad but you cannot ask questions in bad faith or that are meant to harass the witness.

1.19 PROTECTIVE ORDERS

In general, a party may seek discovery on anything that is relevant to the case. But if you are defending a deposition, you may seek a protective order from the court by showing "good cause" that the requested discovery will create embarrassment, annoyance, or undue burden or expense. (Rule 26(c).) A range of remedies prohibits discovery from requiring disclosure or requiring disclosure but making the disclosure sealed from the public. Here are some examples: 1) a company wants to protect its trade secrets, 2) a plaintiff wants to prevent disclosure of embarrassing medical conditions, or 3) there is a less burdensome way for an opposing party to obtain the information.

1.20 OBJECTIONS

The first rule to remember is that what goes around comes around. If you start objecting to a lot of questions, don't be surprised if opposing counsel does the same to you.

More important, the rules make it easy not to object. You don't have to worry that you have missed something because almost everything can be corrected at trial. You do not need to be an expert on trial evidence to take or defend a deposition. Are you afraid that you don't know the ins and outs of the exceptions to the hearsay rule? Don't worry. Rule 32(d)(3)(B) explicitly states that an objection is waived only if it relates to the "form of a question or an answer." That's it. If you are defending a deposition, don't worry if your witness is asked questions that call for hearsay answers. You have not waived an evidentiary objection regarding hearsay at trial. Moreover, you cannot object on evidentiary grounds because the attorney taking the deposition is permitted to inquire about matters—whether admissible at trial or not—that are relevant to the lawsuit.

It is easy to remember the rule if you understand its rationale. Objections regarding complicated evidentiary issues such as hearsay are automatically preserved until trial so that the attorneys and court can examine the issue carefully in the context of the trial. The intent is to encourage the free flow of information from the witness without interruption. However, what you do waive is the right to complain about the form of a question or answer if you don't object, since a timely objection at the deposition would allow the attorney to correct the problem.

For example, if the opposing attorney asks your client (a doctor), "Do you agree you should have taken the time to see if the two drugs you prescribed could have had a fatal interaction and that you failed to do so," you should object to the form of the question. Your client will probably answer "no" because he is focused on the second half of the question ("you failed to do so"), but since the question is compound, the answer "no" could be used by your opponent to suggest at trial that doctor does not think it is appropriate to "take the time to be careful."

By objecting to the form of the question, the opposing attorney must simplify the question so that the answer is clear or run the risk that the trial judge will not allow the answer to an objectionable question that was not rephrased. In any event, the witness must answer the question in whatever way the attorney ultimately decides to ask it. That is, even if you make an objection to the question's form, the witness must answer the question the attorney decides to ask.

Other objections that need to be asserted are those regarding attorney-client privilege or work product. These objections and more will be discussed in Chapter Four.

1.21 MOTIONS TO TERMINATE, LIMIT OR PROTECT

At any time during a deposition, the deponent or a party may move to terminate or limit it on the ground that it is being conducted in bad faith or in a manner that unreasonably annoys, embarrasses, or oppresses the deponent or party. If the objecting attorney decides to file such a motion, he must suspend the deposition "for the time necessary to obtain an order." (Rule 30(d)(3) (A).) Instead of suspending the deposition, filing a motion, and waiting for the court to rule, consider stopping the deposition briefly to see if the court is available by telephone so that the dispute can be resolved. Some judges have a policy to respond to calls where there are discovery disputes during deposition.

> Know your judge's practice. While some judges prefer phone calls to motions, others will be very annoyed by your interruption.

Some problems can be avoided before the deposition begins. If you are defending a deposition and anticipate problems with opposing counsel, you may file a protective order prior to the deposition. Rule 26(c)(1) governs this procedure and provides the circumstances for filing such a motion. Similar to a motion to terminate the deposition, a protective motion can be filed to protect a party or person from annoyance, embarrassment, oppression, or undue burden or expense, including one or more of the following: a) forbidding inquiry into certain matters or limiting scope of discovery, b) designating the persons who may be present at the deposition, c) requiring that the deposition be sealed, and d) requiring that a trade secret or other confidential information not be revealed or limited. (Rule 26(c)(1).)

Likewise, if you are taking the deposition, you may file a motion with the court seeking to ask questions about topics on which you think there will be objections. In either case, the attorneys must attempt to work out an agreement on the dispute before filing the motion with the court.

1.22 WORK PRODUCT PRIVILEGE

Rule 26(b)(3)(A) codifies the work product privilege. It explains that a "party may not discover documents and tangible things that are prepared in anticipation of litigation or for trial by or for another party or its representative (including the other party's attorney, consultant . . . or agent)."

There is an abundance of case law in this area, but the basic idea is that the document is protected from disclosure if it contains "counsel's mental impressions,"[6] or the document can "fairly be said to have been prepared or obtained because of the prospect of litigation."[7] It is important to assert this privilege vigilantly or risk that it becomes waived.

1.23 ATTORNEY-CLIENT PRIVILEGE

This privilege protects conversations between a client and his attorney which were made in confidence for the purpose of obtaining legal advice. For example, if the examining attorney asks a question about your client's conversation with you, you need to object and instruct your client not to answer. Even after your objection, sometimes the examining attorney will ask the witness if he is going to follow your instruction. But the privilege is not completely preserved unless the witness refuses to answer the question after being instructed by you not to answer it.

1.24 SANCTIONS

Under Rule 37(d), if a party fails to attend a properly noticed deposition, the court may impose sanctions, and if the court does, the court must award costs to the prevailing party. Such costs may include attorney fees for time spent waiting for the party to show up at the deposition, travel time, and time spent preparing for the deposition a second time.

---

[6] *Hickman v. Taylor*, 329 U.S. 495 (1947).
[7] *United States v. Adlman*, 134 F.3d 1194, 1196 (2d Cir. 1998).

If a party shows but refuses to answer some questions, the court may award sanctions and must award costs if the refusal to answer questions was not substantially justified. Be aware, then, that if you instruct your witness not to answer a question, you risk paying the other side's costs should a judge determine your reasoning was unjustified.

If a non party witness fails to show, the attorney who requested the deposition will be stuck with paying the court reporter's fee but likely won't seek sanctions from the court since the witness would presumably have to pay them. Seeking costs is no way to make the witness forthcoming when he finally shows up. But, the deposing attorney may well seek the court's help in compelling the witness to attend the next time.

Practice Tip

If you subpoena a witness for a deposition, she may not understand the importance of the deposition. Do everything you can to ensure her attendance by calling her and explaining the procedure.

1.25 WITNESS REVIEW OF THE DEPOSITION

Rule 30(e) provides that a witness may review and make changes to the form or substance of a deposition answer at a later date if such a request is made before the end of the deposition. This is a request that you should always make for your witness. You will usually be asked by the court reporter during the deposition if you want this option for your witness. However, to be safe, simply mention your desire to the court reporter at the beginning of the deposition so you won't forget.

Once the court reporter finishes the transcript, she will send the witness a copy. The witness will have thirty days to make changes provided that the reasons for making them are stated. Usually, there are minor spelling mistakes. However, a court reporter is not perfect, and significant testimony can occasionally be misinterpreted by the court reporter. For example, in a personal injury case, the deponent stated that she was about "thirteen" feet from the accident, but the court reporter transcribed the testimony as "thirty" feet. Such an error would be critical to catch upon reviewing the deposition.

On the other hand, if the witness changes the substance of her testimony and it is not the court reporter's fault, the opposing attorney may seek permission from the court to reopen the deposition to ask the witness about the changes made.

1.26 USING A DEPOSITION AS SUBSTITUTE FOR LIVE TESTIMONY AT TRIAL

Rule 32 governs. Here are its most important points. A deposition may be used to impeach (contradict) a witness' trial testimony. It may also be used as substitute testimony for an unavailable witness. Unavailability occurs when the witness is more than 100 miles from the trial, dead, imprisoned, too old or ill. Be aware that many states have different criteria for substituting a deposition for live testimony at trial. How to impeach a witness with a deposition will be discussed in greater detail in Chapter Seven.

1.27 USING A DEPOSITION TO IMPEACH A WITNESS AT TRIAL

A deposition is one of the greatest weapon's a trial lawyer has during cross-examination. If the witness testifies on an important matter which is inconsistent with his prior sworn testimony in a deposition, you may show this inconsistency to the jury. This technique is discussed at length in Chapter Seven. For now, all you need to know is that when the witness testifies inconsistently, you impeach the witness by reading the relevant part of the deposition that is inconsistent with the trial testimony.

1.28 TAKING A DEPOSITION BEFORE A LAWSUIT OR ON APPEAL

Rule 27 provides a unique circumstance where a deposition may be taken prior to a lawsuit being filed. If a potential party's attorney feels that the testimony of a witness needs to be preserved to prevent a failure or delay of justice, she may file a petition with the court seeking an order authorizing the deposition. The petition must show 1) the petitioner expects to be a party to a lawsuit but cannot bring it or cause it to be brought, 2) the subject matter of the expected lawsuit, 3) the facts of the expected deposition and the reasons to preserve it, and 4) the names and addresses of expected adverse parties.

The need to take a deposition prior to a lawsuit may arise when a party knows that a lawsuit will be filed, but a witness is about to leave the country, move outside the court's subpoena power or has a terminal illness. In such a case, the party would advise the court as outlined above that if this witness' testimony is not preserved, there will be a failure of justice.

The other circumstance where a deposition may be taken outside the confines of a lawsuit occurs when the judgment is on appeal. Rule 27 provides for procedures similar to the ones needed to take a deposition prior to a lawsuit. One situation where this may happen occurs when there is newly discovered evidence, and witness testimony is needed to prove it.

Notes

CHAPTER TWO

Taking the Deposition

There are two possible outcomes [of an experiment]: if the result confirms the hypothesis, then you've made a discovery. If the result is contrary to the hypothesis, then you've made a discovery.

—Enrico Fermi, Nobel Prize winner for Physics in 1938

Much like a scientist who tests a hypothesis, you need to test the theory of your case. If you represent a plaintiff and your case becomes stronger, such a finding will obviously affect the lawsuit's value. If you uncover facts that undercut your theory, the value of the lawsuit will be less, but you may find a way to minimize the damage before trial. Generally, a deposition is the best way to determine your case's strengths and weaknesses, but there are occasions when it is not. Let's first look at the advantages and disadvantages of a deposition and then learn how to take one.

2.1 EIGHT REASONS TO TAKE A DEPOSITION

Cost is a significant consideration in your decision. Expenses for a court reporter can exceed $1,000 for a half-day deposition. In addition, there is a significant burden on your time. Let's look in detail at a deposition's advantages and disadvantages.

Most lawyers see depositions as fact-finding exercises. While this is true, they have a larger purpose. Great trial lawyers use depositions to determine how credible a witness will be at trial. It is a unique situation where you can look the witness in the eye and assess his demeanor. This determination is critical to deciding the settlement value of your case and whether you should go to trial.

Unfortunately, there may be times when you feel pressure from a client to save money by not taking

> You can't rely on a colleague to frame and ask the question in the same manner as you would.

a deposition or by having an associate with a lower billing rate take the deposition. But you are responsible for the ultimate outcome of the case and cannot delegate this task when there is a key witness. Only by seeing the witness in person and hearing his story can you accurately perceive his credibility. While a videotaped deposition by an associate would alleviate this problem to some extent, a face-to-face meeting is the only way to determine how the witness will react to your questions at trial.

Another important reason to take a deposition is to build a record of inconsistent statements from the witness that can later be used to impeach him at trial. For example, in a car wreck case, a plaintiff may testify in his deposition that after the accident the defendant was concerned about his injuries and was helpful in summoning an ambulance. However, at trial, the plaintiff may try to embellish his story and testify that the defendant was not helpful but rather belligerent and angry. If you had not taken the deposition, you would lack the one tool to discredit the plaintiff's trial testimony. Having taken the deposition, you will be able at trial to impeach the witness in the following way.

Example: Deposition Provides Inconsistent Statement

Q. *You testified on direct that the defendant was belligerent and angry at the scene. The truth is that my client was concerned about your injuries and helped in calling for an ambulance.*
A. No.

Q. *Do you remember giving your deposition in this case.*
A. Yes.

Q. *You were under oath?*
A. Yes.

Q. *I would like you to read along silently as I read from page 17 line 2. Isn't it a fact, you were asked the following question? Was the defendant concerned . . . .*

A third reason to take a witness' deposition is to discover the details of a party's claims or a witness' knowledge of events. In short, a deposition lets you confirm what you already know and find out answers to questions you don't know.

It is impossible from interrogatories to gather many details. Through a deposition, an attorney may explore at length the lawsuit's claims that cannot be done in any other way. For example, if a defendant supervisor in an employment discrimination lawsuit asserts in his answer filed with the court that he did not do anything sexually to harass the plaintiff because it was a consensual relationship, only through a deposition can the plaintiff's attorney discover the detailed answers regarding the claimed consent. A deposition allows you to follow-up on answers that simply can't be done with interrogatories. Also, unlike interrogatories, you can get spontaneous answers that are not filtered by opposing counsel.

Likewise, a deposition will help you discover facts that hurt your case. The last thing you want is to be surprised at trial by a credible witness who knows facts that damage your case. If you learn about bad facts during discovery, you usually will have time to find witnesses or documents that can undermine the bad facts. If you find out about the bad facts at trial, it may be impossible to lessen the damage. Moreover, by hearing the witness' bad answers, you will know to avoid asking those questions at trial.

Depositions may also be used to find facts that will be helpful to your case. The other side is never going to volunteer helpful information but, through a deposition, you may find that although a witness has damaging testimony, he also has some helpful information for your side.

For example, in the employment discrimination lawsuit mentioned above, it may be that when you take the supervisor's deposition, he admits that the plaintiff had *always* received excellent performance reviews and that they only went down after the consensual relationship ended, although he denies that event had anything to do with the worse evaluations. Such information would corroborate the plaintiff's theory that her lower performance rating and failed promotion occurred not as coincidence with the ending "relationship" but rather at the end of harassment when the plaintiff finally said "no" to any further sexual contact.

Also, the need to prepare an effective summary judgment motion may require you to take a witness' deposition. It may be that you need to get certain admissions from an adverse witness in order to prove the point you are making in your motion.

Narrowing the issues for trial or mediation is another reason to take a deposition. Often a Complaint and Answer throw in the kitchen sink with allegations and denials. However, depositions of key witnesses often reveal that the alleged wrongdoing or defenses are narrower than they were alleged in court pleadings.

Sometimes you will take a deposition to force a settlement. You may be able to achieve this by showing the witness documents and asking questions that reveal your case's overwhelming strengths. For example, if a defendant hospital were claiming no medical malpractice, a videotaped deposition of the hospital's surgeon briefly showing remorse when confronted with documentation suggesting that there was a mistake may be the tipping point for a quick settlement. As discussed below, a video deposition would be critical to preserve such a reaction that would not show up in a transcript.

Finally, a deposition may be used to preserve a witness' testimony. An attorney may believe that a witness is neutral but might be persuaded to shade his testimony for the other side at a later date. Or, the witness may live outside the court's subpoena range for trial. In such situations, you will not be able to force testimony at trial, and a deposition can be substituted for trial testimony. Preservation may also be necessary if the attorney fears that the witness won't be available for trial due to health reasons. Obviously, there is the risk that if the witness provides hurtful testimony, the attorney has unintentionally preserved harmful testimony that would otherwise not be used at trial.

Deposition Advantages

1. Assess the witness' credibility.
2. Create inconsistent statements for use at trial.
3. Discover details of a party's claims or a witness' knowledge.
4. Gather helpful admissions.
5. Learn bad facts about your case.
6. Narrow the issues for trial.
7. Obtain settlement leverage.
8. Preserve helpful testimony.

Do not feel that you need to limit yourself to just one of the reasons above. For best effect, combine them. There is no reason you can't assess the witness' credibility, discover new leads, and box in the witness with helpful admissions.

2.2 FIVE REASONS NOT TO TAKE A DEPOSITION

Having said this, there are some serious disadvantages to taking a deposition. First, it can be expensive, as mentioned above. Besides the cost of the court reporter, the deposition takes a lot of your time to prepare and takes time away from other important things you could be doing. Is this deposition really worth your time? Moreover, is it really worth double your time? That is, there is a certain tit for tat between attorneys. If you decide to take a lot of depositions, be prepared for opposing counsel to return the favor and take just as many. It is fair to assume that for every deposition you take, you will have to spend the same amount of time defending one.

In addition, by taking depositions, you force the other side to spend time on your case and, therefore, to become better prepared for trial. This is a very significant drawback to taking a deposition. Through the witness' answers, you will inevitably educate the other side about details it might not have taken the time to learn except for the deposition. But for the important depositions, you need the information even if the downside is that the witness and opposing counsel get educated. A good guide, then, is to take only important depositions and not waste your time taking the less important ones.

Another downside to depositions is that you will necessarily reveal your trial strategy through your questions. Even if you are subtle about your theory of the case, the opposing attorney will at least get glimpses through the topics you cover in the deposition and by sensing from your mannerisms which topics seem important.

Moreover, while you are able to assess the witness' credibility, the witness is also assessing your demeanor and strategy. Consequently, the witness will be less surprised at trial, since it won't be the first time he has been confronted by you.

These facts aside, none of the disadvantages should carry the day by themselves except for the most important one: by taking a deposition, you remind the other side to take the depositions of your witnesses. You may inadvertently expose the weaknesses in your witnesses that opposing counsel may not have otherwise discovered if he had not taken their depositions.

Deposition Disadvantages

1. Expensive.
2. Reminds opposing counsel to take depositions of your witnesses.
3. Forces opposing counsel to come to trial much better prepared.
4. Your questions reveal your trial strategy.
5. The witness can assess your demeanor and strategy prior to trial.

2.3 ORDER OF DEPOSITIONS

First, you need to decide the order. Do you want to develop your case from the ground up, or from the top down? Most attorneys start at the bottom and work up, but there is no one right way that applies to all cases.

For example, if you are a plaintiff in a medical malpractice case, you may start by taking the depositions of the nurses and then work your way up to the doctors. This would give you the chance to build the theory of your case with lower level fact witnesses before you question the doctor.

But such an approach alerts the doctor to the questions to expect, since his counsel will have briefed him not only on the questions you have asked but the answers that have been given. It also gives the doctor time to prepare for the moment of truth. By contrast, if you start with the doctor, you may not know all the details of the case, but you will be able to lock down the doctor's testimony before he has time to learn from others' testimony and modify his responses.

There is a definite advantage in taking the deposition of a main witness before that witness has had time to prepare by reviewing documents or learning from other depositions. You can catch the witness off guard because opposing counsel will be hearing the specific areas of your questions for the first time and won't be able to warn the witness ahead of time.

In contrast, working from the ground up is particularly helpful when you don't know who the decision-maker is who took the action which hurt your client. You may need to build your case by getting details from witnesses low in the food chain so you will know what questions to ask the decision-maker when you determine who that is.

The key is to be creative and not approach every case the same. While in most cases, you probably will start with low-level witnesses, don't be afraid to go after the key witness first when you know what questions to ask him.

2.4 TYPES OF DEPOSITIONS

There are various depositions and, whichever type you use, the opposing side cannot object as long as your choice comports with the Rules.

1. Video v. Oral Depositions

In an ideal world, your depositions would be videoed, and your opponent's would not. The reason is that you would have the advantage of using video clips at trial to show how your opponent's witnesses got angry, were arrogant, or paused for a long time before answering a simple question (showing that his answer was disingenuous).

Example: Gates Deposition (*U.S. v. Microsoft*)[1]

In this example, the lawyer asks Gates whether he had a conversation with Microsoft's vice-president Paul Maritz about winning market share for Microsoft's browser. The government had accused Microsoft of using its powers to create a monopoly in this area.

---

[1] For a summary of *U.S. v. Microsoft*, see the Appendix.

Q. Now, did you ever tell Mr. Maritz that browser share was not the company's number one goal?

A. No.

This exchange seems very normal, and Gates appears to have told the truth. However, the video shows Gates pausing uncomfortably for almost a minute before answering this simple question. When the video was played at trial, it caused laughter in the courtroom. This is a perfect example showing that video can capture a crucial moment in a deposition that the written transcript cannot.

> You only get one shot at deposing a witness, so you need to make it count. If possible, always use video.

Likewise, if your witness did any of these things during an oral deposition, your opponent would not be able to take advantage of these mistakes at trial because the deposition of your witnesses would only be taken by a court reporter. Moreover, ideally, you would have infinite financial resources to pay for the added cost of a videographer to video the depositions (i.e. many videographers charge $100/hr. with a four hour minimum).

One more reason to take a video deposition is if you are concerned about opposing counsel's behavior. With the video rolling, you will force opposing counsel to be polite or risk being seen as a jerk by the jury when the deposition is played at trial or seen by the judge in a motion for sanctions for unacceptable behavior.

On the other hand, a video deposition has the disadvantage of preserving your tone of voice and the manner of your questions as well. If you pause a lot between questions, seem disorganized, become angry, or appear nervous, the jury will see this, and your credibility will be diminished.

2. Oral Depositions v. Deposition by Written Questions

While not very common, taking a deposition of a witness or party by written questions can be very useful. Rule 31 provides guidance. The party seeking to take the deposition sends notice to the person and every other party along with questions that are sought to be asked. The opposing party has fourteen days after being served to respond with questions it wants to ask and must serve those on the originating party. The parties have seven days each to serve redirect and recross questions if desired.

You must object to a question that you have been served with within the time for serving responsive questions (14 days) or, if the question is a recross question, within 7 days after being served. (Rule 32(d)(3)(C)).

After all questions have been served, the party who noticed the deposition must then send a court reporter the notice and all the questions that have been submitted. The court reporter then must promptly take the deposition of the deponent by reading him the questions and transcribing the answers, as would be the case in a typical deposition.

There are many disadvantages to a deposition by written questions. If the witness is confused by the question, there is no way for you to rephrase it. Moreover, if the witness gives a vague or limited answer, you cannot follow up. There is also nothing to be done if the witness dodges the question and gives an evasive answer. You will also give the other side the opportunity to draft questions carefully in response to yours.

Nonetheless, this type of deposition is useful in getting business records admitted at trial. For example, you could issue a Notice of Deposition By Written Questions with a subpoena duces tecum (a request for documents to be produced at the deposition) to a custodian of records at a company. The questions you would ask would be those to qualify the documents as business records so that they could be admissible at trial under the business record exception to the hearsay rule. You could also instruct the witness to sign a declaration to the same effect. Then, instead of calling the witness at trial, you could offer the deposition as substitute testimony or the accompanying declaration and documents under Federal Rule of Evidence 902(11) by providing notice of your intent prior to trial.

3. Telephone or Video Conferencing Depositions

You may take a deposition by telephone or video conference if the parties agree or with the court's permission (Rule 30(b)(4)). If the parties do not agree, the court will often permit the deposition unless the opposing party can show a particular reason why she would be prejudiced.

These remote depositions are often done so that attorneys can save the time and expense of traveling where the deponent resides. The only logistical concern is finding a court reporter (and/or videographer) to be present in the deponent's town. The downside to taking a telephone deposition is that you can't see the witness' reactions to your questions and judge how credible she will be before a jury. It can also be hard to question the witness about documents (even if you have mailed them to the court reporter beforehand), since it can be cumbersome to show the witness exactly what paragraph or sentence you want the witness to explain. However, for testimony that is expected not to be very controversial, a telephone deposition is an efficient way to obtain discovery and is very easy to arrange. The video conference allows you visually to assess the credibility of the witness but has the disadvantages of expense and difficult logistics of arranging for video equipment and video streaming.

2.5   GETTING READY TO TAKE THE DEPOSITION

The Boy Scout motto "Be Prepared" teaches scouts that by preparing for the unexpected, they can survive any unforeseen circumstances in the wilderness. The motto serves attorneys equally well. In short, you need to know your case and your opponent's case as well as possible before the deposition begins so that you can handle any surprises. We saw in the Introduction the pitfall of not being prepared. The lawyer questioning Bill Gates did not know the difference between a memo and an e-mail. Being unprepared gives the witness confidence that he is in charge when just the opposite should be the case.

First, send out interrogatories to the other side. While young lawyers spend a ton of time drafting detailed questions, experienced lawyers know that to do so is futile. All the answers will be watered down and filtered by the opposing lawyer. In addition, if you ask detailed questions, the information you put in those questions and the information you seek will tip off the other side to your trial strategy. To illustrate, suppose you ask, "describe in detail what happened at the meeting on April 3rd where the design of product X was discussed and list who was present." You will have alerted your opponent that you consider this an important meeting and will let him focus his witness preparation on this event. Moreover, in return for your question, you will get an objection that the question is overly broad and an answer that is vague and unhelpful.

Consequently, there are really only two types of questions to ask: 1) name witnesses (including experts) that have relevant knowledge about the lawsuit, and 2) contention interrogatories. An example of a contention interrogatory in a car wreck case is: "when you allege contributory negligence in your lawsuit on page three, state the basis for the allegation." (The answer may be, "your client was drunk.")

Second, review the relevant documents in the case. That means studying your client's documents and then examining your opponent's documents. It is essential to get every document you need from your opponent (through requests for production of documents) before taking your first deposition. You can't afford to miss a key opportunity when deposing a witness by not questioning him about an essential document that turns up later because you failed to request it before the deposition.

> Don't even think about deposing a key witness before getting all the documents you need from your opponent.

Don't count on your opponent to produce helpful documents without your having to send a document request. While under the old rules, both sides were required under Rule 26 to produce relevant documents---both good and bad---at a lawsuit's beginning, the rule has been amended so that a party only has to produce documents that support its position. As a result, document requests are now the only means to find the smoking gun from the other side.

> Conduct witness interviews *early*. The sooner you discover your strengths and weaknesses, the better you can attack your opponent.

The next step is essential, but it takes some time and organization. While you are waiting for your opponent to respond to your document requests, meet with the main witnesses aligned with your client. These interviews are critical in determining what leads to follow in preparing your own case. However, these meetings are often difficult to arrange because the client has no sense of urgency.

It is amazing how many clients' first reaction to your request for interviews is one of "Don't bother me now." If you represent a company, the in-house counsel will likely tell you that she wants to keep the number and length of interviews to a minimum because the lawsuit is a distraction and taking valuable time away from employees that could be better spent helping the company to be productive. Once trial approaches, witnesses are more willing to be interviewed, but by then, it is usually too late. Do the best you can to persuade your client that an ounce of prevention is worth a pound of cure. The sooner you know your case's strengths and weaknesses, the better you can attack your opponent's case.

At the very least, meet face-to-face with the two or three key witnesses who know the most about your case. Then, follow up with phone calls for other witnesses.

During this time, you should also interview as many hostile witnesses as possible. The one prohibition is that you cannot talk to witnesses who would fall under the opposing side's attorney-client privilege. Be careful because attorneys take this privilege very seriously. Technically, you could argue that if the opposing party is a business, you have the right to talk to its employees as long as they are not supervisors. But, opposing counsel will likely go berserk if he finds out you are talking to even low-level employees of his client's company. Research the law in your jurisdiction, and even if you have the law on your side, decide if the ensuing fight with opposing counsel is worth it, and bear in mind the likelihood that he may do the same to you.

In any event, when meeting with your witnesses, be aware which conversations are protected by the attorney-client privilege. Again, research the law, but a good rule of thumb is that supervisors are covered while employees are not.

Once you have interviewed witnesses and received responses to your interrogatories and document requests, it is time to proceed with depositions.

2.6 KNOW THE ELEMENTS OF YOUR CLAIMS OR DEFENSES

Knowing the elements of your claims or defenses is fundamental. If you are the plaintiff in a negligence case, make sure you know the elements you need to prove before you begin a deposition. Do you have to prove a breach of a duty? If yours is a medical malpractice case, do you need to prove that the doctors failed beyond a reasonable degree of medical "certainty" or just by a reasonable degree of medical "probability." Once you have researched the law, put that research in your outline so that it will be easily accessible during the deposition.

2.7 DETERMINE YOUR THEORY OF THE CASE

Webster's dictionary defines *theory* as "the analysis of a set of facts in their relation to one another." To arrive at a theory, you must successfully answer this question: "At the end of the trial, what conclusion must the jury be compelled to reach based on the law after hearing all the important good and bad facts?"

In the Simpson criminal trial,[2] O.J. had a powerful theory that the police had framed him. However, in the civil case, the plaintiffs turned this theory on its head. The plaintiffs maintained that the Los Angeles Police Department had no motive to frame O.J. Indeed, the facts overwhelmingly supported the theory that O.J. had a lot of friends at the police department and that, if anything, the police treated him more favorably than the average citizen.

Example: Developing Theory
(Simpson Deposition)

[Plaintiffs' attorney Dan Petrocelli] Q. Did members of the LAPD frequent your house from time to time?
[Simpson's attorney Robert Baker objects] That's pretty vague and ambiguous, too.
[Simpson] A. Yeah, you'll have to be a little more specific because I can't answer that.

Q. Did they ever come to visit you?
A. Yes. . . .One individual [also] used my pool [and brought friends to play on my tennis court].

Q. Did you ever file any charge of harassment against the police at any time before June of 1994?

---

2 For a summary of the criminal and civil trials, go to Appendix One.

A. No.

Q. *Did you ever autograph footballs for officers?*
A. Oh, yes.

Q. *Your son Jason was given an LAPD cap from a police officer?*
A. I would assume so.

Q. *So your dealings with the LAPD were cordial?*
A. Yeah, for the most part, yes.

Q. *As of June 17, Mr. Simpson, did you have any information that caused you to believe that you were being framed or set up by the LAPD?*
A. No.

The plaintiffs' lawyer develops several facts that support his theory that LAPD had no motive to frame O.J. Quite the opposite of O.J.'s claim, their relationship was very cordial.

2.8 UNCOVER YOUR OPPONENT'S THEORY

Equally as important as determining your theory, you must discern what your opponent's theory is. Perhaps the greatest failing of attorneys is their refusal to take the time to analyze critically their case and determine how their opponent is going to try and win the case. One reason for this failure is that attorneys and their clients are in denial about the bad facts in the case. It is ingrained in every client's DNA. By the time a lawsuit is filed, both sides are very self-righteous.

Too many times a skillful attorney on the opposing side will ask a question that crystallizes the strengths of his case in a very profound manner. The question needs to be answered persuasively, and it is too late to help your client if you have not anticipated this moment.

But the attorney who can find out what the truth is has a distinct advantage because that is what will be revealed at trial. You must be objective enough to see the weaknesses in your case, or your witnesses will be surprised at the deposition when asked about bad facts that you have not recognized. When you uncover your opponent's theory, you can prepare your witnesses for the hard questions they will be asked.

2.9 DETERMINE YOUR THEMES FOR THE CASE

Great leaders would not be what they are if they did not understand the importance of boiling down many facts to a memorable theme. President Dwight D. Eisenhower was once troubled by a speech's draft for a national address that he was given to review by his speechwriters. He called the writers into the Oval Office. He shared with them the secret of being a great communicator. He explained to them that before you ever begin to write a speech, you need to be able to fit your bottom line message on the inside of a matchbook cover.

Think of what that lesson teaches. Eisenhower taught his speech writers that before they wrote a draft, explored beginnings and endings, or decided on an order of topics, they needed first to decide what the message was. And then, not only must they decide on a message, but that message should be so clear and concise that they could write it on the inside of a matchbook cover.

The same is true for discovery. Before you embark on depositions, interrogatories, and collecting massive amounts of documents, decide what your case is all about. If you are a defendant in a car wreck case, is your theme that the plaintiff is exaggerating her injuries? If you are the plaintiff, is it that the defendant's carelessness caused permanent suffering? If it is a contract case, is your theme one of broken promises?

By starting with your bottom line message, that message forces you to focus on what is most important in discovery. Your message or theme directs you to take the depositions of *only* the important witnesses. It prevents you from chasing tempting rabbit trails that may be interesting but waste your resources, time, and energy. It also helps you ask the right questions to get important information. Without a clear theme, you may not realize what information is absolutely essential.

Example: Theme
(Simpson Deposition)

One of the plaintiffs' themes was that Simpson was a liar. Petrocelli wanted to get Simpson to lie about as many things as possible in the deposition. A highlight occurred when Simpson swore that he would never wear Bruno Magli shoes which were the shoes that left footprints in the blood at the murder scene. After the deposition, Petrocelli was able to prove that Simpson had bought and worn Bruno Magli shoes.

Q. Did you ever buy shoes that you knew were Bruno Magli shoes?
A. No.

Q. How do you know that?
A. Because I know, if Bruno Magli makes shoes that look like the shoes they had in court [criminal trial] that's involved in this case, I would have never owned those ugly-ass shoes.

2.10 DETERMINE YOUR OPPONENT'S THEMES

Similar to the strategy discussed above for uncovering your opponent's case theory, you need to do the same thing for your opponent's themes. You will immeasurably increase your chances to win when you can boil your opponent's case down to a few key phrases. For the same reasons that your witnesses will be better prepared for a deposition when they know what *your* case is about, they will be more comfortable when you can explain to them clearly through themes what your *opponent* is trying to prove.

2.11 BE SKEPTICAL OF YOUR CLIENT'S STORY

A big mistake to avoid is to buy hook, line, and sinker into your client's story. It is not that clients always lie, but it is certainly true that they are often mistaken about details and frequently exaggerate the wrong the other side committed. More important, clients are almost always in denial to some extent about their wrongdoing. Clients typically will claim that they have done nothing wrong when facts later prove otherwise. You need to learn every important thing about your case as soon as possible so you can develop a theory and theme for the case that will ring true for the jury.

As discussed above, the best way to do this is to interview at the beginning the main witnesses in the case. These interviews do not have to be long and burdensome. They will give you a good feel for the witnesses' credibility and alert you to possible inconsistencies with the initial story your client told you.

A recent study found that nominees to the Supreme Court answer only "between 60 and 70 percent of their questions [at confirmation hearing] in a fully forthcoming manner."

Likewise, be skeptical of the witness you are deposing. Almost everyone has an agenda which effects how truthful he will be. For example, in an ideal world, the most respected judges in the country—those on the Supreme Court—would be counted on to be 100% forthcoming and honest. However, even these judges have been documented to be less than straightforward when it served their agenda.

2.12 CREATE A TRIAL GUIDE

After determining the themes, theories, and legal elements of the case, you need to determine what the most important facts are and how you are going to prove them. Are you going to prove the facts through a witness or a document? Once you decide, make a "Trial Guide" which will govern your case. The trial guide should not be more than one page. Less is more. This trial guide should contain only the most important facts, themes etc. of the case and nothing more.

Keep the trial guide with you at all times. Better yet, put it in a three ring binder and put two other sections behind it. One section will have a one or two paragraph summary of the key witnesses in the case. The other section will have the key documents in the case. Finally, before you make any decisions regarding depositions, consult your trial guide to see what your strategy should be. To illustrate, if the witness isn't going to help you with a key fact, don't waste your time taking her deposition. Below is what the guide should look like.

TRIAL GUIDE	
A. Your Theme	A. Opponent's Theme
B. Your Theory	B. Opponent's Theory

C. Most Important Facts
  1.
  2.
  3.
  4.
  5.
*Reference the source of each fact
  (i.e. does it come from a witness or a
  document)
	C. Most Important Facts
	  1.
	  2.
	  3.
	  4.
	  5.

D. Most Important Exhibits	D. Most Important Exhibits
E. Legal Elements of Claims/Defenses	E. Legal Elements of Claims/Defenses

2.13   DETERMINE CROSS-EXAMINATION TOPICS

Assuming you are taking the deposition of an adverse witness, you need to determine the areas of the topics you are going to question him on. Keep your goal in mind for a summary judgment motion and trial. First, you are trying to learn all the important bad facts this witness will testify about at trial. Second, you are trying to get this witness to help you as much as you can and, to the extent he can't help you, you are trying to get information that will undermine the parts of her testimony that hurt you.

Every witness can be cross-examined at trial on one of the following areas: 1) **c**redibility, 2) **l**ack of knowledge, 3) **i**mplausible statements, 4) **p**rior inconsistent statements, or 5) **s**upport of your case. An acronym to help you remember these areas is CLIPS. And how do you remember the acronym? Imagine the witness is Sampson from the Bible. He gets his strength from his hair. You are going to clip his hair to take away his strength much like you would do against an adverse witness.

One piece of advice before we discuss CLIPS: Although you are trying to find out the weaknesses of the adverse witness during the deposition so that you can later take advantage of them at trial, the reality is that over 90% of cases settle. So, you may decide that it is not enough to discover the weaknesses, but you should make it clear to the witness and opposing counsel through your questioning that you have discovered the weakness to give you leverage for settlement. But, if you use this strategy, be aware that if the case proceeds to trial, you have given up an advantage at trial by sharing with the other side all the weapons you plan to use.

Now, let's look at the "C" of CLIPS. Many witnesses have credibility problems. Are they naturally biased for one side? Are they exaggerating their story? How reliable is their memory? Sometimes the witness will have prior criminal convictions. Explore all these areas in the deposition.

Sometimes your best line of attack is to prove that the witness really does not know much about the facts. This is the "L" of CLIPS. For instance, a supervisor may claim to know that your client is a bad employee, but the reality is that she may have stopped supervising your client three years before the alleged incident leading to your client's firing took place. Question her about her lack of knowledge regarding your client's performance since she stopped supervising him.

A third area ("I") is to see if the witness made prior statements—or makes statements at the deposition—that are implausible. An implausible statement provokes disbelief in the listener. Just because a witness says it's so does not make it so.

Fourth, many witnesses will make statements in the deposition that are inconsistent with what evidence shows in documents or is inconsistent with what they have said to other people. At trial, these statements will become prior inconsistent statements ("P") to those made at trial. One of your goals is to get the witness to talk as much as possible at the deposition because that increases your odds that she will say something inconsistent. This inconsistency can be used at trial to show the witness cannot be trusted because she is mistaken on an important matter or that she has flat out lied.

Fifth, use the deposition to get the witness to confirm facts that support your case ("S"). Almost every witness can help corroborate something good about your case. Many lawyers are in such an attack mode that they forget this helpful strategy. It is best to begin your questioning with this topic, since a witness is more likely to agree with you before you attack her.

Remember

Every witness can be questioned on one or more of these areas (CLIPS):

1. **C**redibility
2. **L**ack of knowledge
3. **I**mplausible statements
4. **P**rior inconsistent statements
5. **S**upport of your case

2.14   PREPARING AN OUTLINE

Start by asking the witness if he understands that the oath in the deposition is the same as the oath taken at trial. Then, confirm that he is competent to give a deposition (i.e. not on medication that is affecting ability to tell the truth) and that you can assume that he understands the question unless the witness tells you differently.

Somewhere near your outline's beginning, write the elements of your claims or defenses. That way, you can refer to them quickly if you need to get a precise answer from the witness.

Then, get answers that reveal all the important bad facts this witness will use against you at trial. In addition, elicit facts that will help you. After you have gotten some helpful admissions from the witness, challenge him with hard questions that might undercut his testimony (see discussion of CLIPS above).

> Conventional wisdom advises you to begin with a lot of background questions. Such a tactic can waste precious time that may be needed elsewhere.

Not surprisingly, it is usually best to get helpful admissions before attacking the witness. Then, end the deposition by getting to some basic background questions (i.e. prior education, jobs, lawsuits etc.) Below is a typical outline.

I.   Witness notification about oath
II. Confirmation of witness' competency to give testimony
III. Elements of cause of action and defenses (for your reference only)
IV. Discover bad facts about your case
V.   Admissions that support your case (the "S" of CLIPS)
VI. Other areas of CLIPS
VII. Miscellaneous questions regarding background

The last category regarding background is necessary because it may lead to other facts that might be used to impeach a witness. Some basic questions to ask the witness are whether or not he has been convicted of a felony in the past ten years. Such information can be presented to a jury. In case you are doubtful that a convicted felon might answer your question truthfully, you can do your own investigation after the deposition, but you will need to get some information to help you. Ask the witness where he has lived in the past ten years. Without much objection, you should be able to ask him his date of birth and driver's license number. But in this age of identity theft, asking a witness for his social security number is probably objectionable.

Furthermore, depending on the witness, you might ask questions about divorce, bankruptcy filings, involvement in other lawsuits, or arrests if they could affect the witness' credibility. Or you might want to explore previous jobs and education if you want to determine expertise or earning capacity.

Many lawyers ask an inordinate number of background questions. Let's look at an example from the Gates deposition.

Example: Lawyer Asks Too Many Background Questions (Gates Deposition)

[*Attorney Stephen Houck*] *Q1. I understand that you are one of the co-founders of Microsoft; is that correct?*
A. Yes.

Q2. When was the company founded?
A.   1975.

Q3. What positions have you held with Microsoft since then?
A.   Partner, chairman, CEO.

Q4. What is your present title?
A.   Chairman and CEO.

The only question that has any relevance is question number four. Questions one through three are pointless. Although the plaintiff's attorney changed topics after question four, many lawyers would have wasted even more time by asking Gates about his high school and college education, his jobs prior to Microsoft, and a description of his duties from 1975 at Microsoft until the present. Such questioning can typically last thirty minutes. Not only are the attorneys gathering meaningless information, but they are wasting energy on unimportant matters.

Finally, don't be a captive to your outline. Listen carefully. You will probably discover new topics to explore that had not occurred to you during preparation. Follow the important leads wherever they take you.

2.15   THERE IS NO SUCH THING AS THE "USUAL AGREEMENT"

As mentioned briefly in Chapter One, there is no such thing as the usual agreement. At the start of a deposition, either the court reporter or opposing counsel will often inquire, "Usual agreement?" This phrase means a hundred different things to a hundred different attorneys. The only thing that is "usual" about the agreement is that it is the same one which that particular court reporter or attorney uses. Simply reply, "I'll agree that this deposition is being taken pursuant to the federal (or state) rules of procedure." With such a response you are not waiving any rights you have, and it will be crystal clear what rules or agreements are governing the deposition.

When taking the deposition, you want to make sure that defending counsel is required to object to the form of the question—as required by the federal rules—so that you can correct it. You would not want his interpretation of the "usual agreement" to mean that he could remain silent and later object at trial because you asked a question whose form was objectionable. How the federal rules affect objections you need to make when defending a deposition will be discussed in Chapter Four.

2.16   REVIEWING THE DEPOSITION

Before the deposition starts, the court reporter will often ask the defending attorney if he wants the witness to review the transcript. The reason is that Rule 30(e) provides that—before the deposition is finished—if the witness or a party requests to review the deposition transcript, the party must be given 30 days after the transcript is completed to review it in order to make changes.

After reviewing the transcript, if the witness makes any changes, the witness must sign a statement listing the changes and the reasons for making the changes. That list becomes part of the deposition.

If you are defending a deposition, always ask the court reporter to allow your witness to review the deposition transcript once it is ready. More important, *you* should review it to protect the witness. There may be substantive answers that need to be changed upon further reflection. More likely, there will be something that the court reporter transcribed incorrectly, that if not fixed by you, could be damaging at trial. For example, the witness may have said he prescribed 40 mg twice daily when the court reporter transcribed the testimony as only daily.

Some attorneys *taking* the deposition request that the witness be allowed to review the transcript. The reason is that at trial, when you impeach the witness' testimony with an inconsistent statement in the deposition, you can also point out to the jury that the witness has read the deposition prior to trial and has signed a statement agreeing with its accuracy.

However, it is better not to remind the witness that he can correct his deposition prior to trial. If the mistake is left uncorrected, your impeachment will not suffer because the witness has not signed the deposition. You will still be able to argue to the jury that the witness was under oath. Opposing counsel will have a hard time on re-direct examination trying to get the witness to explain why he has not reviewed the deposition and made the correction.

2.17   BAD AND GOOD BEGINNINGS

Here is a typically bad way that attorneys begin depositions, followed by a better way. There are many needless questions asked at the beginning that get you distracted by the mundane before you ever begin. Here are some common mistakes to avoid.

Example: Bad Beginning

Q1. Are you represented by counsel?

An unnecessary question. You know the answer to this, so there is no need to put it on the record.

Q2. Is he here in the room with you?

Lawyers ask this question under the mistaken belief that it needs to be clear in the transcript that the witness' attorney is attending the deposition. However, the court reporter will make this clear at the transcript's beginning under a section called "Appearances."

Q3. Do you understand that the court reporter is taking down everything you say?

This is an interesting observation but states the obvious.

Q4. Have you ever had your deposition taken before?
A. No.

If the witness answers yes, you will have some ammunition if the witness later claims at trial that he was confused by the questioning at the deposition. If the answer is "yes," don't ask the following question.

Q5. Has your attorney explained to you the rules of a deposition?
A. Yes.

Some attorneys mistakenly waste time explaining to the witness something like the following: "This deposition is being taken under the Federal Rules of Civil Procedure. I am going to ask you questions, and the court reporter is going to take down your answers. I may show you some documents to identify and talk about. . . ."
These questions state the obvious and aren't necessary.

Q6. Please do not nod your head yes or no to an answer or answer "uh-huh," since the court reporter needs a verbal response.

If the witness is going to shake her head to a question, you will have to remind her when this happens during the deposition. She is just going to forget what you said at the beginning. Don't waste your breath. A perfect example comes from Bill Gates' deposition.
In this example, Gates has a sarcastic tone which is consistent with his attitude throughout the deposition.

Example: Witness Answers with Uh-huh
(Gates Deposition)

[Boies] Q. And that would have been in 1996; that correct?
[Gates] A. Uh-huh.

Q. You have to say "yes" or "no" for the record.
A. Yes. You [the court reporter] don't get "uh-huh's"?
Q. She does, but it doesn't always come out exactly the way you think.

Example: Bad Beginning Cont'd

Q7. It is important that you and I don't talk over each other so that the court reporter can get everything down. So, make sure you let me finish my question before you try to answer it?

Don't ask for the same reason as question six.

Q8. Please make sure you speak up so we all can hear you.

Don't ask for the same reason as question six.

Q9. Now, if you need to take a break, all I ask is that you answer the question before taking a break and consulting with your attorney. Does that sound fair?

In most jurisdictions, a witness cannot consult with his attorney before answering a question unless it is to inquire about the attorney-client privilege, so why instruct the witness about this? An hour into the deposition, the witness is going to forget you ever asked this question. Then, you will have to instruct the witness—and opposing counsel—not to consult with each other. Having given this instruction at the beginning won't give you any leverage later on. Moreover, if opposing counsel is going to ignore the rule, your little lecture is not going to stop him.

Q10. Have you had any alcohol in the past 12 hours? Are you taking any medication? Tell me about your medications. Are you ill? How much sleep did you get last night?

These questions waste time by seeking too many details. All you want to ask the witness is this: "Is there anything that would prevent you from thinking clearly and testifying truthfully today?"

Moreover, some attorneys ask open ended and vague questions which lead nowhere.

Example: Gates Deposition Cont'd

Q. So you understand the deposition process and how it works? Any questions before we proceed into the substance about the procedures?
A. I'm not sure what you mean?

Q. *Well, are you comfortable with the procedures here? Do you have any questions before we proceed about how this deposition works? You have the right to speak to counsel . . . .*

It is pointless to ask if Gates is "comfortable" with the procedures. What witness who is being forced to give his testimony under oath would be comfortable?

Now, let's look at a better way to start a deposition.

Example: Good Beginning

Q1. *Mr. Ratner, my name is Scott Harada. Are you aware that I represent the defendant?*

This question is not really necessary but ensures that the witness cannot later claim that he was tricked because he did not know who was asking him questions.

A. Yes.

Q2. *Do you understand that you are under the same oath today as if you were in a courtroom?*

A. Yes.

This question is the perfect set-up question for impeachment at trial. When you are trying to show that the truth was stated in a deposition and the witness is now lying in court, it is very powerful before a jury to ask the witness, "the testimony you gave at the deposition was under the *same* oath as you took today here in court?"

Q3. *I am going to assume that you understand the questions that I ask you unless you tell me that you don't understand them. Is that fair?*

A. Yes.

The reason to ask this question is that if you impeach the witness at trial, she cannot say, "I did not understand the question." When the witness attempts to do this, all you need to do is refer to this deposition question. This question and the preceding question about the oath are the two most important preliminary questions to ask. If you could only ask two questions, these two would be all you need.

Q4. *Is there anything that would prevent you from thinking clearly and testifying truthfully today?*

A. No.

This question is asked so that the witness cannot claim at trial that she remembers events more clearly now because there were conditions that made her confused at the deposition.

Q5. If at any time you need to take a break during the deposition, please let me know.
A. OK.

This question simply shows fairness and decency on your part to help build rapport with the witness.

Example: Good Beginning
(Simpson Deposition)

Q. My name is Daniel Petrocelli. I represent plaintiff Frederick Goldman in this lawsuit against you. Do you understand that you are under oath?
A. Yes.

Q. You may have to speak up so that the folks down at the end of the table can hear you. Have you ever testified under oath before?
A. Yes.

Q. You understand that even though you're in our law office today, that the testimony that you give under oath here is subject to the same penalty of perjury as though you were testifying in a court of law?
A. Yes.

Petrocelli then asks Simpson whether he has told the truth in other depositions and other trials at which he has testified. Although Petrocelli does not ask Q3 from the previous example that he should have, he certainly asks the most important question about Simpson's understanding of the oath. He also does not fall into the trap of asking needless background questions or explaining deposition rules *ad nauseam*.

2.18 LESS IS MORE

Although you are allowed to take a deposition that lasts up to one day of seven hours (Rule 30(d)(1)), why would you want to? Don't do it just because many attorneys do and the rules allow. First, many lawyers are unorganized, and much time is wasted going over unimportant topics, covering the same ground five and six times, and spending time reviewing documents prior to questioning a witness that should have been analyzed prior to the deposition.

However, even overly organized attorneys can take inordinately long depositions. Unlike the unorganized attorney, this attorney *purposefully* asks a ton of questions because he is too consumed by details. He mistakenly thinks that the more details he collects, the more ammunition he will have. Unfortunately, facts are only good if you

> Set a goal to take a two and a half hour deposition. This will force you to focus on getting the key facts you need and prevent you from getting bogged down in distracting details.

can later find them and use them. The old saying that there are people who can't see the forest for the trees applies all too well to long depositions. The more information (or trees) you collect, the harder it is to see the big picture (the forest). Instead, focus on seeing the forest.

Other attorneys ask many pointless questions to drag out the deposition and then save the important questions for the end. Their hope is that the witness will be worn down and make a mistake when he is tired. However, it is more likely that the witness will answer the question better because he is used to the lawyer's techniques and is more comfortable with the process.

Moreover, the longer the deposition lasts, the less likely you are to ask focused questions that help you. In addition, in order to gain anything from the deposition, you will need to read it. This takes a lot of time. The more depositions you take and the longer they are, by necessity you will need to spend more time studying them. By taking a long deposition, you undercut your ability later to analyze it to get important facts needed for other discovery and trial. In short, a deposition is useless unless you have the time to analyze it, determine what is important in it, and create a written summary.

Finally, the longer a deposition lasts, the more chances a witness has to explain away bad answers that have already been given. Moreover, with each break in the deposition, opposing counsel gets the chance to talk to the witness and coach him in those jurisdictions that permit such advice. The obvious exception to this rule is that if the witness is dodging your questions, take as much time as you need to get the answers you want.

2.19 KNOW YOUR WITNESS

To learn as much as possible about the witness you are about to depose, there are two areas you need to investigate. First, determine those relevant areas the witness has knowledge about so that you can zone in and ask the particular questions needed. You can do this by asking your witnesses what they know about the person you want to depose. You can also get information by asking other witnesses in their depositions about the upcoming deponent's role in the lawsuit.

Second, find out as much as you can about the deponent's personality. Does he have a type A personality? Is he educated or not? Is he meticulous and likely to have kept a lot of records, or is there likely to be very little recorded to help or hurt your case? Is he arrogant or meek? Does he talk a lot, or is he quiet? By learning about your witness' knowledge and his personality, you can tailor your questions to be most effective.

For example, if you learn prior to the deposition that the witness rarely— if ever—kept records, this information will help you during the deposition.

While you might naturally distrust a witness who claims not to have taken notes when it would have been reasonable to do so, your knowledge about the witness will prevent you from getting sidetracked and emotional by pursuing a line of questions to make sure the witness is telling the truth about the lack of notes. Likewise, if you learn that the deponent is a man of few words, then you will know that you will have to ask questions that are constantly eliciting details from him, as opposed to being able to rely on the witness to volunteer information.

2.20 MAINTAINING THE RIGHT ATTITUDE AND HANDLING OBJECTIONS

Not only is it essential for you to learn as much as possible about the witness, you need to begin the deposition with the right attitude yourself. Prepare thoroughly so you will be confident. Your preparation will help you understand the witness' answers so that you will ask appropriate follow-up questions. You should be confident but never arrogant. If you are condescending, the witness will clam up. No one wants to talk to someone who thinks he knows it all or who projects a judgmental attitude.

On the other hand, don't try and be the deponent's friend. That is an easy way to lose the witness' respect. If he sees you as weak, he will think that he can manipulate you and won't answer truthfully. Instead, be calm, confident, and respectful. If the witness respects you, he is more likely to talk and, in the end, he will be more likely to tell the truth.

Example: Asserting Control (Gates Deposition)

As soon as David Boies began questioning Gates, there was a battle for control. Boies was not going to be intimidated by Gates or his attorney. Immediately, Boies signals to everyone that he is going to repeat his question until he gets an answer. Boies' point was that even though Gates did not remember making the statement, the question is: *could* he have made the statement.

Q. *Good afternoon, Mr. Gates. I'd like to begin by following up with Exhibit 356 and Exhibit 355 that I think you have in front of you. First, with respect to Exhibit 356, which is a 1996 Business Week article. I understand your testimony to be that you do not recall giving an interview to the reporter who wrote this. But do you recall saying the statement attributed to you, whether you said it to that reporter or to someone else? And the statement I'm referring to is the statement at the end of the article in which you are quoted as saying: "'One thing to remember about Microsoft,' says Chairman William H. Gates III, 'We do not need to make any revenue from Internet Explorer software.'"*

A. I don't remember saying that.

Q. *Did you say it, sir?*
[*Heiner*] *Objection. Asked and answered.*
A. I don't remember saying it.

Q. *That wasn't my question sir. Did you say it?*
[*Heiner*] *Objection. Harassing the witness.*
Q. *I am not harassing the witness. I want to know whether he had a recollection of – he may not know whether he said it, he may think he didn't say it. I'm trying to clarify what the witness's testimony is.*
[many more objections of "harassing" and "asked and answered" before Boies got the answer he needed]
Q. *Do you have any reason to believe Business Week would make this quote up, sir?*
A. They had made mistakes, but I'm not suggesting that I know that they did in this case.

Throughout the deposition, maintain your composure. Do not get angry or show impatience unless you have calculated that such an emotion displayed for a particular question will help elicit a favorable answer. Instead, show respect toward the witness.

Unlike cross-examination at a trial where you are trying to convey to the jury through your tone of voice that you don't believe the witness and don't respect his story, a deposition is completely different. Here, you are trying to build rapport with the witness so that he will talk to you. To do this, treat the witness with respect. Most people will open up and talk about themselves and what they have done if someone shows them respect and appears genuinely interested in what they have to say. This principle is no less true in a deposition.

If the opposing counsel tries to get you angry with unnecessary objections or the witness attempts to do the same with persistent refusals to answer questions, don't lose your temper. Such a reaction will distract you from your train of thought and cloud your judgment. Instead, if the witness is causing the problem, take your time and calmly ask your question again. If you are having trouble remembering it because of the interruption—a likely possibility—just have the court reporter read your last question to the witness.

In a situation where opposing counsel is constantly making objections, just ask the witness to answer the question. Unless opposing counsel instructs his witness not to answer, the witness must answer the question despite the objection. For example, if opposing counsel objects because he claims your question is compound, you can either rephrase it or simply direct the witness to answer the question you have asked. There is no need to rephrase a question just because there is an objection.

Practice Tip

Here is a great trick. If you think opposing counsel is trying to interrupt your examination with constant baseless objections, ask him to explain the reason each time he objects. He will soon realize that he will save face if he remains quiet instead of trying to make up reasons for frivolous objections.

Example: Staying Calm
(Simpson Deposition)

There was a lot of anticipation prior to Simpson's deposition. Reporters from around the country were waiting eagerly to see what Simpson would say when he was forced to answer questions about the murders of Ron and Nicole since he did not testify in the criminal trial. Imagine how Goldman's attorney, Petrocelli, must have felt when he was met with a flurry of objections—many of them baseless—at the very beginning. After the twelfth question, defense attorney Baker begins objecting. Pay attention to see if Petrocelli gets flustered.

Q. You told the truth [in depositions in other lawsuits]. Right?
[Baker] That's enough. That's enough.
Q. And you told the truth in those [unrelated trials prior to murder trial]?
A. The best I knew it.

Q. Tell me who the parties were.
[Baker] I am going to object. Instruct him not to answer. It's irrelevant and immaterial. **[This is a baseless objection.]**
[Petrocelli] What I would like to do is get a copy of the transcript of his testimony.
[Baker] It's irrelevant, immaterial. Instruct him not to answer.
Q. Now, is this the first time you're testifying under oath since the death of Nicole and the death of Ron Goldman? **[Petrocelli does not get bogged down in arguing about the objections. He states his reason why he would like to know who the parties are and moves on to his next question. He knows that if the fight is important, he can come back to the question or seek relief with the court.]**
A. Yes.

Q. You've never been questioned under oath about the events surrounding Ron and Nicole's death. Is that right?
[Baker] That's been asked and answered. Instruct him not to answer the question. **[The objection is valid because the preceding question asked for the same information. Nonetheless, since the question did not harass Simpson**

because it was being asked only a second time, the objection was probably made to show Petrocelli that Baker would not be a pushover and also to disrupt Petrocelli's rhythm.]

Q. *When you gave an interview on Ross Becker recently, you were not under oath, Correct?*

A. Correct.

Q. *But the subject matter of that video was your side of the story with respect to the deaths of Ron and Nicole, Right?*

[Baker] *I am going to object. That's a characterization that you're making.* [There is no such objection as "characterization." If Baker were implying the question was argumentative because Petrocelli used the word "side" to imply it was not the truth but a self-serving version, the objection might have some merit.]

Q. *You may answer.*

A. I answered the questions that were asked me, basically, yes.

Notice that Petrocelli never lost his temper, nor did he get into long arguments with opposing counsel. He showed Baker that he was not afraid to deal with objections and pressed on with his questions.

Remember

Your mindset is important, so be:

1. Confident,
2. Respectful,
3. Patient,
4. Non-judgmental, and
5. Calm.

2.21 HANDLING LEGITIMATE OBJECTIONS

While you should not be distracted by baseless objections, you need to be alert for legitimate ones. Don't be overwhelmed by this challenge. First, don't worry about objections---even legitimate ones---if you won't need to use the exchange later on. But when you get to the important parts of your questioning, pay special attention. If there is an objection to a key question, determine if it is valid. You don't want to later find out that you can't use a key answer at trial because you failed to rephrase an objectionable question.

To illustrate, if opposing counsel objects that your question to an expert witness assumes facts not in evidence, think carefully about whether you need to rephrase the question to overcome the objection. If you need to, ask opposing counsel which facts in your question he is objecting to. Or, perhaps your question to a friendly witness is objected to because it is leading. If you will need to use the answer in a motion or at trial later, you need to rephrase your question because you can only ask adverse witnesses leading questions.

2.22 OBJECTIONS MAY SIGNAL AN AREA TO ATTACK

Sometimes opposing counsel will object because you are touching on a sensitive area. It may be an area where you expect objections but it might also be in an area that you have stumbled on accidentally. His objection may offer clues to a topic that needs more investigation. Look at the witness' and counsel's body language. Have they tensed up in any way? Is counsel's tone of voice different from other objections he has made? If counsel has been quiet for some time, why is he objecting all of a sudden? Think through these questions. In short, counsel's efforts to limit your questioning may be all the evidence you need to explore deeper an area you once thought was unnecessary.

2.23 LISTENING IS THE GREATEST SKILL

It might seem strange to discuss listening in a chapter devoted to questions used at deposition, but listening is the most important skill to have. If you are listening, you are observing. And through observation, you can understand what is being said so that you can assess the situation and ask the right questions. Perhaps the greatest quality a poet or writer has is the ability to observe. A writer cannot convey ideas if he is not first able to observe and understand the subject matter he is writing about. Likewise, a lawyer needs to be an astute observer and listener to be persuasive.

> Henry David Thoreau was such a good observer of nature that he could tell the type of tree in a forest not by looking at it but, instead, by listening to its leaves rustle in the wind.

Effective listening is very active and requires a lot of concentration. Unfortunately, we have formed bad habits because everyday hearing, like seeing, is very passive and requires very little effort. Watching and listening to television, hearing a conversation on a phone and listening to a friend tell us about his day are very passive activities. In the example below, because Boies listened carefully to Gates' answer, he was able to follow up with an important question that most lawyers would have failed to ask.

Example: Listening Carefully
(Gates Deposition)

Boies is asking Gates about the effect his negative comments made to the media concerning Netscape had on Netscape.

Q. Do you think it [statements by Gates made to media] **adversely** [3] *affected Netscape's business prospects?*

A. I think the general work that we were doing to do strong Internet software had an effect on Netscape, but I don't think quotations like that had any **direct** effect.

Q. Now, you're putting in the word "direct effect," and I know that you're a very precise person from the statement you've already made today. So, I'm going to ask you what you mean by the use of the word "direct" there that you put in the answer that wasn't in the question. What do you mean by "direct"?

A. Well, I said earlier that there are analytical observers like analysts, and they tend to look at technology companies and deliver pronouncements about them. And, you know, some of them will be positive about a company, and some will be negative about a company. It's possible in looking at the general activities of Microsoft, one of those analysts formed a certain conclusion about Netscape and published that conclusion and that that might have had an effect. And so you could say that analysts may have had an effect. And analysts look at what Microsoft does, primarily in the products, not as much what we say as what we do in shipping our products. **[Gates still does not answer the question but sidesteps it by talking about products]**

Q. What I'm asking you about, of course, right now is the effect of what you were saying or what was attributed to you. And I do want to come to the effect that your products had on Netscape as well. But right now I want to talk about the effect of what was attributed to you. And what I'm asking you is whether you believe that the publication of statements like those attributed to you **adversely** *affected Netscape's business prospects.*

A. I'm not aware of any specific effect. And my general experience is that when competitors have made statements about us, that doesn't have an effect, rather that the people who do analysis or the actual products get shipped are what cause effects on our business.

At the beginning, Gates answered that his disparaging statements to the media had no "direct effect" on Netscape. Boies believes this answer is a lie because soon after Gates gave his interview, investors reacted very negatively to Netscape, since Gates' opinion carried a lot of weight. Boies listens carefully and notices that Gates qualifies his answer by saying his comments had no "direct" effect. Boies wants to make sure there is no wiggle room for Gates to later claim that he never suggested in his deposition that his comments did not have

---

[3] Throughout the book, words in the transcript have been put in bold to highlight the point being made in the discussion that follows.

any effect on Netscape, only that they did not have a direct effect. By carefully listening to Gates' answers, Boies is able to follow up and lock Gates into an answer that declares he is "not aware of any specific effect" his comments may have had. Of course, Boies could have followed up more with Gates since Gates used the word "specific" instead of "direct" as Boies had asked him about, but Boies felt he had won enough of the battle that it wasn't worth wasting time asking Gates what he meant by the word "specific" instead of "direct."

Throughout his deposition, Gates avoided directly answering questions by changing words slightly in his answer from the words used in the question. For example, when Boies asked Gates when did you "*first* make a projection of how much money Microsoft would receive from advertising revenue in connection with the browser," Gates answered that Microsoft "*looked* at charging" in 1996. Noticeably, Gates did not say that Microsoft *first* looked at charging in 1993. Consequently, Boies would spend ten minutes or more trying to get Gates to answer this simple question. When Gates' attorney objected, "asked and answered," the following exchange took place.

Example: Listening to Answer (Gates Deposition)

[Gates' attorney] *Certainly asked and answered.*

[Boies] *You may be right. But because he keeps changing the language he uses, and I know from prior answers that usually when he changes the words, he means something by it, I need to have it tied down.*

Practice Tip

Listen carefully and be persistent when a witness does not answer your question directly.

2.24 TYPES OF LISTENING SKILLS

At first glance, what follows may seem obvious. But by reviewing distinct listening skills, we can distinguish what type of listening works in different situations.

Informative listening is what you did in lectures at law school. Your goal was simply to understand the lecture. A necessary ingredient to your understanding was to comprehend the vocabulary being used and the ideas being presented. Likewise, in a deposition, make sure you understand the concepts and words the witness is using.

Being well-prepared for the deposition as previously discussed will go a long way in helping you master this skill at the deposition. However, if you don't understand, don't be embarrassed to ask the witness to explain. Likewise, concentration is important. Your mind needs to be focused on the witness' answer and not distracted by the upcoming question you are trying to formulate in your mind while the witness is answering.

Relationship listening is a second skill. Unlike a lecture in a law school (informative listening) where you probably could have cared less if the professor felt that you were hanging on his every word, in a deposition, relationship listening is very important. Another term for relationship listening is empathy. Webster's dictionary defines empathy as "understanding, being aware of, being sensitive to, and vicariously experiencing the feelings, thoughts, and experience of another."[3]

Your goal is to make the witness feel that his message is being understood, but also that you understand why he believes as he does. A witness is much less likely to talk if you are condescending or if you show no interest in what he says. You can make him feel understood by using phrases such as "I hear you saying," "I understand," and "I can see where you are coming from."

Showing empathy works because most people are self-centered. They usually think what they did was right and are willing to explain their reasons to those that will listen.

In addition, use body language and eye contact to show the witness you are interested. One mistake many attorneys make is that they keep their eyes on their notes and do not make significant eye contact with the witness. Instead, keep eye contact with the witness and show interest even if you don't like what he is saying. Lean forward; don't sit with your arms crossed or in any manner which shows disinterest. Instead, nod your head and smile when appropriate to convey agreement. A pleasant tone of voice is another way to show empathy. If you are sincere, everything else will take care of itself.

Practice Tip

To build rapport with the witness, show empathy. That does not mean you need to sacrifice your integrity by being sympathetic. To illustrate, if a police officer unjustifiably assaulted a suspect, you should understand his motives and reasons (empathy) without agreeing with his feelings or actions (sympathy).

---

[3] Webster's Ninth New Collegiate Dictionary at 47 (Merriam-Webster Inc. 1985).

What makes a deposition challenging is that you must not only empathize with the witness but simultaneously employ a third skill: critical listening. Critical listening is needed to determine a speaker's believability. Aristotle described the three qualities of a speaker in *The Rhetoric:* ethos, logos, and pathos. Ethos is speaker credibility, logos is logical argument, and pathos is psychological appeal.

First, determine whether the speaker has ethos or credibility. Ask yourself whether the speaker is knowledgeable in the area he is talking about. Since you will most often depose adverse witnesses, critically listen to the answers to determine if the witness is really as knowledgeable about his testimony as he claims to be. If you see weaknesses, you can ask appropriate follow-up questions to reveal the lack of knowledge.

Also, a vital essential of ethos is determining whether the witness is trustworthy. While the witness may be an honest person, he may not realize that he lacks sufficient expertise to talk about a particular subject. Or, as is unfortunately often the case with many expert witnesses, they are experts in their field, but they are untrustworthy because they have slanted their opinions to help the side who hired them.

Next, examine the logos of what the witness is saying. Are the arguments logical? Is the witness making reasonable inferences or making implausible statements? This will be discussed in greater detail in the chapter on Expert Witnesses. For your typical fact witness, the key is to listen to see if his version of events is consistent with common sense. That is, will jurors believe this witness, based on their collective wisdom gained through life's experiences?

Finally, listen and watch to determine the pathos, or psychological persuasion, of the witness. For example, the plaintiff in a car wreck may have been injured but is such a bad communicator that he can't convincingly convey the pain and suffering he went through. Or, you may find that the witness is compelling and would easily move the jury to see the damage that was done to him.

The last listening skill is called discrimination. Discrimination helps determine a word's meaning by the change in pitch, volume, or pace of a speaker's voice. Listen for these subtle changes. You will likely be able to tell whether the witness is forthcoming, truthful, or withholding information.

2.25 OPEN-ENDED QUESTIONS

In order to get information from the witness, you need to use a heavy dose of open-ended questions. These questions generally begin with the following: who, what, when, where, why and how. The five "w's" and the "h" form the basic words used to question. They are also the standard words used

I keep six honest serving men,
(They taught me all I knew);
Their names are What and
Why and When,
And How and Where and
Who.

—Rudyard Kipling

by reporters to uncover information for a story. Not surprisingly, such questions are a deposition's bread and butter. Once those questions have been used, follow up with: describe, explain, can you give some examples, tell me more about, and is there anything else?

Below are some examples of open-ended questions for a plaintiff in an employment discrimination lawsuit.

Example: Open-Ended Questions

Q. **Who** do you believe discriminated against you at work?

Q. **What** makes you think you were treated unfairly?

Q. **When** did the discrimination occur?

Q. **Where** were you when you overheard your boss' secretary admit the company was looking for a female to hire?

Q. **Why** do you think you are more qualified than your coworker Mary Smith?

Q. **How** many instances of discrimination are you complaining of?

Q. Can you **give some examples**?

Q. **Describe** the details.

Q. **Explain** further what you mean.

Q. Is there **anything else**?

2.26 THE INVERTED PYRAMID TECHNIQUE

Not only must you ask the right questions, but there must be a starting and ending point for them. Imagine an inverted pyramid. This image has been used by English teachers for decades to explain how to write a paragraph. The paragraph starts with a topic sentence at the top of the inverted pyramid and then becomes more specific and detailed until it concludes with the last sentence at the bottom of the inverted pyramid.

The same imagery works for deposition questioning. You start at the top of the inverted pyramid with a very broad question that suggests the topic of the area of questioning (open-ended questions). Then, you ask the witness to explain her answers (clarifying questions), and then you ask more specific questions that become narrower until you reach the bottom, and your questions on that topic have been exhausted (locking down questions).

Example: Inverted Pyramid

Top of inverted pyramid:

Q. Describe any injuries you have from the accident.

Bottom of inverted pyramid:

Q. How many days did your bruised right ankle hurt after the accident?

Sometimes getting to the pyramid's bottom takes great patience. The investment of time is worth it if the line of inquiry is important to your case. If not, it is a devastating distraction that prevents you from exploring other areas in the limited time allowed. For example, in the Simpson case, it was paramount for the plaintiff to get Simpson to explain how he had gotten the cut on his left hand. At the criminal trial, the theory had been that he had cut it during the knife attack on Ron Goldman when Goldman fought back. The cut explained the discovery of Simpson's blood on the scene. Prior to the criminal trial, Simpson had explained that he had cut it while in Chicago on the night of the murders. Goldman's attorney asked over 300 questions regarding the cut.

Example: Inverted Pyramid
(Simpson Deposition)

Q. *Did you have any recent cuts on your body on the seventeenth of June?* [top of pyramid]
A. On my finger I had a recent cut.

Q. *Did you cut it on one of the broken pieces of glass?* [about 300 questions later]
A. Yeah.

Q. *On what piece?*
A. Can we take a break. . . Jesus Christ. [Simpson wipes a tear from his eye]

Petrocelli concluded that Simpson's story sounded "hollow." As the last question was asked above, Simpson's "face was tight and the veins at his left temple were bulging. Then, Simpson stood, fumbled for the microphone, threw it on the table, and left the room."[4]

2.27 SILENCE IS THE KEY

One of the best tricks to elicit information is to remain silent after asking an open-ended question. Unfortunately, this goes against our misguided training as lawyers which taught us that the more we talk and argue, the more persuasive we are. In a deposition, you need to turn the tables on the witness. It is not beneficial for you to talk. You want to hear what the witness has to say.

After the witness answers, try pausing before you ask your next question and look at the witness like you are still expecting more information. There are two reasons this trick works. First, no one likes silence. The witness has an urge to fill the void with

> "Lenin could listen so intently that he exhausted the speaker."
>
> —Isaiah Berlin

---

[4] Petrocelli, *Triumph of Justice* 156 (Crown 1998).

explanations. Second, the silence makes the witness feel that he has not fully answered the question, so he tries to provide more information. Obviously, don't overuse this technique, or it will look contrived.

As we will see in Chapter Three, opposing counsel is very fearful of this tactic of silence because he has told his witness repeatedly, "Don't volunteer any information unless you are specifically asked for it!" One important factor in gauging a deposition's success is how much you get the witness to volunteer information.

Example: Getting the Witness to Volunteer

Q. *Tell me why you feel discrimination prevented you from getting the promotion.*
A. I was better qualified than any of the other candidates, and my supervisor never gave me a chance.

Q. *[pause for a few seconds]*
A. Neither Mary nor Sally work hard. They never do their share and, besides, I have been at the company for twenty years, and they just arrived a few years ago. Just because they socialize more with other employees than I do doesn't mean that they are better than me.

By remaining silent, the attorney gets the witness to volunteer details that would not have been known otherwise. More important, the witness admits that he does not get along well with coworkers and feels entitled to the promotion just because he has been there longer than others—good reasons why he may not have been the best candidate.

2.28 CLOSED QUESTIONS

On the other hand, use closed questions to clarify the witness' answers and get specific information (i.e. toward the bottom of the pyramid). While an open question tries to elicit many facts from the witness, the key to using a closed question successfully is to ask the witness a question with one particular fact. Open and closed questions are contrasted below. Do not use these closed questions unless you want to get specific information.

Open

1. **Who** did you talk to about the harassment?
2. You mentioned that your supervisor harassed you about the project you completed in May. Tell me **what happened**.
3. Does **anyone** else **know** about the harassment? [**"anyone" and "know" are very broad**]

Closed

1. Other than Ms. Jones in human resources, did you talk to anyone else **in management** about the harassment?
2. You mentioned that your supervisor harassed you about the project you completed in May. What do you mean **by the word "harassed."**

3. Did anyone **see** your supervisor harass you?

The bold words in the closed examples direct the witness to a very specific piece of information that you want.

2.29 BOX THE WITNESS IN

It is vitally important that you pin the witness down with his own answers so that there are no surprises with his testimony at trial. (This is particularly hard to do with experts, a concern which will be discussed later in Chapter Five.) By asking short specific questions, you force the witness to commit to a version of events that he will be hard-pressed to change at trial without suffering a blistering impeachment.

A good way to visualize this technique is to imagine a sheet of paper containing a wide variety of facts. Try to draw a box around the set of facts which will govern the lawsuit. For example, in a disability discrimination lawsuit, imagine that the defense attorney wanted to box in the plaintiff to find out the parameters of his claims.

Example: Box the Witness In

Q. *Well, my question is, did your supervisor ever require you to do jobs that exceeded your physical limitations?*
A. Yes.

Q. *What occasions were those?*
A. Large copy jobs that required a lot of standing.

What question would you next ask to box the witness in? The tempting follow-up, "Tell me about the copy jobs," does nothing to box the witness in. However, the following questions do.

Q. *Any jobs other than copy jobs?*
A. No, not really. [Now, you have limited the plaintiff's claims to copy jobs]

Q. *Let's look at the copy jobs.*
A. Yeah, one I remember was in February of '06, a very large copy job.

What question would you next ask? If you weren't listening to the answer carefully, you might say, "Let's talk about the February job." However, the observant lawyer would realize that the witness had answered in the plural ("one I remember"), so you would need to discuss the other copy jobs.

Even if you were aware the witness had answered that there were multiple jobs, don't ask details about the February job until you have determined how many jobs there were. The reason is that if you explore the February job in detail, you may forget to come back and ask if there were other projects. It is more efficient to get the broad picture first (i.e. how many jobs were there) and then become very specific in your questioning regarding each job.

Q. *What were the other copy jobs?*
A. There was one back in 1997.

Now that the attorney has established on his imaginary sheet of paper that there were *probably* only two occasions, he should mentally draw a box around the facts by asking a question that leaves no doubt about the claims in the case.

Q. *So, is it fair to say that there were only two copy jobs where your supervisor asked you to go outside of your physical limitations?*
A. Yes. [Now, it is time to explore each copy job in detail.]

Q. *Let's talk about the first copy job in 1997. What kind of project was it?*

> If you wait until just after a break to ask the big question, the witness will look very foolish asking for another break. Enjoy watching him squirm.

Another way to box the witness in is to ask your most important question *after* a break. This is a wonderful secret. Here is the reason why it works. If you ask a witness an important question about a smoking gun document, he may give a perfunctory answer and ask for a break which he is entitled to do. After meeting with his lawyer during the break, he will be thoroughly prepared for your follow-up questions. On the other hand, if you wait until immediately after a break, the witness is stuck.

2.30 MAKE THE WITNESS COMMIT

If you are focused in your questions and the witness is cooperative, it is fairly easy to box a witness in to a certain set of facts that will control the case. However, oftentimes the hardest thing to do is to make a witness commit to a certain fact. This is particularly true with experts who are very adept at not answering questions in a straightforward manner. Even lay witnesses will often avoid answering a simple question that will hurt them but, instead, will start talking about matters that are closely related to the question. The witness' hope is that you will forget the precise question you asked and that you will move on.

There are two skills you need to solve this problem. First, make sure you are listening to the witness' answer. If you don't listen, you won't be aware that the witness is avoiding the question. Second, you need to repeat your question until the witness answers it. If your question is simple, the witness will eventually have to answer. However, if your question has several facts in it, it is difficult to pin the witness down.

Example: Lawyer Repeats Question to Force Witness to Answer (Gates Deposition)

Here, Gates had been avoiding answering Boies' question for over ten minutes about the comments Gates had made to the press regarding Netscape. However, Boies was not going to give up until he forced Gates to answer the question. He did this by continually repeating the question. Even Gates' attorney began to show exasperation at Boies' persistence.

Q. You said you didn't know of any effect. And I just wanted to be sure that your answer was meant to apply to the full breadth of my question.
A. The full breadth of your question?

Q. Yes, sir. And if that's confusing to you, as I say, I will put the question as many times as I need to to be sure that I get it clear to you. My question – unfortunately, I'm going to have to quote it again.
[Gates' attorney] There's no need. There's really no need.

Despite Gates' attorney's protest, Boies repeated the question again until he got the answer he needed.

2.31 SUMMARIZING IMPORTANT TESTIMONY

When taking a deposition, have the mindset that your case will go to trial even though the probability is that it will settle. You need to be ready just in case. For example, you will notice that witnesses often give rambling answers—expert witnesses do this on purpose—that bury a helpful admission in a complicated answer that would be useless at trial. For example, if you try to impeach that witness at trial, the impeachment may not be very precise, given that the admission is mixed up with the rest of the answer. If this is the case, simply clarify the helpful admission.

Example: Summarize Helpful Testimony

Q1. On May 20th, did you ever have a meeting with Mark Johnson?
A.   Well, that was a really busy day. I got to my office early that morning. I took a cab to the airport and then flew to Chicago. Once I landed, I went straight to the hotel. I did some work on the upcoming sales meeting in my room. I remember getting a fax delivered to the room, had some lunch, and had a meeting.

Q2. So, is it fair to say you met with Mark Johnson on May 20th? [Attorney tries to clarify helpful answer]
A.   Yes.

The problem with the first response is that the witness does not answer the question until the very end, and, even then, it is unclear if the meeting was with Mark Johnson. If you were at trial and the witness testified that he did not meet with Mark Johnson on May 20th and you had not asked Q2, your impeachment would probably be unsuccessful, since it is not clear that the meeting was with Mark Johnson.

By summarizing the answer in the second question, you have highlighted the contrast for an impeachment at trial. Now, if the witness testifies untruthfully, all you have to read is the second question and the second answer.

2.32 STYLE OF QUESTIONING

Use whatever style you use in everyday life. It is that simple: be yourself. Unfortunately, this advice is rarely given. Some professors will teach that you should be a chameleon who can change colors whenever necessary to succeed. For example, you should be aggressive or kind, deferential or controlling, dumb or smart, down to earth or arrogant, or any number of other things in order to succeed.

> Being aggressive is the most unsuccessful style of questioning.

But you can't be something that you are not. However, with a little awareness, you can recognize what you do when you have your best conversations in daily life. These common qualities include: being respectful, listening, making eye contact, not talking too much, and showing sincere interest in what the other person is saying.

2.33 OBJECTING TO A NON-RESPONSIVE ANSWER

As discussed in Chapter One, objections to a non-responsive answer are waived if the objection is not made at the deposition (Rule 32(d)(3)(B)(i)). If you ask a question and get an answer that gives more information than the question asks for and you don't like the additional information (i.e. it is self-serving for the witness), you need to state, "Objection, non-responsive."

Below is an example from *Jones v. Clinton* where Paula Jones sued Clinton for sexual harassment.[5]

Example: Objecting to Non-responsive Answer

Q. Did you [Clinton] ever have sexual relations with Jane Doe 2?
A. No.

Q. At any location?
A. No.

---

[5] For a summary of the Jones lawsuit and the Clinton impeachment proceedings, go to the Appendix.

Q. What were her qualifications to serve as a Judge in the Court of Appeals?
A. She was an intelligent, hard-working person who was a good friend and supporter of mine. And I thought she would make a good judge. The evidence is that she did, I think.
[Fisher] Objection, non responsive beginning with the words, "The evidence is."

The importance of the "non-responsive" objection is clear when we examine how this excerpt would play out at trial had the objection not been made. If Fisher had failed to make the objection, the jury would have heard that Clinton not only appointed her because of her qualifications, but that the appointment was justified by "evidence" after the appointment that she was a qualified judge.

2.34 ENDING THE DEPOSITION

When you finish asking your questions, simply say, "Pass the witness." That phrase is used because it is the same one used at trial to signal that your examination is over. But you can say anything as long as you indicate that you are finished so that opposing counsel can begin if he wants. Although the words are not significant, the action is. Be sure that you don't have any more questions to ask because you only have one shot. You will not be able to depose this witness a second time unless you get permission from the court. Rule 30(a)(2)(A)(ii). Such a request will not be considered unless you can show a need based on newly discovered information.

Practice Tip

Take a break just before the end of the deposition to review your outline and documents to make sure you have asked all the important questions. You will not get a second chance once the deposition is over.

2.35 CHALLENGING SITUATIONS AT A DEPOSITION

Below are some common situations that arise during a deposition with tips on how to deal with them. More challenging problems that arise with unprofessional attorneys and very difficult witnesses are discussed in detail in Chapter Six.

1. Witness Misspeaks

Sometimes the witness makes a bad word choice and mistakenly gives you the answer that you want, but you know that it is a mistake based on the witness' other statements. In the example below, the defense attorney was taking the deposition of the plaintiff, who was an eighty-year-old father whose son had died at age fifty from an alleged fatal overdose of prescription drugs. The father claimed that doctors prescribed drugs that slowly killed his son over time.

In contrast, the doctors argued that the drugs were perfectly safe and that the plaintiff died from an acute overdose by taking too many pills at once. The medical examiner's report was inconclusive regarding the cause of death. A central issue to plaintiff's claim, then, was any proof that plaintiff was progressively deteriorating over a long period of time, as opposed to the defendant's theory that the plaintiff was healthy until the day he died when he took too much medication.

Example: Witness Misspeaks

At the father's deposition, the defense attorney asked the key question very early on:

Q. *How was your son on Christmas.[shortly after doctors prescribed his medication]?*
A. Oh, he was—he was himself. He was himself, you know, but—and he stayed that way. He—you know, he stayed that way up until the 4th day in May[the day before he died].

This answer was very harmful to the plaintiff because it undercut his theory that the drugs had slowly caused his son's death. When getting such a helpful answer for your side, should you just end your questioning and "pass the witness"? You should decide whether the witness has really just misspoken or whether he firmly believes what he has just said. Take into account the witness' demeanor and whether he has made other statements inconsistent with the "mistake."

In this case, the father had written a letter a year after his son's death which gave some detail about his slow deteriorating condition in the months prior to his death. Thus, the witness either misspoke or lied in the letter.

If the witness seems firm in his belief, then you should ask as many questions as you want in this area, since the witness is not going to correct what you thought was his mistake. However, if the witness actually misspoke, as is likely in this case, do not ask any more questions on this topic but ask other important questions on other topics. If you stop abruptly, you may signal to opposing counsel that the witness has misspoken. For instance, he may have been asleep at the switch when you asked your question and would not realize the need to ask follow-up questions unless you suddenly stopped asking questions.

You really have nothing to lose by moving onto another topic. At the end, if opposing counsel asks questions to correct the witness' mistake, you can ask follow-up questions. If opposing counsel does not ask questions, you will have a sworn admission that is consistent with your theory of the case that "he was himself" until the day before he died.

In this situation where the witness misspoke, if you had asked follow-up questions, the answers would have been devastating:

Q. *Why do you think the doctors caused your son's death?*
A. Well, when he came home from the hospital in December, he was fine, but he slowly got worse and worse. Just a few days before he died he was shaking all over and was extremely tired.

In the same lawsuit, the deceased's daughter (thirty years old) had a claim for mental anguish for the loss of her father. Her deposition presented the same situation for the attorney. One issue very helpful for the defense was the family's disinterest in helping the deceased take his medication (the decedent was extremely bipolar). The family accused the doctors of giving the wrong doses, but the doctors had a valid defense: they prescribed the right doses, but the patient did not follow their instructions and did not get the necessary support from his family.

At the daughter's deposition, the defense attorney got a significant admission when she admitted that she did not talk to her father about his mental illness. Furthermore, she gave these answers.

Example: Attorney Mistakenly Asks Follow-up Question After Good Answer

Q. *Had you ever talked to your father about his problem with taking medications or remembering to take them?*
A. No.

Q. *So is it fair to say you have no idea whether or not he was taking his medication correctly?*
A. Yes.

However, the attorney pressed the issue too much and asked unnecessary follow-up questions which undercut his success:

Q. *Then I guess my question is in those times throughout the years when he was paranoid and having problems when you were an adult, **why wouldn't you ask him if he needed to see a doctor or needed to take more of his medication or less of it?***
A. I mean—I mean, of course—I mean, you're going to ask that. I mean, I don't think I ever said I didn't ask—you know, I didn't ask at all. I never said that. **Of course you're going to ask.**

By asking the question again in such a direct way ("why wouldn't you ask him"), the attorney highlights for the witness the previous bad answer and gives the witness the opportunity to correct it.

In this next example, the plaintiff alleged in his Complaint that there were violations of the Privacy Act due to the unauthorized disclosure of his confidential medical information. Plaintiff alleged that he had been treated with disdain by his co-workers and colleagues and was the subject of ridicule and humiliation by his managers.

At the plaintiff's deposition, the following exchange occurred.

Example: Getting Admission From Witness

Q. Do you believe the defendant has disclosed information about your disability to the wrong people or co-workers?
A. No.

Here, the defense attorney has obtained the admission he needs from the witness to prevail on summary judgment: namely, plaintiff admits that there was no privacy act violation. However, some attorneys who believe that every line of questioning needs to be followed to its logical end might end up with the following exchange.

Q. You are not still asserting your claim as stated in your Complaint that the defendant subjected you to ridicule or disdain because of violations of your privacy?
A. Oh . . No. Yes, I couldn't advance at my job because co-workers learned of my disability and made fun of me.

Q. I thought you just said that you had no knowledge of the defendant disclosing information about your disability
A. Well, what I meant was . . . .

Unlike the situation above, there will be times when the witness is not misspeaking but exaggerating or lying. In those situations, ask several questions so that the witness is firmly locked into the lie.

In this next example, the plaintiff claims he was discriminated at work. You have evidence that he has filed similar complaints in the past. When the witness lies and says that this is the only time he has complained, have him explain in detail why. Then, when you impeach him at trial with inconsistent evidence of prior complaints, his lie will be more egregious.

Example: Lawyer Has Witness Give Details Regarding Lie

Q. So, you have never made discrimination complaints against other supervisors at your current job?
A. No.

Q. Never made them against supervisors at other jobs?
A. No.

Q. Why was this situation the first time you had ever made a complaint?
A. Well, because . . . .

Practice Tip

If the witness misspeaks and gives you a helpful admission, don't follow up with more questions. But if the witness lies or exaggerates, follow up.

---

2. Requests for Documents Used By Witness to Prepare

Almost every deposition has this question: "What documents did you review in preparation for this deposition?" The witness answers with a list of documents, and then the deposing attorney asks the defending attorney to produce the documents.

Federal Rule of Evidence 612 governs this situation. It states that when a witness uses a writing to refresh her memory, "an adverse party is entitled to have the writing produced at the hearing, to inspect it, to cross-examine the witness thereon, and to introduce in evidence those portions which relate to the testimony of the witness."

Depending on the jurisdiction, the defending attorney might be able to object on the ground that if the witness reviewed documents selected by the attorney, the list of documents reviewed is protected by the work product privilege. That is, if the witness were to reveal the documents reviewed, it would reveal which documents the attorney thought were important.

However, many federal district courts have ruled that Fed. R. Evid. 612 trumps the work product privilege. The same analysis applies if the witness were to have reviewed a document protected by the attorney-client privilege. For example, let's assume the witness reviews a summary of the case's strengths and weaknesses prepared by her attorney. Although that document is clearly protected by the attorney-client privilege, many courts have held that if the witness used the document to refresh her memory, the document must be turned over.

There are two lessons here. For the defending attorney, when you are preparing your witness, assume that anything you show her is discoverable. So, only show the witness documents that have already been produced or that you don't mind producing if the above situation occurs.

Second, if you are the deposing attorney, ask the witness what documents she has reviewed and if she has them at the deposition for you to review. If the defending attorney objects, you could stop the deposition and call the judge to get a ruling or file a motion to compel after the deposition. However, a more practical solution would be to simply move on and when you get to the important areas in your deposition, ask the witness, "What documents did you review to refresh your memory about this topic?" Such a question does not suggest that you are asking how the witness' attorney helped prepare her for the deposition. Of course, if the witness were to answer, "some documents my attorney gave me to review," and opposing counsel objected to disclosure, you would be stuck with deciding whether to seek relief from the court. What you decide should be based on weighing the inconvenience and delay of seeking a court ruling against the documents' value.

Example: (Gates Deposition)

Q1. *I assume you've reviewed written materials in connection with your preparation for the deposition today; is that correct?*

A.   I was shown some written documents.

Q2. *Did you review documents that were prepared especially to prepare you for this deposition as opposed to documents that were generated in the normal course of Microsoft's business?*

A.   No.

The question that needed to be asked was whether Gates' *attorney* had shown him particular documents in preparation for the deposition that refreshed his memory. If Gates' had said yes, then, the attorney taking the deposition would have had to make a decision based on the discussion above as to whether to file a motion compelling production of the documents after the deposition.

3. Request for Production of Documents during a Deposition

Oftentimes the deposing attorney will ask the witness at a deposition to produce documents at a later date.

Q. *You just mentioned that you considered the draft employee evaluation from two years ago in arriving at your decision to fire the plaintiff. Would you mind providing me a copy of that evaluation when you get back to your office?*

A. Yes, I think I can find it.

The courts are split as to whether the attorney above can compel the witness to produce the document. But remember that what goes around comes around. If you make such a request, opposing counsel may likely do the same during your client's deposition. If you are defending a deposition, there is no need to object if you believe that the attorney would be able to get the documents through a subsequent request for production of documents or a subpoena.

When taking the deposition, the best practice is to follow up with the attorney at the close of the deposition and then confirm the understanding in a short letter. If the document is not produced or you feel the opposing counsel is dragging his feet, then it is easy enough to prepare a short request for production of documents.

4. Opposing Counsel Instructs Witness Not to Answer

Opposing counsel will often instruct his witness not to answer a question for a variety of reasons, some legitimate and some not. Let's look at an example from the Simpson deposition. In the following example, Petrocelli was asking Simpson about some self-serving statements he made in an interview on a video about what happened on the night of the murders. The video was sold to the public for $29.95.

Example: (Simpson Deposition)

Q. When you gave an interview to Ross Becker recently, you were not under oath, correct?
A. Correct.

Q. Did you tell the truth?
A. Best that I knew it, yes.

Q. Would you have said anything differently if you were under oath?
[Baker, Simpson's attorney] It's argumentative. Don't answer that question.
[Petrocelli to Baker] Are you instructing him [not to answer the question]?
[Baker] Yes.
[Petrocelli] Can we have a stipulation that if you instruct him not to answer, he will abide by your instructions?
[Baker] Yes.

When an attorney instructs his witness not to answer a question, you cannot get a court to force a witness to answer unless the witness has told you that he will follow his attorney's advice. Therefore, you must ask the witness, "Are you going to follow your attorney's instruction not to answer the question?" If the witness says, "yes," then you have met the conditions needed to bring a motion before a court seeking an order to compel the witness to answer.

However, Petrocelli's stipulation is very helpful. By getting the stipulation from Baker that his client will be presumed to have followed his instruction not to answer, Petrocelli does not have to spend time asking Simpson the follow-up question whenever Baker instructs Simpson not to answer. This strategy helps save time and also protects Petrocelli in case he were to forget to ask the follow-up question and later wanted to file a motion with the court to compel an answer.

Many more problems are discussed in Chapter Six, but, for now, let's turn our attention to witness preparation in the next chapter.

☲CHECKLIST

Pros of Deposition

1. Assess witness' credibility.
2. Create inconsistent statements for trial.
3. Discover important details.
4. Gather helpful admissions.
5. Learn bad facts about your case.
6. Narrow issues for trial.
7. Obtain settlement leverage if your witness is good or opponent is bad.
8. Preserve testimony.

Cons of Deposition

1. Increases expenses.
2. Reminds opponent to take depositions of your witnesses.
3. Forces opponent to prepare for trial sooner.
4. Reveals your trial strategy.
5. Causes witness to be more comfortable on cross at trial.

Order

1. It's usually better to start with most important witness to catch him off guard.
2. Start with low-level witnesses if you are unsure of the important facts in your case, and you need to gather information.

Video, Oral or Written Questions

1. Video is always better if you can afford it.
2. Deposition by written question is inexpensive way to authenticate business records for trial.

Getting Ready to Take Deposition

1. Review client's documents.
2. Send interrogatories to opponent.
3. Request documents from opponent.
4. Interview main witnesses.
5. Know legal elements of claims and defenses.
6. Uncover theory of case for both sides.
7. Determine themes of case for both sides.
8. Be skeptical of client's story.
9. Prepare outline.

Contents of Deposition Outline

1. Goal is to find out how witness can hurt you (bad facts) and how you can undercut testimony if necessary (good facts).
2. In addition to learning bad facts, adverse witness can be questioned on at least one of five areas (CLIPS):
    —credibility
    —lack of information
    —implausible statements
    —prior inconsistent statements
    —support of your case
3. Ask questions that will support your case before you ask antagonistic questions.
4. Focus on no more than three or four topics.
5. Put legal elements of claims and defenses in outline for easy review.

Sample Outline

I.   Witness notification about oath
II.   Confirmation of witness' competency to give testimony
III. Elements of cause of action and defenses (for your reference only)
IV.   Discover bad facts about your case
V.   Helpful admissions (the "S" of CLIPS)
VI.   Other areas of CLIPS
VII. Miscellaneous questions regarding background

Taking the Deposition

1. Don't waste time on background questions.
2. A good beginning simply confirms that witness understands oath.
3. A short organized deposition is best.
4. Be confident, calm, and show respect.
5. Build rapport with witness.
6. Listening is most important skill.
       —show empathy toward witness to encourage witness to talk
       —determine if witness is believable by critical listening
7. Primarily use questions with who, what, when, why, where and how.
8. Use inverted pyramid to start with broad questions and then more specific ones.
9. Choose topics carefully since time is valuable.
10. Use focused (closed) questions to pin witness down when necessary.
11. Pause after witness answers to see if he will volunteer.

12. Repeat question if witness avoids answering it.

13. Ask most important question immediately after break.

Most Common Mistakes New Attorneys Make

1. Lecturing witness about rules of deposition instead of building rapport.

2. Spending too much time on background questions.

3. Looking at notes to formulate next question instead of making eye contact with witness and listening to answer.

4. Moving on to next question instead of realizing that witness has not answered pending question.

5. Exploring ten topics when only three are necessary.

6. Letting objections interrupt flow of questions.

Challenging Situations

1. If witness misspeaks and the statement is to your advantage, don't follow up since you will alert the witness and her attorney to the mistake.

2. If witness exaggerates, get details to highlight the exaggeration.

3. If witness reviews documents prior to deposition that refresh her memory, many courts will require her to produce them to the examining attorney.

4. If a witness refers to a document during an answer that the examining attorney has not seen, the attorney often will ask the witness to produce the document to him at a later date. Even if the witness says "yes," the courts are split as to whether this agreement is binding.

5. If opposing counsel instructs his witness not to answer a question, confirm with the witness that she is going to follow her attorney's advice.

Notes

CHAPTER THREE

Preparing Your Witness

The fight is won or lost far away from witnesses. It's won behind the lines, in the gym, and out there on the road, long before I dance under the lights.

—Muhammad Ali

Many clients think that a lawyer can save them from mistakes during a deposition or that the mistakes can be corrected later. Such conventional wisdom could not be more wrong. First, there is little a lawyer can do during a deposition to prevent a bad answer. Second, while it is true that the witness can make changes to the transcript after the deposition, any substantive changes can be used against the witness with devastating effect at trial. For example, at trial, opposing counsel could accuse the witness, "You changed your sworn deposition only after you consulted with your lawyer and realized that what you said the first time would really hurt your case."

In short, for all intents and purposes, deposition testimony *is* trial testimony. A bad deposition can't be fixed and can ruin a case. Indeed, Ali's quote about boxing is quite true for depositions. Primarily, the deposition is won or lost depending on how well you prepare your witness. Nothing can be done to win the deposition once it starts.

Unfortunately, the typical lawyer meets with his witness for thirty minutes or less prior to the deposition. The lawyer quickly explains how a deposition works and then goes over a few key questions and answers. Such practice is totally unacceptable and unprofessional. The reason is that cases are settled by the perceptual value of the deposition. To illustrate, if the plaintiff gives a bad deposition, the lawsuit's value drops dramatically.

Is that the plaintiff's fault, or yours? Did you prepare him well for the deposition? Attorneys too often take the easy way out and will explain that the plaintiff just "came across badly" while not admitting that, with better preparation, the plaintiff would have been more believable.

For a short deposition, a good rule of thumb is that you should spend *at least* one hour in a meeting with the witness where facts are discussed and another hour in a meeting preparing for deposition. You will need to spend more time with expert witnesses discussing the facts and their opinions. If you expect the deposition to last more than two hours, you should spend even more time. The truth is that you need to spend as long as it takes to get your witness ready.

Conventional wisdom also states that if you explain to your witness all the do's and don'ts learned from mistakes of previous witnesses, then your witness won't repeat them. One book published by the American Bar Association put this conventional wisdom into a list of rules for a witness to follow. It instructs that it is a list that "no lawyer should forget to bring to the woodshed the next time she is preparing a client."[1]

The list is known as "130 Rules for Every Deponent." The problem is most witnesses could not remember ten rules, much less 130.

A closer look at the 130 rules shows just how absurd the conventional wisdom is. Not only is the number of rules preposterous, but many are so contradictory that a witness would be hopelessly confused even if she were able to remember them. The confusion starts early in the list:

RULE 2: Listen to the question. Pause. Think as long as necessary before answering.

RULE 3: Don't pause too long before answering.

Witnesses who are told to pause before answering often will pause before answering even the simplest question. Such pauses convey the impression that the witness has something to hide because she is having to pause and think of an answer that is different from the truthful one that would have come naturally without a pause.

RULE 11: Answer 'yes' or 'no' if appropriate.

Rule 12: Don't answer 'yes' or 'no' to a yes-or-no question if the question cannot be answered accurately with yes or no.[2]

How is a witness supposed to know when to apply rule 11 instead of rule 12? There are many more examples:

RULE 21: Be positive, assertive, confident, certain, strong, and precise.

RULE 22: Or be quiet.

RULE 28: Don't volunteer.

RULE 29: Where appropriate, volunteer.

RULE 82: Be yourself.

---

[1] Priscilla Schwab and Lawrence Vilardo editors, *Depositions* 65 (ABA 2006).
[2] Id. at 66.

It is hard to be yourself if you are trying to follow over a hundred rules.

RULE 110: Bring what you need: checklists, key documents, notes.

RULE 111: Bring only what I tell you to bring.

RULE 124: Relax, but keep that edge.

RULE 125: Don't relax. Stay wary and vigilant.

And after being given 127 rules to follow, you are given this one:

RULE 128: Break the rules if you have a good reason.[3]

So many rules cause a witness to believe that she can't be herself but must act and answer in a way that is different from what comes naturally. She becomes so afraid of answering a question incorrectly that she won't answer the simplest questions for fear she is admitting something that will hurt the case.

In the following example, Boies questions Gates about an e-mail that Gates sent to Gary Stimac, an employee at Microsoft who was considering taking a job at IBM.[4] He qualifies his answers, is evasive, and does not answer simple questions. Perhaps Gates was inundated with rules to follow during witness prep, and he was trying to sort through all the rules before answering the questions.

Example: Witness Does Not Answer Simple Questions (Gates Deposition)

[Boies shows Gates an e-mail he wrote to Stimac]

Q. *This relates to a conversation you had with Gary Stimac, is that correct?*

A. Not strictly. [There is no need for Gates to qualify his answer here; he should just answer the question.]

Q. *Does it relate in part to that?*

A. Yes.

Q. *And did Mr. Stimac tell you [in the e-mail] that he was thinking about taking a job with IBM?*

A. I think he did.

Q. *And did he tell you that one of his concerns was whether IBM's relationship with Microsoft would be a problem?*

A. I see that in the e-mail. I don't remember it specifically. [There is no need for Gates to qualify his answer by saying that he doesn't remember. The question is asking what Gates said in the e-mail]

Q. *Do you remember people at IBM being concerned about IBM's relationship with Microsoft being a problem?*

A. No.

Q. *Do you remember Mr. Stimac telling you [in the e-mail] that he was concerned about*

---

[3] Id. at 66-72.
[4] A summary of the trial can be found in the Appendix.

whether IBM's relationship with Microsoft would be a problem either here or—or at any other time?

A. No, I don't remember that.

Q. In response to that you say that you told him that "the Java religion coming out of the software group is a big problem." Do you see that?

A. Uh-huh.

Q. Did you tell Mr. Stimac that [in the e-mail]?

A. I don't remember telling him that. **[Again, Gates does not answer the question. Boies is asking Gates about the e-mail, not what Gates may have told Stimac in addition to the e-mail. If Boies had felt it was important to nail Gates down on this issue, he could have followed up. However, Boies wanted to get to the heart of the questioning which follows.]**

Q. Now, when you talk about the Java religion coming out of the software group, you were talking about IBM's software group, correct, sir?

A. I'm not sure.

Q. Well, this sentence immediately follows Mr. Stimac purporting to be concerned about whether IBM's relationship with Microsoft would be a problem and immediately precedes a sentence in which you say you told him that IBM refused to buy anything related to Backoffice.

A. Yeah. That doesn't relate to the IBM software group.

Q. But it relates to IBM, correct, sir?

A. Yes.

Q. This whole paragraph relates to IBM; correct, sir?

A. Primarily. **[Again, there is no need to qualify the answer.]**

Q. So when you say that you told Mr. Stimac that the Java religion coming out of the software group is a big problem, do you really have any doubt that you were talking about IBM's software group?

A. Well, there was a lot of joint work between IBM's people and Sun's people and other companies, and so it's very hard to draw a line between the IBM software groups and other people's software groups. **[This is another disingenuous answer.]**

Q. Does that mean that it is your testimony here under oath that when you refer to the software group in this sentence, you don't know whether you were talking about the IBM software group?

A. I'm certainly talking about software groups that IBM is at least a part of. **[Gates finally answers the question but can't help himself and still qualifies his answer.]**

Throughout his deposition, Gates hedged any answer he could. While he thought he was being clever, others saw that he could not answer a simple question. When a witness can't answer a simple question, a jury will always believe he has something to hide even if he doesn't.

3.1 THE WITNESS INTERVIEW

Conduct a witness interview and the deposition preparation at separate meetings. Otherwise, the goals of the two meetings can become confusing for the witness. Ideally, the witness interview will occur long before there is any hint of a deposition. That way, the witness won't be distracted by the upcoming deposition. At the witness interview, your main goal is to learn what the witness knows and does not know. It is okay to admit to the witness that you are just learning about the case and need his help. This often causes the witness to be more helpful to you.

> Bring to the meeting any relevant document that has the witness' name on it or mentions him so it can be reviewed.

Does the witness need to meet or talk with other witnesses to help him remember what happened? Often this is useful. If the meeting will help uncover the truth, it is a good idea. If it will result in witnesses coming up with the same "story," you have obviously made a huge mistake. If the witnesses meet together, you must be very vigilant to prevent a uniform story that is not true. Demand that they tell the truth. Also, reassure them that differences in opinions and memories are normal.

Also, unless you are present and all the witnesses are your clients, the discussions are discoverable. To illustrate, at a deposition, the witness could be asked: 1) whom did you talk to about this deposition and 2) what did you and the other witness talk about.

A second goal is to calculate how believable the witness' story is. It is also a chance for the witness to become comfortable with your litigation style and competence.

3.2 THE DEPOSITION PREP MEETING

Here, the goal is for the attorney to teach the witness how to tell the truth in a confident manner and to protect the witness from opposing counsel's tactics that would undermine that goal.

First, relieve your witness' anxiety. Before you launch into your questions, ask if he has any. He probably will have a couple from this list: how long will it take, can they ask me anything, what do they want from me, what if I make a mistake, what is your role, and do you have a strategy?

By the deposition prep meeting, you should know the case inside and out. Success in a deposition is a simple matter of putting in the time to prepare. You must know the *entire case* inside and out. The witness must know the *key parts* of his testimony inside and out. Project confidence. Relieve the witness'

> Preparation is the key. Lincoln said: "If I were given the task of chopping down a tree and was told it would be an eight-hour job, I'd be sure to spend the first six hours sharpening my axe.

fears by telling him that he is a small piece of a large puzzle. Even if the witness is one of a few key players, you can relieve his anxiety by making him feel that the whole case does not rest on his shoulders. Usually, there is at least some other evidence to support your case in the form of witnesses or documents.

The worst thing an attorney can do is lecture the witness about the do's and don'ts of a deposition (see discussion above). Instead, use your trial guide to help you focus on what is most important. Chapter Two explains the trial guide in detail, but it is reprinted here for your convenience. Remember, don't show the witness any document—particularly the trial guide—that you are not afraid for the witness to turn over if asked at the deposition what documents he relied on to prepare for the deposition.

TRIAL GUIDE	
A. Your Theme	A. Opponent's Theme
B. Your Theory	B. Opponent's Theory

C. Most Important Facts
  1.
  2.
  3.
  4.
  5.
*Reference the source of each fact (i.e. does it come from a witness or a document)
	C. Most Important Facts
	  1.
	  2.
	  3.
	  4.
	  5.

D. Most Important Exhibits	D. Most Important Exhibits
E. Legal Elements of Claims/Defenses	E. Legal Elements of Claims/Defenses

Even if you had a short and correct list of the mistakes to avoid, a lecture is not the proper format. Instead, make sure the witness is involved in the discussion with you. To do this, pepper your conversation—not lecture—with questions to make sure the witness is engaged. For example, you might ask the witness not only if he understands what you just said, but ask him if he has any questions.

Since the witness is probably just trying to get through this meeting as quickly as possible, he likely won't have many questions for you other than how a deposition works. But he is more likely to engage you the more opportunities you give him. Also, ask if there are questions he is concerned about being asked.

A response by the witness would provide a great launching pad into further discussion about what to expect at the deposition and how to meet it.

To make the witness comfortable, nothing is more important than to have the witness practice answering the tough questions. You can only do this if you have studied your case and made a concerted effort to see the case through the eyes of opposing counsel. For example, determine the weaknesses in your case and the line of questioning your witness can expect. You can provide your witness even better information if you have seen opposing counsel's strategy from previous depositions.

In addition, determine the important documents in the case. Don't let the witness see them for the first time during a deposition when he is nervous. Review them ahead of time, and you will go a long way toward relieving the witness' anxiety. But realize that anything you show is probably discoverable by opposing counsel (see discussion below on privilege). One trick is to show your witness many documents and then just focus on a few. That way, when opposing counsel asks what documents were reviewed, the witness can truthfully refer to a large stack of documents. Even if opposing counsel discovers the documents, it is no big deal, since he probably already knew about them, and the reward of getting your witness prepared is worth the risk of disclosure to the other side.

Furthermore, tell your witness not to create any notes between now and the deposition. Although the witness might be tempted to compose an outline to help his memory, such a document becomes discoverable.

Another trick to help your witness relax is to describe opposing counsel's personality. Is he soft spoken, belligerent, unprepared, aggressive, straightforward, deceptive, vague, organized, or does he jump around from topic to topic? Whatever the case may be, your witness will be more at ease if you can analyze opposing counsel's strategy—or lack thereof—and instruct your witness how to react.

You may have heard the saying about someone who talks too much. If you were to ask him what time it is, he would tell you how the watch was made. Volunteering information is one of the worst things a witness can do. Opposing counsel's goal is to get as much information as possible. The more information your witness gives to the attorney, the more likely the witness is going to reveal important information that the attorney did not know to ask about. Witnesses are under the mistaken belief that if they volunteer facts, the deposition will end sooner. But just the opposite happens. Armed with additional

> We are masters of the unsaid words, but slaves of those we let slip out.
> —Winston Churchill

information, opposing counsel will simply ask more questions.

For example, if the attorney asks, "Where do you live?", answer, "Chicago." There is no need to volunteer that you live near downtown in a two bedroom apartment in a high-rise and the address is _____. For more complicated questions, tell your witness that if he speaks more than a couple of sentences he is probably talking too much.

Moreover, teach the witness through examples specific to your case that he can comfortably respond, "I don't understand the question," "I don't remember," and "I don't know." Most witnesses are fearful that they are supposed to be able to recall events that occurred months or years before. They will be very relieved when you assure them that such a feat is usually impossible and not expected of them. Also, tell the witness that if he gets too uncomfortable, he must answer the question but it is then up to him— not you—to ask for a break.

The most important rule you can teach your witness is: "Tell the truth. You know what you know. You don't know what you don't know. Don't guess!" Instructing your witness to "tell the truth" is not only the legally and morally right thing to do, it is also the best thing for your case. The sooner you learn about a problem, the easier it is to fix. Besides, if the other side proves before a jury that your client has lied, your case will be severely damaged—much more so than if your client had revealed to you the truth that she thought would hurt her case.

Teaching your witness not to guess is critical. If your witness guesses and is wrong, that wrong guess has now become a lie. To illustrate, suppose your client is at a meeting and the question is whether Robert discussed "X." (he didn't). If your client guesses "yes," it was discussed when he is not certain, then opposing counsel will be able to assert your client is lying when Robert and a document showing the minutes of the meeting reveal that there was no such discussion. If opposing counsel can suggest that your witness has lied, your case will be weakened considerably.

Since these instructions are so important, mention them at the beginning and end of your meeting because that is when people pay most attention.

In addition, alert your witness to questions that contain superlatives such as "always" and "never." Superlatives are used by lawyers to box a witness into a corner. Your witness needs to be very careful before answering such questions.

Finally, opposing counsel will often ask the witness if he has met with his attorney prior to the deposition. Some witnesses freeze because the question is phrased in a somewhat accusatory fashion and so they will lie and say, "no." Remind your witness that it is perfectly fine that you have met with him. Also, instruct him not to talk to others about the deposition, as that may draw more people into the lawsuit should the witness be asked if he spoke with people other than his attorney.

Remember

The most important rule you can teach your witness is: "Tell the truth. You know what you know. You don't know what you don't know. Don't guess!"

3.3 COACHING

"The adversary system benefits by allowing lawyers to prepare witnesses so that they can deliver their testimony efficiently, persuasively, comfortably, and in conformity with the rules of evidence."[5] But, the lawyer's duty "is to extract the facts from the witness, not to pour them into him; to learn what the witness does know, not to teach him what he ought to know."[6] Indeed, the District of Columbia Bar issued an ethics opinion concerning the preparation of witnesses for trial. It concluded that "a lawyer's suggesting actual language to be used by a witness may be appropriate, as long as the ultimate testimony remains truthful and is not misleading."[7]

In short, if the substance of the witness' testimony comes from the witness' version of events instead of from you, you have not improperly coached the witness. Let your conscience be your guide when deciding how much advice you want to give your witness. Also, when there are moments when the witness is questioning how to phrase something or becomes frustrated, you can assist him in coming up with a phrase he is comfortable with but also remind him simply to "tell the truth." Obviously, don't cross the line and say, "You've got to say _____ or we can't win."

Practice Tip

To make sure you don't improperly coach the witness, imagine that the witness is secretly recording your advice. Don't say anything you would not be proud of if one day it were made public.

---

[5] Richard C. Wydick, *The Ethics of Witness Coaching*, 17 Cardoza L. Rev. 1 (Sept. 1995).
[6] *In re Eldridge*, 37 N.Y. 161, 171 (N.Y. 1880).
[7] District of Columbia Bar, Legal Ethics Comm., Op. No. 79 (1979).

For a very interesting and detailed discussion of those times attorneys cross the line into prohibited conduct, read *The Ethics of Witness Coaching*.[8] That article provides multiple examples and research to analyze how and why attorneys improperly coach witnesses. For the purposes of this book, all you need to know is the obvious: never sacrifice your integrity to win a case. In addition, being honest actually helps you win, not lose. Nothing will destroy your case sooner than a witness who shades the truth. Nine times out of ten, the truth will eventually come out, and your witness' credibility—not to mention your own credibility even if you are an unwitting participant—will be destroyed.

3.4 NON-RESPONSIVE OBJECTIONS

Prepare your witness for the primary objection the examining counsel will make: objection, non-responsive. The attorney will make this objection when he thinks the witness has not answered the question he has asked. One possibility is that your witness is dodging the question. If opposing counsel keeps asking the question, you might want to jump in and simply tell your witness to answer the question. It depends on the situation.

But it is often the case that your witness has answered the question well and opposing counsel simply doesn't like the explanation given. So, to get the answer he wants, opposing counsel will say, "objection, non-responsive" and ask the question again hoping to get a different answer. Teach your witness to stick to his guns and not change his answer just because there is an objection.

3.5 PRIVILEGE

A critical step in preparation is having your client review documents that will refresh her memory about the case. But be careful not to show the witness privileged documents, and be aware that the other side may very well be entitled to review any documents your witness reviews in preparation.

The reason for this caution is the interplay between Rule 30(c) and Federal Rule of Evidence 612. Rule 30(c) states that the examination at a deposition is like that at trial, while Evidence Rule 612 states that a court—in the interests of justice—may require a witness to produce documents used to refresh her recollection prior to testifying or when testifying. While there is a wide range of judicial opinions, the safe way to proceed is to assume that anything you show your witness in preparation for the deposition is discoverable.

---

[8] Richard C. Wydick, *The Ethics of Witness Coaching*, 17 Cardoza L. Rev. 1 (Sept. 1995).

3.6 ENLIST THE HELP OF A TRIAL CONSULTANT

Witness performance can have a lasting impact on the case. Dan Petrocelli, the plaintiffs' attorney in the civil wrongful death case against O.J. Simpson had this to say about the defendant: "Simpson did not live up to his billing as a charming, seductive communicator. He didn't look good as a witness. He slumped in his chair, stared vacantly, delivered answers robotically, and showed no energy, no punch. He did not take this deposition as an opportunity to sell his innocence."[9] Likewise, Bill Gates did little to help his case by the way he arrogantly refused to answer simple questions and appeared evasive.

The truth is that lawyers are sometimes not the best qualified people to prepare a witness. Not surprisingly, many great trial lawyers have a trial consultant to help them for all aspects of a trial, including preparing witnesses for depositions. A trial consultant can be critically important in getting key witnesses ready for deposition and trial. Gates and Simpson could have certainly benefitted from an effective trial consultant.

While lawyers are very effective in preparing a witness by focusing on the substance of the testimony, attention also needs to be paid to having a witness actually convey information in a clear and persuasive manner. There is an enormous difference between *telling* a witness that she needs to give "more concise" answers vs. *teaching* her how to give concise answers. Some attorneys struggle to assess and teach communication skills adequately. On the other hand, trial consultants have formal training in psychology and communication science which can greatly assist in this area.

There are several reasons that trial consultants are not used in cases. First, some attorneys are very effective at witness preparation. Others are unwilling to admit their weakness in this area. Also, companies have the mindset that they cannot afford a top-level witness to take time away from work for the extra training provided by a trial consultant. In addition, some clients are reluctant to pay a trial consultant's expenses on top of attorney's fees. But making the time for a witness to get properly prepared and paying a trial consultant's fee may be the best decision you make if it prevents a horrible deposition that sinks your case.

Finally, some companies fear that if the practice session is videoed, the video may get leaked even though there are likely safeguards in law (check your jurisdiction) and technology to prevent such an occurrence. In any event, you should at least explore the use of a trial consultant for witness preparation when practical. To give readers a sense of the invaluable insights a

---

[9] Daniel Petrocelli, *Triumph of Justice* 178 (Crown 1998).

trial consultant can provide, Bill Kanasky Jr., Ph.D. from Courtroom Sciences Inc. (**http://www.courtroomsciences.com/**) shares his thoughts below.[10] Dr. Kanasky is one of the nation's top experts on witness communication.

3.7 VOLUNTEERING INFORMATION

The most common and preventable witness blunders include volunteering information, guessing and not listening or thinking effectively. Let's take each in turn.

Volunteering information occurs when the scope of a witness' answer exceeds the scope of a question from opposing counsel. This common mistake occurs for three reasons. First, witnesses who are anxious and unfamiliar with the legal environment tend to fall back on their work and social communication skills to help them "survive" the testimony. At work, home or with friends, it is perceived as friendly, helpful and efficient when someone offers extra information following a direct question. Therefore, novice witnesses inadvertently volunteer excessive information, thinking that it will be helpful, unknowingly causing tremendous potential damage. Second, many witnesses purposely try to anticipate the next question or questions, in an effort to bring the testimony to a close more quickly. These individuals erroneously conclude, "The more I say, the faster this uncomfortable process will be over with." Nothing could be further from the truth, as an opposing counsel will actually question a "chatty Cathy" witness longer than a witness who volunteers less information. Third, witnesses experience an intense, internal urge to explain away answers to simple, direct questions. They feel that if they don't, they are letting down the team and hurting the case. The classic, "Yes, that is true, but here is why" type of answer from a witness is particularly damaging, as the unsolicited explanation fuels opposing counsel's attack.

3.8 GUESSING

Guessing comes in many forms, and witnesses often take educated guesses instead of stating that they "don't know," "don't remember" or "don't have any personal knowledge of that." Why

---

[10] Bill Kanasky Jr., Ph.D. is Director of Litigation Psychology at Courtroom Sciences, Inc. (CSI), one of the top litigation consulting firms in the country with offices in Dallas and Chicago. In addition to his duties at CSI, Dr. Kanasky is a highly sought after speaker on witness communication at major corporate law departments, law firms and national organizations.

do witnesses so often opt to guess rather than admit not knowing something? Two reasons: embarrassment and intimidation. Many witnesses feel embarrassed if they can't provide an answer to what is perceived as an important question, and attorneys are experts at creating this powerful emotional reaction. The standard trick is to say to a witness, "You've been an employee at Company X for 15 years and you can't answer my important question? My client has a right to an answer. Let me repeat my question, and let me remind you that you are under oath." At this very point, 99 percent of witnesses take an educated guess, simply because they feel compelled to correct the perception that they don't know. They end up feeling obligated to provide "something," regardless of its accuracy or relevance.

Intimidation is also a powerful tool. Attorneys can raise their voices, increase the pace of questioning and become sarcastic or aggressive towards witnesses and "bully" them into answers. When this occurs, a witness becomes scared, rattled and very uncomfortable. The witness then provides an educated guess in an effort to give the attorney "something" so that he will back off. Regardless of the cause, guessing is a devastating witness blunder, which leaves an attorney and a client vulnerable. Guesses are rarely accurate, and a savvy attorney can use a witness' guesses against him or her, heavily damaging that witness' credibility and believability.

3.9 NOT LISTENING OR THINKING EFFECTIVELY

In today's high-speed, instant-gratification society, people are now cognitively hard-wired to listen and think simultaneously when communicating with others. In other words, when someone asks a question, the respondent automatically begins to think about his or her response in the middle of the questioner's inquiry, rather than listening to 100 percent of the question, then thinking 100 percent about his or her response. From a neuropsychological standpoint, a respondent is extremely vulnerable to error, as concentration and attention are split between two activities—listening and thinking—instead of dedicated to one cognitive activity. While this pattern is efficient and friendly in the workplace or social settings, it is extremely dangerous in a legal environment.

Listening and thinking simultaneously as a witness results in poor answers because the witness does not hear the question in its entirety. What happens next is that the witness answers: 1) a different question than what was actually asked, which makes the witness appear evasive; 2) a question incorrectly, for example, inadvertently accepting the questioner's language and agreeing with a statement that isn't true; 3) a question that shouldn't be answered in the first place—questions to which an attorney would raise form or foundation objections; or 4) a question beyond the scope of the inquiry, which volunteers information and makes the witness appear defensive.

3.10 COMMON EMOTIONAL MISTAKES WITNESSES MAKE

There are four potent psychological landmines that will damage your witness's credibility every time: Anxiety, Anger, Arrogance, and Apathy. One or more of these factors routinely results in major headaches for trial attorneys attempting to prepare their witnesses for deposition or trial testimony. The good news: all of these are detectable and fixable. Let's take a closer look.

1. Anxiety

By far the top barrier to effective communication, anxiety can conceal a witness's true character, motivation and credibility. Even worse, the physical and psychological symptoms of anxiety send a message of "I am not prepared, I am scared, I am intimidated, and I have no confidence in my answers." To achieve the perception of credibility, witnesses need to be confident, assertive, and professional—and anxiety will destroy all three, and thus destroy credibility. Some level of anxiety is normal, and perhaps good, as we want the witness to be "on his toes" during questioning. The Answer: thoroughly evaluate the witness's anxiety levels and find the source; often the source of the anxiety is deep-rooted and is completely unrelated to the case.

2. Anger

Many witnesses are pretty ticked off that they have to go through the legal process, and many are furious because they feel that the case has no merits. Angry witnesses are very dangerous, as they can exhibit volcanic and random outbursts, a tendency to "jump the gun" in defending themselves, and an overuse of sarcasm. Plaintiff attorneys love angry defense witnesses, as their anger severely impairs their communication skills and subsequently wipes out their credibility. Courtroom Science Inc. interviews over 5,000 jurors annually who say: "poise, composure, and professionalism = credibility." The Answer: give the witness the opportunity to vent and process his anger before his testimony preparation; let him blow off steam, let him heal, and then proceed with preparation.

3. Arrogance

Want to get a jury really mad at you? Have your witness display arrogance…works every single time. This is a major problem with higher level witnesses (i.e., C-level executives, managers, celebrities, physicians, etc). The strategic (and economic) cost of arrogance is _very_ high, as the testimony becomes immediately and permanently poisoned. On paper, these should be the most credible and effective witnesses of all, given the high levels of intelligence and professional achievement involved. The problem is that in the business world, a good dash of arrogance may not only be beneficial to one's career, it may even be necessary for professional survival. The Answer: carefully remove arrogance (without interrupting confidence/assertiveness) and carefully insert a dose of humility (but only a moderate amount).

4. Apathy

So your witness has no passion? No conviction? No motivation? Guess what?—he has no credibility either. Apathy typically occurs because the witness doesn't care about you, your case, or the consequences. Apathy is particularly problematic with witnesses that are no longer tied to the defense (i.e., former employees). This makes sense, as the witness has to do all of the work, go through the grueling litigation process, put up with all of your phone calls and demands, and then receive no reward in the end. Sounds fun to me, where do I sign up? The Answer: make the process worth their while; create internal and emotional rewards that will be appealing.

Anxiety, anger, arrogance and apathy all negatively impact your witness's credibility at the jury level, even if he is telling the truth! All too often, these factors are ignored, underestimated and given little or no attention in the witness preparation process. In fact, the vast majority of these problems are first detected during the deposition, when everything is on the record and each mistake hurts.

3.11 SPECIAL CONSIDERATIONS FOR CORPORATE REPRESENTATIVES

For the moment, let's interrupt Dr. Kanasky's discussion so that another important issue can be discussed. Under Rule 30(b)(6), a party may name as the deponent a corporation, partnership, association, or other entity as long as reasonable particularity of the subject of the deposition is given. The named organization must then provide a witness who is capable of testifying about the information. The deposition notice typically asks for a representative to provide information on a vast array of a company's policies and procedures. This type of deposition is so common that it is commonly referred to as a "30(b)(6) deposition."

However, while the deposition may be common, preparing a witness for one presents special challenges. Sometimes the witness for the 30(b)(6) deposition is testifying to routine matters. Other times, the stakes are very high. The corporate representative may be the one who has made the decision to hire you as his attorney or certainly has influence over a decision to keep you hired after the deposition. Not only is your financial interest at stake, but the fate of the lawsuit can rest upon whether or not the corporate representative is believable.

Unfortunately, there is no way to prepare such a representative for a deposition in the short amount of time that most attorneys allow. An afternoon meeting—or worse, a meeting an hour before the deposition—simply can't get your witness adequately ready. This is particularly true when a corporate rep. is arrogant. Telling a witness one or a hundred times not to be arrogant isn't effective. The reason is that people who are arrogant often don't see themselves that way. Throughout this book we have seen examples from Bill Gates' deposition. Although he was technically a defendant, and not a corporate representative, he is the perfect example of an arrogant person who is the face of his organization. His demeanor did more to hurt his case than any answer he gave.

In a high stakes case, a trial consultant can put a witness through a sophisticated training program that focuses on the non-legal aspects of testimony (legal communication science, litigation psychology, non-verbal communication, emotional control, and attorney psychological tricks/ traps). A consultant can also educate him about the way jurors make and do not make decisions. A witness is usually very surprised to find out that jurors highly value the rep's attitude, tone and body language, rather than the intricate parts of his answers. In other words, a witness needs to understand that he will never convince jurors that he is correct through substance alone and that arrogance is the top killer of credibility.

In the remainder of this section, let's return to Bill Kanasky Jr., Ph.D from Courtroom Sciences Inc. Below, he shares his thoughts on the challenges facing attorneys with this difficult type of deposition.

There are three special challenges in preparing a corporate representative to testify. First, when corporate representatives are designated, they feel that they are being put into a "know it all" position, which is not realistic or practical. While the amount of study time and preparation time dwarfs that of a regular fact witness, 30b6 witnesses need to be told that they are not required to know <u>every</u> detail of the company's history and operations (it is impossible). They need to demonstrate the skills of a leader by clarifying what is delegated to whom and why. They need to be seen as confident leaders who know how to organize talent and keep lines of communication flowing. They do not have to suddenly become an expert at finance, operations, IT, sales, marketing, or any other functional area. If they try to be an expert on every topic, they will not come across as credible or believable.

Second, many, if not most executives got to their positions of status by being more aggressive than their colleagues. Along the way to the corner office they learned that conflict-seeking and even occasional aggression gets rewarded. They may have a personal style that is genteel or diplomatic, but when push comes to shove under cross they are very likely to revert to the idea that the best defense is a good offense, resulting in intense defensiveness and argumentativeness. Those traits do not promote credibility or believability during sworn testimony. Third, they despise litigation and hate attorneys—even their own! They see legal issues and attorneys as necessary evils that are extraordinarily expensive. These emotions affect their willingness to take advice in witness preparation sessions and to be calm during a deposition.

If you could tell a corporate representative only one thing in order to prepare him for a deposition, it should be: "You don't have to be perfect on substance; but you MUST be perfect on demeanor and professionalism." (i.e., anything related to substance can be "fixed" with more questioning; but if a corporate representative comes across as arrogant, angry, scared, anxious, or apathetic, the entire corporation will be perceived that way at trial. The corporate rep's demeanor and professionalism is the

face and heartbeat of the entire corporation). Put another way…
"deposition testimony is indeed trial testimony."

There are three common mistakes corporate representatives
make in a deposition. First, they try to win with every answer
instead of just answering the questions honestly. Second, they do
not utilize their rights as a witness: 1) asking for questions to
be restated/rephrased; 2) being patient before answering; and 3)
asking to review a document before answering. Third, they forget
that their demeanor/character is just as valuable as the substance
of their answers.

3.12 EXAMPLES FROM GATES DEPOSITION

Finally, let's look at a few more examples from the Gates deposition.
While the entire deposition is a treasure trove of what not to do as a witness,
here are some of the highlights.

Example: Gates Is Not Sincere
(Gates Deposition)

You want your witness to come across as sincere and likeable. However,
in the heat of the deposition it is easy to forget about this goal. Below, Gates
comes across as a smart-aleck as opposed to a sincere witness. The video
portion of this deposition is discussed in Chapter Ten (clip 7) and can also be
seen at **http://winningatdeposition.com/**.

*[Attorney Stephen Houck] Q. The Microsoft computer dictionary, 1997 edition, defines
killer app as follows, and it gives two definitions. And I'll be very complete this time,
Mr. Gates. The first definition is, "An application of such popularity and widespread
standardization that fuels sales of the hardware platform or operating system for
which it was written." Do you agree with that definition?*
A. Are you saying to me that there is more in there and you're just reading me
part of it?

Q. I'm going to read you the second definition as well.
A. So you're asking me about it without reading me the whole thing?

*Q. No, sir. There's two definitions. You're familiar with dictionaries, I take it?
Sometimes they have more than one definition of a term; correct?*
A. Sometimes terms have more than one meaning, so it's appropriate that
dictionaries would give the two different meanings. And generally before
you'd ask somebody if they agreed with the dictionary, you'd actually give
them the benefit of reading them what is in the dictionary, not just a part of it.

Q. I read you the first definition and asked you if you agreed with that definition.
A. I don't think it's the only definition.

Q. *Is that an accurate definition?*
A. I'd like to hear what the other –

Gates was asked a simple question that had no trickery in it. But he thought he would be clever and try to show that the lawyer was asking a deceitful question. Even when the lawyer recited the entire definition below, Gates still did not give a straight answer.

Q. *I'll read it to you. The second definition is "An application that supplants its competition."*
Q. *Let me go back and read you the first definition again, now that you've heard both of them. The first definition reads as follows: "An application of such popularity and widespread standardization that fuels sales of the hardware platform or operating system for which it was written."*
A. I already told you that my definition of killer app is a very popular application. **[Gates does not answer the question.]**

Q. *Is this definition accurate?*
A. I told you, when I use the term "killer application," in particular when I use it in a piece of e-mail, what I mean by it— I'm sure there's people—**[Gates still does not answer the question.]**

Q. *I understand. You've told me that, but there's another question on the table. Do you have any disagreement with this definition?*
A. I think most people when they use the word "killer app" are not necessarily tying it to any relationship to hardware. **[Gates still doesn't answer the question.]**

Example: Gates Refuses to Answer Simple Question (Gates Deposition)

Boies questioned Gates on his knowledge of Netscape's revenues. Given Microsoft's dealings with Netscape, this was something he certainly had some knowledge about. In fact, after this excerpt, Gates admitted that he had asked his assistants to get this information for him. Notice how his refusal to answer simple questions makes it seem as though he was being deceitful.

Q. *And in 1996 what were Microsoft's revenues compared to Netscape's revenues?*
A. I don't know Netscape's revenues.

Q. *Approximately, sir?*
A. Approximately what? **[too argumentative]**

Q. *Approximately what were Netscape's revenues compared to Microsoft's revenues?*
A. You want me to guess at Netscape's revenues?

Q. *I want you to give me your best judgment and estimate as a chairman and CEO of*

Microsoft, sir. If you call it guessing, you can call it whatever you want. What I want is your best estimate under oath as you sit here?

A. I know that Microsoft's revenues would be dramatically higher than Netscape's, but I—I really won't want to hazard a guess at Netscape's revenue in particular.

Q. As you sit here now, can you give me any estimate or range at all of what Netscape's revenues were in 1996?

A. Zero to 200 million.

Q. As you sit here now, can you tell any estimate or range of what Netscape's revenues are today?

A. I think zero to 500 million. **[This answer and the preceding one are needlessly argumentative and absurd on their face.]**

Q. Can you be any more specific, that is, can you narrow the range at all?

A. Yeah. 200 million to 500 million.

Q. Can you narrow the 1996 range at all? The 1996 range you gave me was zero to 200 million.

A. 30 million to 200 million.

Q. Is that the best you can do as you sit here now?

A. Well, the chance of my being wrong goes up as I narrow the range.

Example: Gates Argues with Boies
(Gates Deposition)

The attorney David Boies was asking Gates about an interview he gave to reporters where he talked negatively about Netscape. Netscape had complained that Gates' public comments had negatively affected its business.

Q. Let me ask you a different question. Do you believe that the publication of this article and, in particular, the publication of the statement attributed to you . . .'Our business model works even if all Internet software is free,' close quote, . . .quote, 'We are still selling operating systems. What does Netscape's business model look like if that happens? Not very good,' close quote. Do you believe that the publication of that statement affected Netscape?

A. I know when people have been quoted in the press, competitors, saying how—what trouble Microsoft is in and how much better their products are . . . .

Q. [Boies]I'll move to strike the answer as nonresponsive. [to the court reporter] Would you read the question again please? (The following question was read: "Q Do you believe that the publication of that statement affected Netscape?")[Gates] What do you mean "affected Netscape"?

Q. Are you telling me you don't understand the question, sir?

A. Yes, that's what I'm saying to you.

Q. Okay. By "affected Netscape," I mean adversely affected Netscape.

A. **Like hurt their feelings, somebody cried, or somebody in reading the article smiled?**

Q. Are you saying that you don't understand what I mean by "adversely affected Netscape"?

A. No, I don't know what your criteria is. I think it's likely somebody may have read it and disagreed with it.

Q. Do you think it adversely affected Netscape's business prospects?

A. I think the general work that we were doing to do strong Internet software had an effect on Netscape, but I don't think quotations like that had any direct effect.

Gates would have been much more believable and likeable if he had just answered a simple question. His smart-aleck answer in bold above and his pretending not to know the "criteria" of a simple phrase, "adversely affected," undermine his credibility. While Gates might get some pleasure from being a difficult witness at the deposition, he would not be rewarded for such behavior by the judge at trial. Gates' bad deposition cost Microsoft millions of dollars.

☰ CHECKLIST

Preparing the Witness

1. Conduct two meetings: the first is fact finding and the second is preparation for the deposition.
2. Most attorneys don't prepare enough. Two hours minimum are needed.
3. Don't lecture witness but have a conversation instead.
4. Use your trial guide to help you focus on what is important.
5. Practice answers to difficult questions.
6. Tell witness: "Tell the truth and don't guess!"
7. Tell witness that you can handle any bad fact if you know it soon enough. But if witness lies, it will destroy the case.
8. Assume any documents you show witness will have to be turned over if other side requests at deposition.

Witness' Common Substantive Mistakes

1. Problem: volunteering information.
   Solution: tell witness if he uses more than two sentences, he is probably talking too much.
2. Problem: guessing.
   Solution: teach witness that he should not feel obligated to guess if he doesn't know the answer.
3. Problem: not listening to question.

Solution: teach witness to listen to entire question instead of thinking about his answer while attorney is in the middle of the question.

Witness' Common Emotional Mistakes

1. Problem: showing anxiety

   Solution: thoroughly evaluate the witness's anxiety levels and find the source; often the source of the anxiety is deep-rooted and is completely unrelated to the case.

2. Problem: becoming angry.

   Solution: give the witness the opportunity to vent and process his anger before his testimony preparation; let him blow off steam, let him heal, and then proceed with preparation.

3. Problem: being arrogant.

   Solution: carefully remove arrogance (without interrupting confidence/ assertiveness) and carefully insert a dose of humility (but only a moderate amount).

4. Problem: displaying apathy.

   Solution: make the process worth their while; create internal and emotional rewards that will be appealing.

Special Considerations for Corporate Representatives

1. Allow extra time to prepare witness.
2. Relieve witness' anxiety that he must know everything.
3. Corporate reps tend to be aggressive which is disastrous in deposition.
4. Corporate reps don't like lawyers and are often unwilling to take advice.
5. Corporate reps forget that their demeanor in answering questions is just as important as the answer.
6. Corporate reps try to win with every answer instead of answering honestly.

Notes

CHAPTER FOUR

Defending the Deposition

People who make no noise are dangerous.
—*Jean de La Fontaine*

Not so long ago, federal depositions were a true free-for-all. Attorneys defending depositions would offer a speaking objection to a question that would coach a witness as to the correct answer. For example, an attorney might object, "Your question is trying to trick my client. She has always said that she was fired because of her race *and* her gender." In addition, immediately after a question was asked, attorneys would often instruct their witness "if you remember," "if you know," or "if you understand" before the witness had a chance to answer the question. Or, a witness would sometimes consult with her attorney after a difficult question to make sure that she would answer it correctly.

Commenting on a 3,000 page deposition, Justice Powell observed that "discovery techniques and tactics have become a highly developed litigation art—one not infrequently exploited to the disadvantage of justice."[1] But now federal rules (and likewise most state rules) have been modified to strictly prohibit coaching at a deposition. Rule 30(c)(2) declares, "an objection must be stated concisely in a nonargumentative and nonsuggestive manner."[2]

Unlike the past, today "there is no proper need for the witness's own lawyer to act as an intermediary, interpreting questions, deciding which questions the witness should answer, and helping the witness to formulate answers."[3] Some states have gone even further than the amended federal rules. For example, Texas limits objections specifically to two words: "objection, form."[4]

---

[1] *Herbert v. Lando*, 441 U.S. 153, 179 (1979) (Powell, J., concurring).
[2] See *McDonough v. Keniston*, 188 F.R.D. 22, 23 (D. N.H. 1998) (speaking and "coaching objections are simply not permitted in depositions . . . .").
[3] *Hall v. Clifton Precision*, 150 F.R.D. 525,528 (E.D. Pa. 1993).
[4] See TEX. R. CIV. P. 199.5(e).

Consequently, the French poet Jean de La Fontaine's quote above applies perfectly to defending depositions. The silent lawyer is the dangerous one because that means he has prepared his client so well that there is no need to coach the witness improperly during the deposition.

There are two main situations where improper coaching occurs. One is where the attorney helps the witness answer the question. The other is where the witness is coached during a break. For now, let's look only at the first situation. Both scenarios are discussed in detail in Chapter Six.

Example: Improper Speaking Objection (Simpson Deposition)

Petrocelli is questioning Simpson about clothes that were found in a duffle bag in the Bronco driven on the famous chase. Petrocelli wanted to determine if the clothes were O.J.'s. because O.J. had claimed that he had intended to visit Nicole's grave before killing himself. Nevertheless, there was also evidence that O.J. intended to flee the country—which would obviously be inconsistent with suicide. If Petrocelli could establish that the clothes were O.J.'s and were packed for a trip, it would help prove that Simpson was trying to run away because he was guilty. Simpson had given several evasive answers prior to the exchange below.

Q. In other words, if these [clothes] were found in or near your bag in the Bronco, you can't say that they're not your items. Correct?
Baker: Wait a minute. If they were found in or near—

Petrocelli: Yes.

BAKER—his bag in the Bronco—

Petrocelli: Yes.

BAKER—you can't say that they're your items, and I am going to instruct him not to answer based on the pictures because you can't tell from the pictures whether they're his, whether they're A.C.'s or someone else.

Petrocelli: Who's talking about A.C.? He never mentioned A.C. Why did you mention A.C., Mr. Baker?

Baker: My depo isn't being taken.

Petrocelli: Exactly. That's my point.

Baker: I don't care what your point is, and I'm trying to respond to your question.

Petrocelli: My point is, stop trying to suggest answers. The witness can speak for himself. Just make an objection.

Baker's suggestion that the clothes could have been those of A.C. (Al Cowlings, who drove the Bronco in the famous low speed chase) was improper coaching. He was trying to give—or remind O.J.—of an explanation why the clothes might be in the Bronco if O.J. were going to commit suicide instead of flee from the police.

Since you really can't do much *during* a deposition to protect your witness, your success is dependent on how well you prepare the witness *before* the deposition begins (see Chapter Three). Nonetheless, there are still several things an attorney can provide for his client during a deposition.

4.1 PROTECT YOUR CLIENT

Before we get to the needed objections you should make, let's look at one of the most overlooked tasks of successfully defending a deposition. Many attorneys are so worried about making the correct objection that they forget to make sure their client is conveying the truth convincingly. Your successful witness preparation can go down the drain if you fall asleep at the switch during the deposition. Listen carefully to your client's answers. Make sure that he is not misstating the facts. Sometimes a witness will misunderstand an entire line of questioning and give damaging testimony. Or a witness will start shading the truth in a deposition because he gets nervous and feels the need to protect others or himself.

Other times, a witness will be less than candid because the examining lawyer's tone of voice is accusatory. You may find that a witness simply does not listen to the question. In any of these situations, it is your job to ask for a break and find out why your witness is not being as persuasive as he needs to be.

Another category of problems occurs when your witness' body language betrays his testimony during a videoed deposition. Is your client slouching, looking bored, tired, impatient, or arrogant? It is your job to correct these problems by asking for a break.

4.2 PROCEDURAL OBJECTIONS

Let's first look at some procedural objections that can be made. Rule 32(d)(1) states that "an objection to an error or irregularity in a deposition notice is waived unless promptly served in writing on the party giving the notice." For example, if you object that you have not been given reasonable notice or that the designated location is improper, then you need to provide a written objection and be ready to file a motion to quash prior to the deposition if an agreement cannot be worked out with opposing counsel.

Other procedural objections include objecting to the manner of taking the deposition, the oath, or to opposing counsel's conduct.[5] A further objection is to the qualifications of the court reporter or videographer.[6] In all of these instances, the objections must be made "timely." In short, as soon as there is a problem, you need to object. It is likely you could go an entire career without needing to object to any of the procedural issues in this paragraph except for opposing counsel's conduct which, unfortunately, you may run into more than you would like. Handling difficult opposing counsel will be discussed in Chapter Six.

4.3 SUBSTANTIVE OBJECTIONS

There are not many substantive objections to worry about, since the significant objections can be asserted at trial. The reason is that the Rules explicitly provide that an objection to a witness' competence "or the competence, relevance, or materiality of testimony is not waived by failure to make it before or during the deposition, unless the ground for it might have been corrected at that time."[7] It is very rare that an objection could correct one of these problems. Whether testimony is competent, relevant, or material is a decision best made at trial by the judge. Only she can decide if such testimony is admissible at trial because it is trustworthy and proves an issue in dispute.

In fact, one would be hard pressed to find an example where a deposition objection could have cured problems related to competency, relevancy, or materiality. To illustrate, assume that defense counsel wants to take his expert's deposition because he knows the witness won't be available for trial. If you think the expert is not qualified to give an expert opinion, there is no need to object to his deposition answers because you can raise your objections later. Only the trial judge can determine the expert's competency to testify. Is the witness offering admissible and relevant testimony? Again, this is a decision for the trial judge. Indeed, Rule 32(d)(3)(A) "avoids burdening the deposition with a number of objections."[8]

The rule's purpose is to discourage objections. You do not even need to object to inadmissible testimony such as hearsay because such objections are not waived. Likewise, if testimony is more prejudicial than probative and might be excluded under Federal Rule of Evidence 403, save your objection for trial. Remember the guidance of Rule 26(b)(1). Subject to limitations such as the burden and expense of responding to a request, a party is entitled to discover

---

[5] Rule 32(d)(3)(B).
[6] Rule 32(d)(2).
[7] Rule 32(d)(3)(A).
[8] 8A Charles Alan Wright & Arthur R. Miller, Federal Practice and Procedure § 2153 (2d ed. 1994).

relevant evidence, even if it is inadmissible at trial, as long as it "is relevant to any party's claim or defense and proportional to the needs of the case. . . ."

Nonetheless, you must keep your guard up for questions that seek to invade a privilege or have an objectionable form. For example, if your client answers a question that reveals attorney-client communications, he has waived the privilege. Be vigilant, then, throughout the examination for any questions that call for such information.

Second, you need to listen to the form of the question. An objection is waived if it relates to the form of the question or answer.[9] The rationale is that it would be unfair to object at trial to the form of a question when it could have been easily fixed at the deposition if an objection had been made.

The most common objections to a question's form are: 1) compound question, 2) argumentative, 3) ambiguous, 4) misleading/vague/unclear, 5) asked and answered, 6) calls for speculation, 7) mischaracterizes prior testimony or evidence, and 8) lack of foundation. An examiner may also object "non-responsive" to a witness' answer that avoids the question.

Common Objections to a Question's Form

1. Compound question
2. Argumentative
3. Ambiguous
4. Misleading/vague/unclear
5. Asked and answered
6. Calls for speculation
7. Mischaracterizes prior testimony or evidence
8. Lack of foundation

When asserting these objections, you have a choice whether to say, "objection, form" or give the underlying reason, "objection, ambiguous." Clearly under the Rules, you are permitted to describe the reason as long as it is "concisely stated in a nonargumentative and nonsuggestive manner." Rule 30(c)(2).

Even though you are allowed to give the underlying reason, generally, the best strategy is to simply say, "objection, form." There are several reasons for this approach. First, opposing counsel certainly cannot complain that you are coaching your witness.

---

9 Rule 32(d)(3)(B)(i).

Second, it allows you to make a split second decision to object without having to state the reason or reasons for it. To illustrate, a question may call for speculation and/or be compound. However, when you hear it, you know it is objectionable but you need more time to figure out exactly why. By saying only the word "form" instead of blurting out a reason that may turn out to be wrong (i.e. speculation instead of compound), you give yourself time to later assert the correct reason at trial. If your reason is wrong at the deposition and the judge overrules you at trial, you can't tell the judge, "what I really meant was _____."

Third, if you give a reason such as compound or ambiguous, you are helping opposing counsel reframe a confusing question in a better way that will often hurt you. A confusing question gets a confusing answer. A reframed question allows the examiner to get the precise information he needs. Of course, if opposing counsel asks you for the reason for your objection, you must give it to him. But usually he will just prefer that his question get answered without wanting to hear the reason for your interruption. Having said that, often the best tactic is to not object at all. That way you don't in any way alert opposing counsel to his bad questions.

Nonetheless, there may be occasions when you want to give the reason for your objection as allowed by the Rules. For example, if a question is intended to trick the witness because it is purposefully ambiguous, you might want to give the reason for the objection. In such a situation, you are preserving an objection so that the question and answer can't be used against your witness at trial, and you have the added benefit of alerting your witness to the question's problem.

On the other hand, it would be improper to make objections with explanations that are *unfounded* in an attempt to alert the witness to particular questions. For example, if you made several objections to form because the questions misstated evidence when they did not, opposing counsel would be justified in being upset. In addition, you would certainly cross the line if you said, "objection, the question is ambiguous in that it suggests that the witness did not give timely notice to human resource personnel of how she was harassed by her supervisor."

In any event, even if you object to the question's form, the witness must still answer the question if the deposing attorney wishes. If the deposing attorney thinks your objection is valid, he may rephrase his question to overcome it. It is the examiner's choice.

Finally, there are three reasons not to object even if you can. First (as stated above), an objection to form alerts the examining attorney that he should ask a more precise question that will often get him a better answer.

Second, an objection may alert opposing counsel that he has touched on a sensitive area that you are concerned about. Your objection may cause him to ask a lot more questions than he ever intended to.

Third, if you start objecting a lot, you will confuse your witness. A witness' natural instinct is to get tense when you make an objection. Then, the witness tries to figure out what you meant by the objection and how he should change his intended answer. If you are constantly objecting, the witness may believe he is failing at the deposition even if your objections are valid. Whatever the reasons for your objections, from the witness' perspective, your objections are a distraction and a signal of your fear. As a result, the witness becomes more nervous. Calm and thoughtful answers are replaced by rushed and emotional ones. In short, don't unnecessarily become a distraction to your witness.

Practice Tip

Keep a poker face. That is, whether examining counsel is asking a boring question or the most sensitive one, don't let your expression reveal your opinion. Likewise, if your witness is doing badly, don't let your facial or body language reveal this to opposing counsel. He may not be aware of the problem you sense. Don't unintentionally alert him to go after the jugular.

Examples follow of some objectionable questions discussed above where you need to object to the form.

Example: Compound Question

A compound question asks about two or more facts in a single question that causes the answer to be unclear.

Q. *Did you go to the meeting on March 1st and did you talk to Keith Young?*
A. No.

Since the question asks about two facts—attendance at the meeting and whom the witness spoke to—it is unclear from the answer whether the witness is answering "no" that he did not attend the meeting and did not talk to Young, or that he attended the meeting but did not talk to Young, or that he talked to Young but did not attend the meeting.

Although your objection should not explain the underlying reason for it (i.e. the details), it is okay to do so if opposing counsel requests more information from you so that he can correct the mistake you perceive. After all, that is why you are making the objection. Here is how the above example may play out.

Q. Did you go to the meeting on March 1ˢᵗ and did you talk to Keith Young?
[Defending Attorney] Objection, compound question.
[Deposing Attorney] What's wrong with the question?

[Defending Attorney explains underlying reason] The question inquires about two facts: the meeting on March 1ˢᵗ and a conversation with Keith Young and can't be answered with a simple "yes" or "no."

Practice Tip

Don't object unless it helps you. Opposing counsel may ask a confusing question that elicits a confusing answer. In such a situation, if you object, you will only help your opponent ask a better question.

Example: Argumentative Question
(Simpson Deposition)

An argumentative question does not seek an answer but instead frames the question in an argumentative way that usually becomes a personal attack on the witness.

Q. Well, at the time you had that gun out in that Bronco, though, you knew you were going to be arrested, and you knew-
A. I could care less.

Q. —and you knew the police were hunting for you.
A. And I could care less about what the police was thinking. It was how I was feeling, and that's why that gun was out, is because I felt I was in a lot of pain and I couldn't handle it at the time. I didn't feel I could handle it at the time.

Q. Was the pain of losing Nicole so great that you were prepared to deprive your children of their parents? **[Possibly argumentative]**
Baker: Don't answer that. That is outrageous.

Petrocelli: I am trying to understand the witness—
Baker: I don't care what you're trying to do. That's an outrageous argumentative question, and he is not going to answer it.

Petrocelli: You instruct him not to answer?
Baker: You bet.

Q. Well, let me ask you this: Before you went in that Bronco, had you made arrangements with anyone for the care of your children?
A. Well, yes.

Q. What arrangements did you make?

A. What arrangements. There are certain people that I asked to, you know, see if they can help if anything came up with my kids.

Q. You mean to help in case you killed yourself. Is that what you mean?

A. That was a possibility, yes.

Q. I just want to understand what you're saying. When you say "if anything came up," I just want to make sure I understand what you're saying.

A. Yes.

Whether a judge would rule that the question was argumentative depends on its sincerity. If Petrocelli were sarcastic when he asked the question, a judge would find the question argumentative. However, if a judge credited Petrocelli's explanation that he was "trying to understand the witness," then the objection would be overruled.

Example: Ambiguous Question

An ambiguous question has at least two possible interpretations.

Q. How many home repairs did you do last year?

Here, it is unclear if the question is asking how many repairs the witness did "personally" or how many he paid someone else to do.

In the Simpson deposition, the following objection took place.

*Q. As of June of 1994, is it true that you had generally **favorable** relations with the Los Angeles Police Department?*

Baker: I don't know what you mean by that, and I don't know that he can characterize his relations.

Q. You can answer.

Baker: No, don't answer. That question is overbroad, vague and ambiguous.

Q. Did you think you had a good relationship with the LAPD as of June 1, 1994?

Baker: His state of mind relative to his relations with the LAPD, it's irrelevant and I am going to instruct him not to answer that question.

Petrocelli: Okay.

Q. Before June 1 of 1994, had you ever been arrested by the LAPD?

A. No.

The question was ambiguous because it is unclear what Petrocelli meant by the word "favorable." Did it mean that Simpson had never been arrested or that he was friends with the police? After the objection, Petrocelli corrected his mistake and made the following questions more clear. First, he asked about arrests and then he asked about friendships with the police (not shown above).

Example: Unclear/Vague/Misleading Question

An unclear question is so confusing that the witness cannot understand what information the question asks to be provided. It can also include compound and ambiguous questions and is considered the catch-all for questions that confuse the witness. In addition, misleading questions misstate facts—either intentionally or unintentionally—so that the witness cannot give a clear answer.

Below, the lawyer asking the question mistakenly believes that the doctor saw the patient on the 13th of May when it was his partner who did the examination that morning.

Q. Doctor, when you saw my client on the 13th, why didn't you order a blood test?

This is a misleading question—albeit an unintentional one—that you should object to. In order to avoid the appearance of coaching, you should simply say, "objection, misleading" and wait for opposing counsel to ask you why you think it is misleading. Even if he does not ask you, your witness has been alerted that the question is misleading and he should think more carefully before answering.

In the Simpson deposition, the defense attorney for Simpson properly objected to a vague question.

Q. Did members of the LAPD frequent your house from time to time?
Baker: That's pretty vague and ambiguous, too.
Simpson: Yeah, you'll have to be a little more specific because I can't answer that.

Petrocelli: Q: Did they ever come visit you?
A. Stop—

Baker: In an unofficial capacity come visit him for a social call, is that the question?

Petrocelli: Correct, Mr. Baker, and all of this is before June 12, 1994.
A. Yes. And even after they've stopped and talked to me at my driveway and stuff, yes.

There is a fine line to avoid crossing when asserting the objection "misleading" or "unclear." The reason is that the issue is whether the witness can understand the question, not the attorney. If you needlessly object too much, a court may find that you are coaching the witness by repeatedly alerting him to questions that need special attention.

Example: Asked and Answered Objection (Simpson Deposition):

The objection is mistakenly asserted below.

Q. *You put three photographs of your family in the black bag which you got someplace in the house at Rockingham. Right?*
A. That's correct.

Q. *And what did those photos depict?*
A. My family.

Q. *By "family," who are you referring to?*
A. Sydney, Justin, Nicole, Jason, Arnelle.

Q. *Each photo had all of them in it?*
A. No. It was kind of a mixture.

Q. *So your four children plus Nicole.*
A. Yeah.

Q. *And yourself.*
A. And myself, yeah.

Q. *And what was your purpose in putting those photos into the black bag?*
A. Because I wanted pictures of my family with me.

Q. *With you at the Kardashian house?*
A. Wherever I was going, but, yes, at the Kardashian house.

Q. *Did you anticipate taking them to jail?*
A. No. I didn't anticipate being arrested.

Q. **Why** *did you want to bring the pictures with you to the Kardashian house?*
Baker: Asked and answered. Don't answer that.

Petrocelli: Q, Did you contemplate that you would be killing yourself?
A. No.

Q. *At that point in time?*
A. No.

Notice that Baker objects incorrectly since Petrocelli had asked several questions about the photos in the bag but not "why" he wanted to bring them to the Kardashian house. In any event, there is really no point in objecting the first time you think a question has been repeated as Baker did here. Despite the objection, the witness must answer. But if the same question has been asked repeatedly, object "asked and answered." If you think the repeated questioning has become harassing to your witness, you may stop the deposition and seek a protective order from the court.

But what generally happens is that instead of suspending the deposition, the defending attorney will instruct his witness not to answer the question, and the deposing attorney will move on to other topics. Usually, the deposing attorney has obtained the information he needs and is ready to move on anyway. Yet, if the question is about a key point, deposing counsel won't move on until he gets an answer. You need to make sure the questioning has become harassing or you run the risk that deposing counsel will win a motion to compel if you instruct your witness not to answer. Consequently, you need to calculate whether opposing counsel will file a motion after the deposition and the probabilities of its success. The fight in court should be a last resort.

Example: Lack of Foundation Objection

A witness must have firsthand knowledge to testify at trial. That is, he must have personally seen or heard something to testify about it. Otherwise, there is no foundation for his testimony.

Q. Mr. Brown, was the driver talking on her cell-phone when she ran the red light?
[Defending lawyer]: Objection. Lack of foundation.

[Examining lawyer]: Explain your objection.

[Defending lawyer]: This witness did not see the accident but only heard about it.

Another situation arises when a lay witness is asked to give an improper opinion. One instance arises where a witness is asked a question he is not qualified to answer. An example of a proper lay opinion would be whether or not the plaintiff was angry or intoxicated. The witness is qualified because the typical person can reliably reach this conclusion based on life's experiences. An improper opinion would be that the plaintiff was driving 55 m.p.h. (you would need evidence of a properly calibrated radar gun or some other facts to establish a proper foundation).

Second, a witness may not be asked to give an opinion that is only for the jury to determine. To illustrate, a lay witness can testify that the plaintiff ran the red light but not that he was negligent (a decision for the jury).

4.4   ASSERTING THE ATTORNEY-CLIENT OR WORK PRODUCT PRIVILEGE

Rule 30(c)(2) permits an attorney to instruct his witness not to answer a question "when necessary to preserve a privilege." Two applicable privileges are the attorney-client privilege and work product doctrine (commonly referred to as a privilege.)

The attorney-client privilege has the following elements: 1) it must be asserted by a client or one seeking to become a client, 2) the communication must be made to a lawyer or his subordinate, 3) the communication was made in connection with the lawyer performing his duties, and 4) the communication was made in the absence of third-parties and was for the purpose of getting legal advice.

The work product doctrine encompasses documents or items prepared in anticipation of litigation or trial by or for that party's representative (including his attorney, consultant, insurer, or agent). Since the attorney-client privilege is the one that comes up more often, it will be discussed below. The same guidelines work equally well for asserting the work product doctrine. That is, if the objection is asserted, opposing counsel may inquire whether the elements to assert the work product privilege have been met.

Example: Asserting the Attorney-Client Privilege

Assume the defendant is taking the plaintiff's deposition in a car wreck case.

[Defense Attorney] Q. Tell me about all the conversations you have had regarding this accident in the last week.
[Plaintiff's Attorney] Objection. Attorney-Client Privilege. I instruct the witness not to answer this question.

[Defense Attorney] What's your concern?
[Plaintiff's Attorney] I spoke with my client this morning prior to the deposition.

Note that a few examining attorneys will then ask the witness if he is going to follow his attorney's advice not to answer the question since the witness has the right to waive the privilege. However, such a question is going to be thwarted by the witness and will only antagonize the defending attorney.

In any event, the vigilant plaintiff's attorney has saved the day and objected properly. However, the question then becomes what can the opposing attorney do. Once the objection has been made, usually the attorney will simply rephrase the question as follows: *"Other* than those conversations you may have had with your attorney, please tell about any conversations you have had regarding the accident in the last week." The defending attorney has no reason to object to this rephrased question.

An aggressive deposing attorney may want to probe the validity of the attorney-client privilege further. If you are the deposing attorney and are tempted to do this, remember that turnabout is fair play, and you are inviting such questions when the tables are turned. Nonetheless, here is how the probing might be done.

Example: Determining If There Is an Attorney-Client Privilege

Q. *Without telling me the substance of any conversations you have had with your attorney, just tell me how many times you have spoken in person with him in the last week?*

A. Once.

Q. *Was that this morning before the deposition?*

A. Yes.

Q. *Was anyone else present?* [This question is asked to see if the privilege was waived because a third party was present when the conversation took place.]

A. Only his secretary. [Since an attorney's staff is not considered a third party, the privilege has not been waived]

Q. *Were you seeking legal advice?* [If conversations involved non-legal matters, they are not protected]

A. Yes.

Q. *Let me ask you, have you had any conversations with people other than your attorney this week . . . .* [Attorney focuses on other conversations since privilege has not been waived.]

4.5 INSTRUCTING A WITNESS NOT TO ANSWER AND PROTECTIVE ORDERS

There are three instances when an attorney can tell his witness not to answer a question: 1) to protect a privilege, 2) to enforce a court order limiting evidence, and 3) to prevent questions asked in bad faith, to annoy, embarrass, or oppress the witness. See Rule 30(c)(2) and 30(d)(3)(A). The first instance has been discussed above. An example of the second instance is when a court has ordered a limitation on discovery (i.e. no discovery will be allowed on Company A's trade secrets), and the deposing attorney insists on asking questions regarding this prohibited area.

While it is quite a bit easier to determine when a deposing attorney has crossed the line into areas of a privilege or violation of a court order, it is trickier to determine whether questions are asked in bad faith to annoy or harass. Let's face it, by their very nature, depositions are annoying and harassing for your witness. When is the line crossed and what do you do? One good sign that the line has been crossed is when personal questions are asked that have nothing to do with the case. Do questions about your client's divorce have any relevance in a breach of contract case? Probably not.

But questions about your client's financial problems—even though they are annoying—are a much closer call. If the plaintiff is seeking punitive damages, asking about a defendant's finances is fair game. However, what if the plaintiff believes the motive for breaching the contract was the defendant's financial problems? Or, what if plaintiff simply wants to know how much your client has in the bank account to see if he can pay a judgment? Theoretically, these lines of inquiry may be relevant but will routinely be met with vigorous objections. If you think this will be an issue at a deposition, be armed with case law supporting your position. Often the issue is resolved because insurance will pay for the lawsuit, and most states allow discovery of insurance limits.

In addition, another objection is that the deposition is covering the same ground over and over again. Such an objection is probably too vague to prove that the deposition is being conducted in bad faith.

The solution to an inappropriate question is to instruct the witness not to answer and then suspend the deposition "for the time necessary to obtain an order." See Rule 30(d)(3)(A). But sometimes, once your objection is made, opposing counsel will simply move on to other areas of questioning. Here is how three different scenarios usually play out.

Example: Instructing Witness Not to Answer (Scenario One)

Let's assume that the plaintiff is suing your client for breaking an employment contract. Your client is a developer whose business is a sole proprietorship.

Q. Tell me about the allegations your wife made in your divorce.
[Defending counsel] Objection. This question is harassing, and I instruct the witness not to answer.

Q. All right, **[Attorney pauses, decides the battle is not worth fighting and moves on.]** *Let's talk about your interpretation of the employment contract.*

The Rules presume that the defending attorney will file a motion for a protective order to limit the deposition after it has been concluded. However, it may be that the deposing attorney feels satisfied with the other questions he got answers to, and the heat of the moment has passed. Here, there is no need to file a motion for protection with the court because the deposing attorney has clearly dropped the topic and moved on to permissible questions.

Example: Instructing the Witness Not to Answer (Scenario Two)

Q. I'd like to ask you some questions about your divorce. How much child support are you paying?
[Defending counsel] Objection. This questioning is harassing, and I instruct the witness not to answer the question.

[Deposing counsel]. I think I am entitled to ask the question to determine his financial ability to pay a possible judgment.

[Defending counsel]. I disagree. How much child support he has to pay, to whom, and for whom is completely harassing.

[Deposing counsel]. I am entitled to an answer. Let me ask it again. How much child support are you paying?

[Defending counsel]. Objection. I will file a motion to limit questioning in this area with the court. You can either ask questions on another topic and come back to this topic if the court denies my motion, or I will end this deposition now until the court can rule on my motion.

[Deposing counsel]. All right, I'll move on.

Unlike Scenario One, it is clear that deposing counsel feels that he is entitled to answers to his questions. If a motion for protection is denied, the court may at its discretion award costs to the losing side for the expenses the prevailing party has in asserting its rights by way of motion or objection.[10]

Example: Instructing the Witness Not to Answer (Scenario Three)

Q. *Tell me about the allegations your wife made in your divorce.*
[Defending counsel] Objection. This question is harassing, and I instruct the witness not to answer.

[Deposing counsel] I disagree. This line of question goes to his character and his likelihood to tell the truth. I insist that the witness answer the question now. I have travelled from across the state to be here today, and I don't want my time wasted anymore.

[Defending counsel] Let's call the court and see if the judge is able to handle this. Otherwise, I am going to instruct my client not to answer until I can get a ruling from the court.

> Know your judge's practice before calling. While the issue may be important to you, he may consider it a waste of his time.

Given that the costs of being wrong are higher since the deposing attorney has travelled a long way to the deposition, calling the judge for help may be prudent. But remember that this remedy should be used very rarely. The Judge could be in a trial or doing any number of other important things.

---

[10] Rule 37(a)(5)(A) and (B).

4.6 ATTORNEY'S EMOTIONAL SUPPORT

Aside from the procedural and substantive objections, the most important thing an attorney can provide is emotional support. Remember, a deposition creates a lot of anxiety for the deponent. Although good preparation will go a long way toward ensuring a successful outcome, you can help guarantee such a result by helping your client stay relaxed during the deposition. One opportunity you will have to help is to sit next to your client during the deposition. Although she will be sitting to your side at the table, make sure that you are a little forward in your chair so that she always sees you.

Your body language is important. Your client will look at you often during the deposition. You must appear confident and interested. Unbelievably, many attorneys have their laptops open to work on other matters. After all, it doesn't take much vigilance to listen for an objectionable question that asks about a privilege. But your witness will pick up on your inattentiveness and lose her confidence and concentration. If through your body language, you express alertness and patience, your witness will mirror that behavior. Likewise, when you make an objection, if you do so calmly, your witness will notice and more likely remain calm during her answers.

During breaks, don't overload your witness with information or present her an oral report card of how good or bad she is doing—even if she asks for one. Your job is to remain supportive even if the deposition is not going well. This is not to say that you fail to provide needed guidance that is allowed under the Rules, but you do so in a way that is constructive. If you do anything to undermine your witness' confidence, your actions will be reflected in the witness' answers to subsequent questioning.

4.7 CLARIFYING QUESTIONS

Finally, if your witness makes mistakes during the deposition, you will have the opportunity at the end to ask your witness questions so that she can correct her mistakes. It is best to correct a mistake immediately. The procedure goes like this. After opposing counsel has finished his questions, he will say, "Pass the witness" or "I have no further questions." If you don't have any questions, simply say, "I will reserve my questions until time of trial." This is the phrase that most attorneys use. You really don't need to say anything, but you need to indicate to the examining attorney that you don't have any questions to ask.

The bigger decision is whether you ask your witness questions. If you don't think your witness will be at trial, it is a must that you put on a full direct to get the evidence in. But you might feel the need just to ask a few questions to clear up vague or incorrect testimony your witness gave.

This strategy prevents your witness having to make written corrections to the deposition. Also, the sooner a mistake is corrected, the less mileage the opposing side can get by trying to prove that the testimony was not a "mistake" but a statement under oath that is untrue.

The one risk—and it is a significant one—in asking questions at the end is that opposing counsel can ask follow-up questions about the topics you inquired about. So, you must weigh the reward of correcting a mistake against the risk that the witness' deposition will continue, and more information will be uncovered by opposing counsel's second round of questions.

4.8 WITNESS REVIEW OF THE DEPOSITION

Rule 30(e) provides that a witness may make changes to a deposition transcript if such a request is made before the end of the deposition. You should always make this request. You will usually be asked by the court reporter during the deposition if you want this option for your witness. However, to be safe, simply tell the court reporter at the beginning so you won't forget.

Once the court reporter finishes the transcript, she will send you or the witness (depending on your choice) the original deposition. The witness has thirty days to make changes. There will be a page at the back of the deposition for changes and the witness' signature. The witness should state the page and line number that is being changed and give the reason why.

Usually, there are minor spelling mistakes. However, a court reporter is not perfect, and significant testimony can occasionally be misinterpreted by her. For example, in a personal injury case, the deponent said that she was about "thirteen" feet from the accident, but the court reporter transcribed the testimony as "thirty" feet. Such an error would be critical to catch upon reviewing the deposition.

On the other hand, if the witness changes the substance of her testimony and it is not the court reporter's fault, the opposing attorney may seek permission from the court to reopen the deposition to ask the witness why the changes were made. An example would be if the witness answered "yes" but now realizes that the question was asked in the negative and that the answer should be "no."

Nonetheless, just because a prior answer is changed does not mean that the prior answer is erased from the record. At trial, opposing counsel can still impeach your witness with the original answer and can often get mileage out of the fact that a change was made only after the witness realized how bad the answer was and talked to his attorney. The point is that bad answers in depositions live on forever. There is no substitute for preparation.

CHECKLIST

Primary Goals of Defending Deposition

1. Protect your client.
   Listen carefully. Make sure client is answering questions persuasively and truthfully. Ensure that client's body language and temperament are not betraying answers in video deposition.
2. Object to important questions that are improper.

Objections in General

1. Speaking objections are not allowed.
2. Coaching a witness is not allowed.
3. Relax, most objections to the admissibility of evidence are not waived.
4. Be vigilant and object to questions that invade the attorney-client or work product privileges.
5. If it will help you, object to the form of the question.
6. Even if you object to the question's form, the witness must still answer the question if the deposing attorney wishes.
7. If the deposing attorney thinks your objection is valid, he may rephrase his question to overcome it. It is the examiner's choice.

Objections to Form of Question

Check the practice in your jurisdiction. You may be limited to saying only "objection, form," but you may be allowed to give the reason. (i.e. "objection, compound question."). The common objections under the Rules are:

1. Compound
2. Argumentative
3. Ambiguous
4. Misleading/vague/unclear
5. Asked and answered
6. Calls for speculation
7. Misstates evidence or prior testimony

Reasons to Say "Objection, form" Instead of Giving the Reason

1. Examining counsel can't complain you are coaching.
2. It allows you to make a split second decision to object without committing to a reason for it.

3. If there are several reasons to support an objection and you give the wrong one, you cannot later assert the correct one.

4. Stating the reason may cause examining counsel to ask a better question.

Exception: state the reason to preserve the objection and alert the witness to a particularly tricky question.

Three Reasons Not to Object

1. An objection alerts examining attorney that he should ask a more precise question that will often get him a better answer.

2. An objection may signal opposing counsel that he has touched on a sensitive area that you are concerned about which will lead to more questions.

3. A lot of objections may confuse your witness. A witness' natural instinct is to get tense when you make an objection. Then, the witness tries to figure out what you meant by the objection and how he should change his intended answer. As a result, the witness becomes more nervous. Calm and thoughtful answers are replaced by rushed and emotional ones.

Attorney-client Privilege Objection

A. Elements of Privilege

    1. Must be asserted by client or one seeking to be client.

    2. Communication must be made to lawyer or subordinate.

    3. Communication was made in connection with lawyer performing duties.

    4. Communication was made in absence of third-parties and purpose was legal advice.

B. Asserting Objection

    1. Object to question (i.e. "Objection. Attorney-client privilege").

    2. Instruct witness not to answer question.

Work Product Privilege Objection

A. Elements of Privilege

    1. Documents or items prepared in anticipation of litigation or trial

    2. By or for that party's representative (including his attorney, consultant, insurer, or agent)

B. Asserting Objection

    Same steps as attorney-client

When to Instruct Witness Not to Answer

1. To protect privilege
2. Enforce court order limiting evidence
3. Prevent questions asked in bad faith, to annoy, or embarrass witness

Clarifying Questions at End

1. If you don't think your witness will be at trial, it is a must that you put on a full direct after opposing counsel's examination to get the evidence in through the deposition.
2. If your witness will be at trial, you might just ask a few questions to clear up vague or incorrect testimony given by him. This strategy prevents your witness having to make written corrections to the deposition. Also, the sooner a mistake is corrected, the less mileage the opposing side can get by trying to prove that the testimony was not a "mistake" but a statement under oath that is untrue.
3. Remember that anytime you ask clarifying questions, opposing counsel may follow up with more questions that may hurt your case.

Reviewing the Deposition

1. Always ask court reporter to allow witness to review transcript.
2. Make request at beginning of deposition so you don't forget.
3. The witness has thirty days to make changes.
4. Reasons for changes must be stated.
5. If significant changes are made, opposing counsel likely can reopen deposition and ask more questions.

CHAPTER FIVE

The Expert Witness

Truth is ever to be found in the simplicity, not in the multiplicity and confusion of things.

—Isaac Newton

At first glance, taking an expert's deposition can appear very challenging. The two main reasons are that you will certainly have less expertise than the expert, and the expert is usually a professional witness. Don't be overwhelmed. There are a few easy tricks to master which will guarantee success. However, before we learn these secrets, let's look at a couple of preliminary issues.

5.1 DAUBERT REQUIREMENTS

In order to testify at trial, an expert must meet the criteria set forth in *Daubert v. Merrell Dow Pharmaceuticals, Inc.*, 509 U.S. 579 (1993). The criteria include the following: whether a theory or technique can be (and has been) tested, whether it has been subjected to peer review and publication, the known or potential rate of error, and whether the theory or technique is generally accepted.

There is no need to get caught up in the *Daubert* criteria since most experts will easily satisfy them. If you are defending an expert and opposing counsel objects after the deposition to his qualifications (known as a *Daubert* challenge), courts will generally hold a hearing prior to trial to determine the merits of the expert's opinion.

5.2 COMPENSATION OF EXPERTS

Rule 26(b)(4)(E) declares, "Unless manifest injustice would result, the court must require that the party seeking discovery pay the expert a reasonable fee for time spent in responding to discovery under Rule 26(b)(4)(A) or (D)." That is, if the defendant corporation wants to take the deposition of the plaintiff's designated expert, it has to pay the expert's hourly rate for the deposition time. Some courts have also interpreted this Rule to mean that the requesting party must also pay for the expert's reasonable preparation time for the deposition.[1]

Despite the rule's clear explanation, occasionally each side pays all the expenses for its own experts. It depends on the custom in your jurisdiction.

5.3 COMPENSATION OF TREATING PHYSICIANS

Another issue occurs when an injured plaintiff lists his treating doctors as possible fact witnesses to testify how they treated his injury. If you are a defense attorney and decide to depose the plaintiff's treating doctor, the question arises: who pays for it? Treating physicians do not have to prepare expert reports and are not treated as experts under Rule 26(a)(2)(B).

What often happens is that once you notify plaintiff's counsel that you would like to take the deposition of plaintiff's treating doctor, plaintiff's counsel will get available dates for the doctor's deposition and deposition fee. The price will likely shock you, particularly if the treating doctor charges an exorbitant price because he does not like depositions. Depending on your jurisdiction, you could argue that since the doctor is not a retained expert, all he is entitled to is the standard $50 for witnesses pursuant to 28 U.S.C. § 182(b) and (c)(2).

There are a variety of opinions whether a treating doctor is only entitled to the standard witness fee[2] or an hourly fee.[3] More often it is just easier to pay the hourly fee than to fight it. Do you really want to get into a financial argument with the doctor whose deposition you are about to take? Imagine the mood the doctor will be in if you prevail on your request to the court that the doctor should only get $50 instead of the several hundred dollars he is requesting. Do most doctors think their afternoon is only worth $50? Remember, you are trying to get at least a little helpful information from this doctor. Even if the court orders a fee more than $50 but less than the doctor has requested, you have only won a battle but will still lose the war with the doctor.

On the other hand, if you are the plaintiff's lawyer and you are trying to take the deposition of the doctor who treated your client, the doctor will be much more sensitive about his fee. Explain to him your client's limited resources, the merits of your case, and that a short deposition will probably avoid a trip to the courthouse for trial later on. Also, accommodate his schedule in any way that you can (i.e. at his office after his workday is complete). You will find that the treating doctor will often become very reasonable.

---

[1] *Knight v. Kirby Inland Marine Inc.*, 482 F.3d 347, 356 (5th Cir. 2007).
[2] See *Demar v. United States*, 199 F.R.D. 617 (N.D. Ill. 2001) (surveys a variety of opinions).
[3] See *Hoover v. United States*, 2002 WL 194734 (N.D. Ill. Aug. 22, 2002).

5.4 LOCATION

For a non-retained expert who is not an agent or employee of a party (i.e. a police accident reconstructionist), the location of the deposition is within 100 miles of his employment or residence. See Rule 45(c)(3)(A)(ii). Experts who have been retained or who are a party's agent or employee of a party do not fall under Rule 45. For these experts, the attorneys will work out an agreement that considers cost, convenience and litigation efficiency.

To illustrate, if a retained expert is hired a lot, he will be very accustomed to travelling to the city where the lawsuit has been filed. An expert that is not hired a lot and has a busy work schedule will probably want his deposition taken at his office. There are also travel costs to consider for the attorneys. In short, attorneys try and make the burden for each side equal. So, if the plaintiff's experts are going to fly to the city where the lawsuit is filed for a deposition, it is expected the defendant's experts will do the same.

5.5 PREPARING TO TAKE THE DEPOSITION

The most efficient way to prepare is to ask *your* expert what questions you need to ask the *opposing* expert. After all, the subject area will be difficult to grasp, and only by talking to your expert can you make it a level playing field when you go to deposition. Have your expert teach you what you need to know so that you can intelligently ask questions and understand the answers at the deposition.

Have your expert go through the opposing expert's report paragraph by paragraph and explain the strengths and weaknesses of each paragraph. Then, have your expert review the opposing expert's curriculum vitae and explain to you its strengths and weaknesses so that you can explore the weaknesses at the deposition.

Gather all the key information you can about the expert. A good place to start is Westlaw or LexisNexis. For example, LexisNexis has Expert Research on Demand (formerly known as IDEX) which provides information regarding *Daubert* challenges, deposition transcripts, trial testimony, verdicts, settlements and other valuable information.

Scour the Internet for your opposing expert. Is there anything on Facebook that reveals he belongs to groups that might undercut his credibility? Has the Board he belongs to in his specialty taken any adverse action against him? For many doctors, there are various websites that have patient reviews that will be revealed through any Internet search of the doctor.

Look into specialized litigation groups that have their own databases such as DRI, a large organization of defense attorneys, and AAJ, an organization of plaintiff's attorneys. Finally, a lot of experts have their own websites. It is shocking to find what proclamations they put on their website that you can use to undercut their credibility.

Also, collect an expert's previous depositions and trial testimonies. Under Rule 26(a)(2)(B), an expert must disclose in his report a list of all cases in the previous four years in which he has testified either at deposition or trial. Contact the attorneys who took the expert's deposition in the cases listed. The attorneys are often very responsive in sending you transcripts. This step is important because you want to determine if the expert has testified differently in a significant way on the same issue in your case. Don't forget to ask the attorney what he thought of the expert. He may gladly turn over his entire investigative file to help you out.

The opposing expert must also provide a list of his own publications. Have your expert review those publications to determine how good they are. It is often the case that the publications are not directly on point to the subject matter of the expert's opinion. Such information can be used to undercut his authority for arriving at opinions that hurt your case. In addition, check the sources the expert refers to in his report. Many times the articles or treatises the expert refers to are not credible.

Finally, when you notice the deposition, request the expert to bring to the deposition the articles he has relied on. The tool to do this is a subpoena duces tecum. Simply state in your notice to the expert that the notice includes a subpoena duces tecum and list on a separate page in the notice the list of documents you wish the expert to bring. The reason to do this is that some of the articles that your expert needs to review may be difficult for him to find.

Remember

Investigate the opposing expert by doing the following:

1. Search for transcripts, verdicts, disqualifications and settlements involving experts through Westlaw and LexisNexis.
2. Examine the expert's website, Facebook page, and scour the Internet for information.
3. Search databases of litigation groups such as DRI and AAJ.
4. Contact other attorneys to get their opinion of the expert and copies of prior depositions that have been disclosed under Rule 26.

5.6 EXPERTS RARELY CONCEDE ANYTHING

The first thing you will learn about an expert is that he can be very hard to pin down. Indeed, it can be very difficult to get him to commit to anything other than his ultimate conclusion. For example, if you ask him if today is Monday, he will probably say, "It depends what part of the world you are in." An expert will emphatically declare his final opinion but less strongly how he got there. The reason is that an expert never wants to get boxed in by assumptions that—if later changed—would force him to alter his opinion. The expert is getting paid a lot of money to help the other side, and he will do everything he can to come through on his commitment. Let's look at an example where an expert only admits to an assumption when he is confronted with his own sworn testimony in a prior lawsuit.

Example: Cross-examination of Dean Schmalensee (*U.S. v. Microsoft*)

In this example, David Boies is trying to get Microsoft's expert, Dean Schmalensee, to admit to a simple type of methodology which even a lay person would admit to.[4] However, the expert—as is true with most experts—does not want to give an inch in the deposition for fear of letting down his client by making any concessions at all.

Q. *Now, would you also agree that* **the standard way** *of approaching that question, that is, the question as to whether a firm has monopoly power, is to first define a relevant market and then look at what the share of that market is, and then if the share is sufficiently high, to look at conditions of entry?*

A. That is, as Professor Fisher [a government expert] indicated in his testimony, one approach. It provides some information. Market share, particularly in areas where market boundaries are difficult to draw or are fluid, is not terribly informative. That is an approach. It is useful in some circumstances. **[The expert will only concede that it is "an" approach, not that it is the standard way.]**

Q. *Well, more than being an approach, would you agree that that is the traditional and most common approach?*

A. I haven't done a survey. I have, of course, written on its utility for the last 20 years or so, and there are some circumstances in which it is not particularly informative, as Professor Fisher has said, and some where it is. It is **an approach** that has been used for a long time. **[Again, the expert will only admit that it is "an" approach.]**

Q. *Let me put before you and offer in evidence plaintiffs' exhibit 1526, which are*

---

[4] For more details regarding this lawsuit, go to the Appendix.

excerpts from testimony that you gave in the Bristol case [another lawsuit] that you referred to. . . . Let me direct your attention, Dean Schmalensee to page 541 and lines 11 through 19, and the question and answer there, which I will read . . . (reading): "question: how does an economist such as yourself go about determining whether a seller of a product has monopoly power in a given product market?
*Answer: there are a number of approaches depending on the availability of data. The **traditional and most common approach** in an instance where one can define a relevant market in the antitrust sense, is to first look at shares of that market and then if shares are large, to move on to consider conditions of entry." Now, recognizing that there may be cases in which you want to take a different approach, would you agree that the **traditional and most common approach** is the approach that you have identified here?*

A. When, as that indicates, one can define a relevant market in an antitrust sense, **yes.**

In the example, only after being confronted with his prior sworn statement, does the witness admit the obvious: the starting point for determining if there is a monopoly is to first determine the relevant market. This expert would not have admitted this fact if he had not been confronted with his prior sworn statement. Why would the expert not admit such a simple fact, particularly if he had said so under oath in the past?

Experts often won't give up an inch of ground in certain areas, even if the inch doesn't really matter. As seen below in the section on "confirm favorable facts," an expert will have to concede the truth of certain favorable facts to your side or he will look foolish. Your job is to explore at a deposition and determine which facts the expert will concede.

This next example is not from the Microsoft trial. Assume that the plaintiff's expert witness is claiming that the doctors were negligent in increasing the prescribed amount of drugs the patient was taking which caused a toxic build up in his blood stream, resulting in death. As the defense attorney representing the doctors, you are trying to get the expert to commit to whether it was the increased dosage that was prescribed or a build up over time of taking the drugs at any dosage level that caused the death.

Example: Attorney Tries to Challenge Expert's Assumptions (Hypothetical Case)

Q. *So, it's the increase in dosage prescribed by the doctor on March 18th that led to the overdose which led to his death?*

A. That's the highest probability, yes, sir.

Q. *You would agree then that if he had been prescribed this increased dosage but did not take it, then the increased dosage did not cause his death.* [Given the prior answer, the logical answer to this question should be: "Yes, if he did not take the larger amount of drugs as prescribed, then, the alleged negligent increase in the prescription could not have caused the death.

However, if the expert admits this, the case may well be over if there is proof that the plaintiff often did not take his pills.]

A. It wouldn't have eliminated the possibility. It would have re-enforced that it was a continuation of the process that began with the initial prescription a few months earlier.

Q. *So now you're saying that it could have been caused by the [lower] dosage that was prescribed in January?*

A. It is a possibility that I have to consider. The probability is that it was probably a change in dosage.

Q. *Based on a reasonable degree of scientific probability, did those dosage amounts in January—could they have led to an overdose?*

A. And I said it needs to be considered and could have. [The witness wants to avoid saying that it was a "reasonable degree of scientific probability" and effectively does that because it would undercut his theory that it was the negligent increase in dosage that caused the death.]

Q. *But to a reasonable degree of scientific probability, could those dosages have caused his death in May assuming there was no increase in March?*

A. And I said it needs to be considered and could have. [Again, witness does not answer question.]

Q. *But to a reasonable degree of scientific probability, could those dosages have caused his death in May?*

A. Well, I—well, I have to answer that in a more complex fashion. So let me do that. . . . [Again, witness does not answer question.]

Q. *I'll repeat the question. Well, answer however you want.* [Here, the attorney gets frustrated and momentarily lets the witness off the hook].

A. All right. Fine. Well, to give you an answer, the answer is, yes, we have to consider that in all possibilities because—

Q. *I don't—just so we don't waste a lot of time. I don't want to talk about possibilities. I want to talk about a reasonable degree of scientific probability. To a reasonable degree of scientific probability could the initial dosage in January have caused the death?* [Here, the attorney regains his footing and repeats the question which will force the witness to answer]

A. Yes. And I need to explain that . . . .

Although the attorney forces the witness to answer, it is not the answer the attorney wants. In essence, the expert explains that it doesn't matter whether the patient took the increased pills as prescribed or not, the drugs that were prescribed eventually killed the patient one way or another.

> Experts are masters at dodging questions.

5.7 STYLE OF QUESTIONING

Most experts are arrogant. They also enjoy spouting off their opinions. This combination works perfectly for the examiner who is respectful and sincerely interested in the opinion the expert is so proud of. The examiner should also mix in a dose of feigned ignorance if necessary. The more respect you show and the more you encourage him to explain his reasoning to you, the more you will get him to talk. Time after time, questions such as, "I don't understand, will you explain this to me" are met with a free-flowing response from the expert.

If you have ammunition to use against the witness, use it after you have gained all the favorable information you need. On the other hand, you might want to start off attacking the witness if he is so clearly unqualified or has made a key mistake in his report. You can get the expert on the defensive early. Such an attack may cause him to back down from some of his conclusions before he is able to regain his footing later in the deposition.

5.8 KEYS TO ATTACKING AN EXPERT EFFECTIVELY

Now that we have seen how difficult it can be to get experts to answer simple questions, let's look at some techniques that you can use that will almost always be successful at a deposition (and at trial). We are now going to return to the Microsoft trial and examine the trial testimony of one of the Department of Justice's technical experts, Glenn Weadock. Below, Microsoft's attorney, Rick Pepperman, attacks the government's expert. By looking at his cross-examination at trial, we can learn the needed strategies and techniques to use in a deposition so that the cross will be successful at trial.

1. Confirmation of Favorable Facts

Like with other witnesses, it is best to get the witness to confirm favorable facts before you challenge him. In the following questions, Pepperman tries to get the government's expert, John Weadock, to admit that Microsoft was not trying to create a monopoly by having its Internet Explorer accessible through Windows 98 but made it linked to Windows 98 in order to provide convenience for its customers. The Department of Justice was contending that Microsoft should not have put its browser, Internet Explorer, on computers with Windows 98 operating system, or it should have given consumers a choice of other Internet browsers to use. Microsoft contended it was easier for customers to browse the Internet or Intranet by having Internet Explorer imbedded in Windows.

By taking a focused deposition, Pepperman was able to ask questions at trial with the comfort of knowing that he already knew the answers because they had been provided at the deposition.

Q. And I think you agree with me that the number of organizations that want no Internet access and intranet access is decreasing?

A. Yeah, I think that's probably a fair statement.

Q. At the bottom of page 16 [of direct testimony], you list as one of the reasons why an organization might want to have no web-browsing software on its computer is to, quote, make it more difficult for certain employees to access the public Internet in order to reduce the amount of unproductive time employees spend surfing the net on subjects unrelated to their jobs. Do you see that, sir?

A. Okay, I see it.

Q. Again, sir, web-browsing software might be needed so that employees can access a private intranet; is that correct?

A. Yeah, that's correct. . . .

Q. So, there are companies, sir, you would agree, that don't want their employees accessing the public Internet but still may want web-browsing software [such as Internet Explorer] on their computers so that their employees can access a private intranet?

A. Yes.

Q. And would you also consider as another potential advantage that a user who has experience with the public Internet can use a private intranet without learning an entirely new user interface?

A. Yes, I would agree with that.

Q. And that is because he or she could use the same user interface to browse an intranet that is used to browse the Internet; correct?

A. Supposing for the sake of this discussion that they used the same web browser in both cases, yes, that would be a benefit.

Q. And you agree, don't you, sir, that the number of users who have experience with the Internet is growing rapidly over time?

A. I do.

Q. And isn't it also true, sir, that organizations that want to make it difficult—make it more difficult for certain employees to access the Internet can do so by a variety of means other than by not installing web-browsing software on those employees' computers?

A. Yes, they have several choices.

You will always have success at trial by cross-examining an expert on facts that he must agree with that are helpful to your case. Therefore, at the deposition, get the expert to admit the truth to as many of your favorable facts as possible. The reason this tactic is successful is that an expert has to admit the truth of at least some undisputed facts or he will look like a fool. However, what he will fight you to the death on is the interpretation of the facts. So, ask about facts, but don't ask about his interpretation of the facts or go too far and try to get the expert to admit to facts that are in dispute.

Q1. Does Microsoft, to your knowledge, prohibit those end users from removing the Internet Explorer icon from the Windows desktop?

A.   Generally, no, no, they don't . . . .

Q2. And Microsoft also doesn't prohibit end users from removing the entry for Internet Explorer on the start menu; correct?

A.   That's correct.

Q3. And Microsoft does not prohibit end users from removing the Internet Explorer option on the quick launch menu; correct?

A.   That is also correct.

*Q4. And in fact, **you're not aware of anything** that Microsoft does to restrict organizations' ability to remove the most commonly used means of accessing Internet Explorer; correct?*

A.   **Absolutely not correct. Absolutely not.**

In question four, Pepperman goes too far. There is no way the expert is going to admit that Microsoft does not do "anything" to restrict a customer's ability to remove its web browser, Internet Explorer. That is a central issue in the case. If Internet Explorer had been easy to remove with the click of a button, it certainly would have weakened the government's case that Microsoft was trying to monopolize the browser market by linking its Windows operating system with a web browser that could be removed with a click.

2. Lack of Expertise

There is almost always room to attack an expert's qualifications. Oftentimes, the expert has exaggerated accomplishments on his curriculum vitae (resume). Other times, he has simply listed accomplishments that look better on paper than they really are. Or he may have been more proficient in the past and has no recent experience.

Q. And the plaintiffs have identified you in court papers as one of their technical experts, correct?

A.   I believe that that's the case, although I am not sure I can recall a particular document that uses those terms. But I think that is true.

*Q. You do not, however, consider yourself, sir, to be an expert in the **design** of operating system software, do you?*

A.   No, I do not.

*Q. And you have never worked on the **development** of an operating system, have you?*

A.   No. That is correct.

Based on his deposition, the attorney highlights for the judge that the expert lacks expertise in areas that are central to two issues at trial: Microsoft's design and development of its Windows operating system.

Pepperman continues to hammer in on the theme of inexperience.

Q. *If you could turn to your direct testimony[5] on the second page, paragraph 2, you write, "I am a seminar developer, seminar instructor, author of computer books and videos and computer consultant." do you see that, sir?*
A. I do.

Q. *You have, however, never provided consulting services to a software company concerning the **design or development** of operating software, have you, sir?*
A. No. That's correct. There's lots of different kinds of computer consulting.

Q. *And the subject of which features should or should not be included in an operating system has never been the primary focus of any of the books, articles or videos you have written, correct?*
A. That is correct.

Q. *And, similarly, that subject has never been the primary focus of any of the seminars you have developed or taught, correct, sir?*
A. It has never been the primary focus. The issue of what operating systems look like and what vendors, with particular respect to Windows, include with their operating systems is a subject that comes up in my seminars, but it's not a primary focus, I think was your question.

Q. *That was my question, sir.*
Q. *And it's true, isn't it, sir, that you have never written anything about Windows 98 that has been published in a peer-review journal or publication?*

Q. In a peer-review—no, that is certainly correct . . . .

Notice how Pepperman dissects the expert's qualifications. While on paper, it may look impressive that the expert is a consultant, lectures at seminars, and has written books—even some that are widely read—such "expertise" is really not relevant to the issue at hand regarding operating systems. Many times the articles an expert has published are either not directly on the topic in dispute or have not been subject to peer review (i.e. scientific journals).

Pepperman continues to humble this expert.

Q. *You also state, sir, in paragraph 2 on page 2 of your direct testimony, the last sentence of that paragraph, that you are the, quote, president of Independent Software, Inc. Do you see that, sir?*
A. There are no quotes. You added that.

Q. *I was quoting from it, sir. Do you see where I am referring?*

---

[5] Since this was not a jury trial, the judge accepted a written statement of the expert as direct testimony that was submitted earlier in the proceedings. At trial, the witness swore that the statement was truthful, and it was admitted as evidence. Then, the cross-examination began.

A. Yes, I do.

Q. *You are also the one and only employee of Independent Software, aren't you, sir?*
A. That's correct.

In a few series of questions, Pepperman has established that this "expert" is not an expert in the design of operating software systems, has never written anything on this topic subject to peer review, and is the president of a company that employs one person, himself.

3. Meaningless Memberships and Organizations

Always question the expert about the organizations he brags about in his curriculum vitae (CV). Without fail, experts throw in the kitchen sink and list everything they belong to in order to bolster their perceived expertise. However, many of the organizations do nothing to establish expertise but only sound good on paper.

Q. *The last sentence of that paragraph reads, "my current professional memberships include the American Society for training and development and the association for computing machinery."*
Do you see that, sir?
A. I do.

Q. *I notice that you use the verb "include" in that sentence. Those two organizations are, in fact, the only organizations to which you currently belong, correct?*
A. The only professional organizations—

Q. *Yes, sir.*
A. —or organization of any kind?

Q. *Professional associations.*
A. That's right.

Q. *Now, isn't it true that there are no specific requirements or certification procedures for joining either of the two organizations that you've listed in your direct testimony?*
A. Yes, that is true.

Q. *And leaving aside the general presumption that applicants for these organizations are probably people who work in the industry, all that someone needs to do to join these two organizations is send in a check, correct, sir?*
A. That is true.

Practice Tip

Almost every expert includes meaningless organizations that he belongs to on his CV. Undermine his credibility by showing that the memberships are based simply on writing a check to join.

---

4. Irrelevant Education

In addition to exploring an expert's memberships, his training often is an area of weakness to explore. For example, an expert's educational background may be impressive but not relevant to his claimed expertise.

Q. *And you received from Stanford a bachelor's of science degree in general engineering; is that correct?*
A. That is correct.

Q. *And since graduating from Stanford, you have not received any graduate degrees from any formal universities; is that correct, sir?*
A. That is correct.

Q. *No master's degrees?*
A. I think that was encompassed in your earlier question. [expert is getting defensive]

Q. *And no doctorate degrees, correct, sir?*
A. Again, same answer.

Q. *Isn't it true, sir, that you took only two computer science courses at Stanford?*
A. I think that's correct.

Q. *And one of those two courses was a basic introductory course, something like programming 101?*
A. That is correct.

5. Reasons for Opinion Explained in Detail

An expert's report will discuss in summary fashion his opinion and the reasons for them. However, a deposition is critical to understand the details behind the opinions. You need the details for two reasons. First, it may be that you find that the expert has flawed reasoning when he tries to explain his opinion in detail. Second, the explanations will help your expert develop better counter arguments for his deposition or trial.

A simple way to do this is to show the expert his report at the deposition and have the expert go through each paragraph and explain his conclusions.

Practice Tip

Every expert has to make assumptions and when he does, you can show that if the assumptions were different, the conclusions would be different.

6. Why Does Expert Disagree with Your Expert?

One of the most important things you can accomplish at the deposition is to find out exactly those points the expert disagrees with and the reasons why. Show the witness your expert's report. Go through the important paragraphs and ask the witness why he agrees or disagrees with your expert's findings.

7. Frequency Hired by Plaintiffs or Defendants

Determine how often the expert testifies for the plaintiff or defendant. Usually, the expert will say that he testifies about 60-40 for one side or the other. Upon closer investigation, the facts often show that the expert clearly is hired a larger majority of the time by one side or the other. For that same reason, don't take your expert's word for it when you hire him that he testifies equally or 60-40 for one side. You will be unpleasantly surprised when he testifies differently at his deposition.

Practice Tip

Ask the adverse expert what percentage of his income is derived from being a paid expert. Often, a majority of an expert's livelihood is dependent on being hired as an expert. Such testimony reveals his bias.

---

8. Lack of Preparation for Deposition or Trial

An expert's opinion can also be affected by how much or how little work he has done in preparing his expert report, preparing for the deposition, or preparing for trial. This is an area that you should consider exploring at a deposition. However, note that if you point out omissions the expert has made at the deposition, he may be able to correct them prior to trial and be better prepared when it counts. Let's look at another example from the Weadock cross at the Microsoft trial. Below, the expert's failure to read only one deposition undercuts his credibility.

Q. *The next to last bullet point [of his expert report] reads, "my **review of documents and deposition testimony** (of Microsoft employees and other witnesses) in the months prior to this trial." Do you see that?*
A. I do.

Q. *Now, at the time you submitted your expert report in this case on September 3rd, 1998, isn't it true that you had at that time **read only one of the 98 depositions** that had been taken in this case?*

A. I think that may be true.

Q. *And that one deposition was the deposition of Jim Allchin, a Microsoft employee?*

A. Right.

9. Biased Investigation

You should also determine what investigation the expert has conducted in formulating his opinions. In the example we have been looking at, Weadock interviewed several companies. Pepperman wanted to find out if the expert's opinion was completely objective or if it had been influenced by the companies he had interviewed. Below is one exchange.

Q. *You also interviewed the Sabre Group, correct?*

A. Yes, that's correct.

Q. *Now, the Sabre Group offers an online reservation service called Travelocity; is that right?*

A. That is correct, yes.

Q. *And that online service competes with Microsoft's Expedia service, correct?*

A. That's my understanding.

Q. *And the Sabre group is also an **outspoken critic of Microsoft**; isn't that right?*

A. I don't know if they are outspoken or not.

Q. *Were you aware that the Sabre group **is a member of Procomp, an anti-Microsoft lobbying group** here in Washington, D.C.?*

A. No, I wasn't.

Q. *Were you—were you aware that the C.E.O. of the Sabre group, **Mr. Michael Durham, publicly criticized Microsoft** on April 30th, 1998 in testimony before the House Commerce Committee?*

A. Gosh, Mr. Pepperman. Lots and lots of people publicly criticize Microsoft. I am not aware of all of them.

Q. *A lot of them made up your focus group, didn't they, sir?*

A. I wouldn't call it a focus group. These are illustrative examples —companies that I had conversation with—one-of-ten areas that I relied upon in my testimony.

Q. *Well, it's true, isn't it, that one of the representatives of the Sabre group, whom you interviewed, told you that, as a matter of company policy, if there is a product available that is comparable to a Microsoft product, **the Sabre group always uses the non-Mircosoft product**, correct?*

A. That is correct.

Pepperman was trying to establish at trial that many of the companies that were complaining about Microsoft's alleged monopoly were biased against Microsoft. By asking relevant questions at the deposition, Pepperman was able to use that information at trial for an effective cross.

10. Nail Down Extent of Opinions

Experts are always trying to add to their opinions at trial. For example, they may come up with additional reasons to support their conclusion or give an alternative conclusion for the first time. While some judges will not allow the expert to go beyond his opinions set forth in his expert report, you need to make sure in the deposition that the expert states clearly all the opinions he is rendering and the reasons for them.

To accomplish this goal, ask the expert near the end of the deposition the following: "Are you going to testify at trial to any opinions you have not given here today? Are there any assumptions or reasons that support your opinions that you are going to testify at trial that you have not stated here today?" If he answers, "yes," explore what those opinions are and what the reasons are.

Sometimes the expert will hedge and say that he may change his opinion depending on other depositions or facts that come to light. That is a reason why you should generally take an expert's deposition at the end of the discovery. That way, he can't hedge his conclusions and you can be certain he won't have a good reason to change his opinion.

The most important areas that should be explored at a deposition are:

1. Confirmation of your favorable facts
2. Lack of expertise (education, etc.)
3. Reasons for opinions
4. Reasons why expert disagrees with your expert
5. Frequency of hiring by plaintiffs or defendants
6. Lack of preparation
7. Biased investigation
8. Making sure expert has told you all of his opinions and reasons supporting them

---

11. Two Areas Not Worth Exploring

Finally, let's look at two areas that are a waste of time to explore. Although questions about an expert's compensation should be asked at a deposition if it is not already known through a discovery disclosure, there is no point in bringing it out at trial since your expert will also be compensated. That is, since your expert is also getting paid, you are not going to get much mileage out of the reality that the fact finder should not believe the opposing party's expert because he is getting paid. However, this is a mistake that many attorneys make at trial.

Q. *The Department of Justice is compensating you for your services at the rate of $100 per hour, correct?*
A. That's correct.

Q. *And that is your normal consulting rate, correct?*
A. Yes, sir.

Another mistake at trial is trying to get the expert to admit that he would slant his opinion in favor of the side that hired him. No expert is ever going to admit this. In the exchange below, notice how well the expert handles such questions.

Q. *Mr. Weadock, do you know who Michael Wilson is?*
A. Yes, I do.

Q. *Who is Mr. Wilson?*
A. He's one of the people who works with the Department of Justice. . . .

Q. *Have you had discussions with Mr. Wilson?*
A. Yes.

Q. *Do you know who wanpt [the initials on an email] is?*
A. I would guess it's Pauline Wan.

Q. *Have you ever had discussions with Ms. Wan?*
A. Yes.

Q. *About midway through the e-mail, Mr. Wilson includes a parenthetical that reads, "I also think he wants to teach b/c he hinted that the teaching course is more prompt at paying his invoices. He hasn't received payment for his February bill for January work—**we need to keep Glenn happy because he's the most efficient, articulate and flexible expert we have.**"*
Q. *The "Glenn" referred to in that parenthetical is you, Mr. Weadock?*
A. I am pleased to say that it appears to be.

Q. *And has Mr. Wilson ever described you in your presence as the Department of Justice's most flexible expert?*
A. Not in my presence. And I think if you look at the context of this memo, he is talking about scheduling.

Q. *But Mr. Wilson is—*
A. **I would hope that Mr. Wilson doesn't mean that I'm flexible in my opinions. Anybody who knows me very well knows that my opinions are generally my own and not easily influenced.**

Q. Mr. Wilson notes in this e-mail that you actually have a scheduling conflict for a meeting that was being scheduled, correct? [The attorney tries to backpedal from accusing the witness of slanting his opinion for monetary gain to soften the failure of his attack]

A. Yeah, I think so.

Q. So in the context of saying you have a scheduling conflict, he's saying that you have the most flexible schedule, correct? That's your understanding? [The attorney has now completely backpedalled]

A. I mean, we'd have to ask him exactly what he means, but that's the way I take his memo.

Most important, notice that the attorney made the mistake of not asking such questions at the deposition. If he had, he would have known that the witness had a good explanation for the e-mail. Further, the attorney would have avoided the embarrassment of trying to make the witness look overreaching and having it backfire on him because it was the attorney who was overreaching.

ⅢCHECKLIST

Daubert Requirements

An expert must meet the following criteria:

1. The technique or theory can be tested (and has been).
2. The technique or theory has been subject to peer review and publication.
3. The known or potential rate of error has been determined and the theory or technique has been generally accepted.

Most experts will easily satisfy these criteria.

Expert Compensation

1. The party taking the deposition must pay the hourly rate of the expert, but attorneys sometimes agree not to.
2. The same is true for treating doctors, even though they are really entitled only to a nominal witness fee.

Location

Generally at witness' office.

Preparation

1. Begin search with Westlaw or LexisNexis to find verdicts, settlements, disqualifications, and transcripts.
2. Examine expert's website and Facebook page.
3. Scour the Internet for information.

4. Search databases of litigation groups such as DRI.

5. Contact other attorneys to get their opinion of the expert and previous deposition transcripts.

Style of Questioning

Be respectful and inquisitive. Expert will respond with free flowing responses.

Keys to Attacking Expert

1. Confirm favorable facts.

2. Examine expert's CV for meaningless memberships and organizations meant to bolster reputation.

3. Make expert explain in detail the reasons for his opinion.

4. Determine the assumptions expert has made to support conclusion.

5. Understand why expert disagrees with your expert.

6. Determine how frequently expert testifies for plaintiffs and defendants.

7. Expose expert's lack of preparation in reaching conclusions.

8. Determine if expert had bias affecting his investigation.

9. Make expert tell you all of his conclusions and reasons supporting them so you won't be surprised at trial.

Two Areas Not Worth Exploring at Trial

1. Don't ask about expert's compensation at trial since your expert is also being paid.

2. Don't suggest that expert would slant opinion based on compensation for the same reason as number one.

CHAPTER SIX

Problems at Deposition

An eye for an eye only ends up making the whole world
go blind.

—*Mohandas Gandhi*

Gandhi's advice could not be more sound for dealing with difficult
opposing counsel and witnesses. If you fight back in the same
way that you are being attacked, nothing will be accomplished.
However, Gandhi did not simply preach passive resistance at all costs. He
also declared, "All compromise is based on give and take, but there can be
no give and take on fundamentals. Any compromise on mere fundamentals
is a surrender. For it is all give and no take." You need to strike a balance.
Compromise only as long as you can still gather the information you need
from the witness and protect your witness' fundamental rights (if you are
defending the deposition).

Let's look at some common situations you are likely to encounter and
how to handle them. First, we will look at problems caused by difficult
witnesses and then those caused by attorneys.

6.1 ATTORNEY CONVERSATIONS WITH EXPERT WITNESS

A very important change to the federal rules occurred in December 2010
regarding the disclosure of communications between an attorney and his
designated expert witness. Rule 26(b)(4)(C) is a significant departure from
the old rule and the current practice in many states. A designated expert is a
witness who can testify at trial. Under the old rule, if the witness had been
designated as an expert and thus not a consulting expert (a witness who
could not testify at trial but could give confidential advice to an attorney),
any communication between the attorney and that expert was discoverable.
Let's look at an example from the Microsoft case under the old rule.

Example: Cross of Weadock (*U.S. v. Microsoft*)

Weadock was an expert hired by the Department of Justice. Here, he is being questioned at trial by Microsoft's attorney.

Q. *Over the last year, has any Department of Justice lawyer ever expressed appreciation for your willingness to conform your views to those of the Department of Justice's?* **[seeks communication not protected under old rule]**

A. Quite the contrary, Mr. Pepperman. As a matter of fact, I made it very clear as a condition of employment when we were having these discussions in —I believe it was October—early October of last year—that if they were to hire me as a consultant, that I would not be bound by any preconceptions and that I would be free to call things as I see them. And, in fact, it's—it's my opinion as a businessman and as a consultant, that that's the greatest value a consultant has to a client, is to call things as they see them. They said, "that's all we want you to do." And they hired me on that basis.

The Microsoft attorney should have expected such an answer. It should not be surprising that an expert who is being paid a lot of money by one side is not going to help the other side with an answer that hurts his client. The following example (not from the Microsoft case) is another scenario that often took place under the old rule.

Example: Attorney Conversations with Expert Under Old Rule (Hypothetical Case)

Q. *Did you meet with Mr. Dodge [defense attorney] this morning prior to the deposition?*
A. Yes.

Q. *What did you discuss?*
A. We discussed my expert report and the expert report from the other side.

Q. *Did Mr. Dodge mention to you any concerns he had about your report?*
A. No.

Q. *Describe in more detail what you talked about.*
A. We essentially discussed my report in brief, and I reaffirmed what I said in it.

Q. *Did you and Mr. Dodge discuss what questions I might ask you?*
A. None that I remember. He just said that I would get asked some questions about my report and plaintiff's report, and he told me to tell the truth.

While under the old federal rule and many current state rules, these scenarios occurred often, the new federal rule specifically protects from disclosure communications between an attorney and his expert witness unless it relates to 1) the expert's compensation, 2) facts or data the attorney provided which were considered by the expert, and 3) assumptions the attorney provided that the expert relied on.[1]

---

[1] Rule 26(b)(4)(C).

Even under the old rule, experts rarely revealed any communications despite the fact that the old rule required such disclosure. Now, the rule protects many of those disclosures. But be aware that an opposing attorney may still discover communications such as facts and assumptions supplied to the expert. Although it is highly unlikely that your expert would reveal these facts under the new rule (see practices under the old rule above), you would still have a duty to correct the record if the witness lied at a deposition. This is not a position you want to be in. So, be careful what facts or data you supply to your expert.

Remember

Take advantage of the Rule Amendments that now protect from disclosure most communications between you and your expert.

6.2 WITNESS GIVES IMPLAUSIBLE ANSWER

There is nothing you can do when a witness gives an implausible answer. This is one of the most common—and frustrating—occurrences in a deposition. Many attorneys become exasperated when this happens. Instead, you should realize that you have achieved victory when you get such an answer. The reason is that it does not matter what the witness says, only if a jury will ultimately believe what was said. Consequently, a jury will see an implausible answer for what it is: an attempt by the witness to deceive. When this answer is shown to the jury, it is as helpful to you as the admission you were trying to get. Let's look at a few examples from the Gates deposition.

Example: (Gates Deposition)

In this example, Boies is showing Gates an e-mail he wrote to a subordinate on Jan. 5, 1996. The Justice Department was accusing Microsoft of attempting to monopolize the market for Internet browsing.

Q. And the first line of this is, "Winning Internet browser share is a very very important goal for us." Do you see that?
A. I do.

Q. Do you remember writing that, sir?
A. Not specifically.

Q. Now, when you were referring there to Internet browser share, what were the companies who were included in that?
A. There were no companies included in that.

Q. Well, if you're winning browser share, that must mean that some other company is producing browsers and you're comparing your share of browsers with somebody else's share of browsers; is that not so, sir?

A. You asked me if there are any companies included in that and now—I'm very confused about what you're asking.

Q. Allright, sir, let me see if I can try to clarify. You say here "Winning Internet browser share is a very very important goal for us." What companies were supplying browsers whose share you were talking about?

A. It doesn't appear I'm talking about any other companies in that sentence.

Gates' answer that there were no companies referenced in the e-mail does not pass the laugh test. Gates is afraid to admit that Microsoft wanted to win the browser share market from Netscape. As Boies pointed out, Microsoft had to be trying to win browser share from *some* company. Gates' refusal to answer a simple question would hurt him later at trial. When this deposition excerpt and others were played by videotape at the trial, the judge—who in this case was the trier of fact as well since there was no jury—shook his head and laughed.[2]

Example: Cont'd (Gates Deposition)

In this example, Boies confronts Gates with a document sent to him by Brad Chase, Microsoft's vice-president.

Q1. Let me go down to the third paragraph of the document and the fifth sentence that says "Browser share needs to remain a key priority for our field and marketing efforts." Do you see that?

A. In the third paragraph?

Q2. Yes.

A. Okay, the third sentence, the third paragraph. Yeah.

Q3. Were you told in or about March of 1997 that people within Microsoft believed that browser share needed to remain a key priority for your field and marketing efforts?

A. I don't remember being told that, but I wouldn't be surprised to hear that people were saying that.

Q4. Immediately before that sentence there is a statement that Microsoft needs to continue its jihad next year. Do you see that?

A. No.

Q5. The sentence that says "Browser share needs to remain a key priority for our field and marketing efforts," the sentence right before that says "we need to continue our jihad next year. That's the way it ends. Do you see that?

A. Now I see—it doesn't say Microsoft.

---

[2] **http://www.cnn.com/TECH/computing/9811/17/judgelaugh.ms.idg/index.html**. *Gates Deposition Makes Judge Laugh in Court.* (accessed March 20, 2011.)

Q6. *Well, when it says "we" there, do you understand that means something other than Microsoft, sir?*

A. It could mean Brad Chase's group. **[Boies gets frustrated with this implausible answer, refuses to accept it and tries to challenge Gates because he is so exasperated with the answer. His efforts go unrewarded.]**

Q7. *Well, this is a message from Brad Chase to you, Brad Silverberg, Paul Maritz and Steve Ballmer [management at Microsoft] correct?*

A. As I say, it's strange that. this—if this was a normal piece of e-mail, it wouldn't print like that. I'm not aware of any way—maybe there is some way that e-mail ends up looking like this when you print it out. **[Gates now tries to dodge the question completely by questioning the document's authenticity]**

Q8. *I wasn't the one that was asserting it was an e-mail. I don't know whether it is an e-mail or memo or what it is. All I know is it was produced to us by Microsoft. And the first line of it says "To" and the first name there is "Bradsi." Do you see that?*

A. Uh-huh.

[Boies then asks several questions to get Gates to admit that all the names on the address line work for Microsoft.]

Q9. *And it says it's from "Bradc" and do you believe that is Brad Chase?*

A. Yes.

Q10. *Now, when Brad Chase writes to you and the others "we need to continue our jihad next year," do you understand that he is referring to Microsoft when he uses the word "we"?*

A. No.

Q11. *What do you think he means when he uses the word "we"?*

A. I'm not sure.

Q12. *Do you know what he means by jihad?*

A. I think he is referring to our vigorous efforts to make a superior product and to market that product.

It is understandable why Boise spent the time to ask more questions in order to get Gates to change his implausible answer to Q6. Who would not have done the same in the heat of the moment? How can Gates possibly deny that "we" does not mean Microsoft? Once Gates declares that "we" does not refer to Microsoft, he is not going to change his answer and thereby look even more foolish than after he gave his original answer.

When a witness is backed into a corner, he still won't confess, but you have won because he will be forced to give an answer that won't be believed.

6.3 WITNESS HEDGES HIS BETS

Some lawyers instruct witnesses to give evasive and ambiguous answers. The goal is to limit the details given so that they can surprise opposing counsel at trial with new facts. The following is such a scenario.

Q. Who witnessed the harassment you suffered at work?
A. All I can remember now is Jonathan.

Here, the evasive witness lies at the deposition by testifying that Jonathan is the *only* witness she remembers when she knows there are really two witnesses. At trial, the witness hopes to surprise opposing counsel by saying, "Now I remember that there was another witness."

However, coaching your witness in such a manner is not only unethical, but it is also impractical. The evasive answer can easily be cured by asking this follow up: "Would anything help you remember if there were other witnesses?" If the witness says "No," then you are done. At trial, you can impeach the witness' sudden recollection of another witness by showing her the deposition transcript which shows "nothing" could refresh her memory.[3]

If you get the opposite answer, simply follow up with the questions that will determine what would help the witness remember. Then refresh the witness' memory with a particular document—if you have it—or follow up with another witness if the deponent suggests that if she were to speak with someone, then that would refresh her memory.

6.4 WITNESS PRETENDS NOT TO UNDERSTAND QUESTION

Perhaps the most frustrating thing in a deposition occurs when a witness pretends to be confused by a simple question. There are four steps to solve this problem every time. Boies provides the perfect demonstration below, and he had to do it quite often with Gates. Below, Boies asks Gates about an e-mail he wrote in January 1996.

Q. What were the non-Microsoft browsers that you were concerned about in January of 1996?
A. What's the question? You're trying to get me to recall what other browsers I was thinking about when I wrote that sentence?

Q. No, because you've told me that you don't know what you were thinking about when you wrote that sentence. Right? What I'm trying to do is get you to tell me what non-Microsoft browsers you were concerned about in January of 1996.

---

[3] Moreover, such coaching is self-defeating since the Rules require a party to disclose the names of witnesses that will support its claim (Rule 26(a)(1)(A)(i)). A judge would not allow the undisclosed witness to testify at trial.

A. If it had been only one, I probably would have used the name of it. Instead I seem to be using the term non-Microsoft browsers. [Boise did not ask Gates "how many," but Gates tries to avoid the question by not answering it, so, Boies repeats the question.]

Q. *My question is what non-Microsoft browsers were you concerned about in January of 1996?*

A. I'm sure —what's the question? Is it—are you asking me about when I wrote this e-mail or what are you asking me about?

Q. *I'm asking you about January of 1996.*

A. That month?

Q. *Yes, sir.*

A. And what about it? [Gates is in full dodging mode.]

Q. *What non-Microsoft browsers were you concerned about in January of 1996?* [This is the third time Boies has asked the exact same question. Look how Gates dodges the question a third time.]

A. I don't know what you mean "concerned."

Q. *What is it about the word "concerned" that you don't understand?* [Step one to take when a witness claims he does not understand a word]

A. I'm not sure what you mean by it. Is there a document where I use that term?

Q. *Is the term "concerned" a term that you're familiar with in the English language?* [Step two]

A. Yes.

Q. *Does it have a meaning that you're familiar with?* [**Step three**]

A. Yes.

Q. *Using the word "concerned" consistent with the normal meaning that it has in the English language, what Microsoft—or what non-Microsoft browsers were you concerned about in "January of 1996?* [Step four (Repeat the question). This is also the fourth time the question is asked]

A. Well, I think I would have been concerned about Internet Explorer, what was going on with it. We would have been looking at other browsers that were in use at the time. Certainly Navigator was one of those. And I don't know which browser AOL was using at the time, but it was another browser. [Here, Boies gets his answer but notices that Gates may still be qualifying his answer because he says he was "looking" at Netscape Navigator and others. Boies follows up with many more questions that Gates dodges. A few of them follow.]

Q. *What I'm asking, Mr. Gates, is what other browsers or what non-Microsoft browsers were you concerned about in January of 1996? I'm not asking what you were looking at, although that may be part of the answer, and I don't mean to exclude it, but what non-Microsoft browsers were you concerned about in January of 1996?* [The fifth time the question is asked.]

A. Well, our concern was to provide the best Internet support, among other things, in Windows. And in dealing with that concern, I'm sure we looked at competitive products, including the ones I mentioned.

Steps to Take When Witness Pretends Not to Understand a Word in the Question

1. Ask the witness what he does not understand about the word (i.e. concerned).
2. Ask if witness is familiar with that word as it is used in the English language.
3. Ask the witness if he is familiar with the *meaning* of that word.
4. Ask witness your original question beginning with this phrase: "Using the word "[i.e. concerned]" consistent with the normal meaning that it has in the English language, what non-Microsoft browsers were you concerned about . . . ?

In the next exchange, Gates does not give Boies the perfect answer because he still qualifies it a bit by saying that he "looked" at certain products. It can be maddening when a witness doesn't answer a question directly, particularly a witness like Gates who failed to do so throughout the deposition. You need to choose your battles carefully. Here, Boies continues to battle. Although, he never gets the perfect answer he wants, he wins the battle as will be discussed below.

Q. *Let me try to use your words and see if we can move this along. What competitive products did you look at in January of 1996 in terms of browsers?* [A variant of the original question that has been asked six times.]
A. I don't remember looking at any specific products during that month.

Q. *Were there specific competitive products that in January of 1996 you wanted to increase Microsoft's share with respect to those products?* [The seventh time]
[Gates' attorney]: Objection.

Q. *Do you understand the question, Mr. Gates?*
A. I'm pausing to see if I can understand it.

Q. *If you don't understand it, I'd be happy to rephrase it.*
A. Go ahead and rephrase it. I probably could have understood it if I thought about it, but go ahead.

Q. *In January, 1996, you were aware that there were non-Microsoft browsers that were being marketed; is that correct?* [Boies is now backtracking and losing ground on the concession he got earlier. Gates probably enjoys trying to frustrate Boies. Watch what happens a few questions later.]

A. I can't really confine it to that month, but I'm sure in that time period I was aware of other browsers being out.

Q. *And were those non-Microsoft browsers, or at least some of them, being marketed in competition with Microsoft's browser?*

A. Users were making choices about which browser to select. [Gates does not answer the question but starts to talk about "users."]

Q. *Is the term "competition" a term that you're familiar with, Mr. Gates?*

A. Yes.

Q. *And does it have a meaning in the English language that you're familiar with?*

A. Any lack of understanding of the question doesn't stem from the use of that word.

Q. *And you understand what is meant by non-Microsoft browsers, do you not, sir?*

A. No.

Q. *You don't? Is that what you're telling me? You don't understand what that means?*

A. You'll have to be more specific. [Boies and Gates argue for another five minutes over terminology before the following and final question on this topic is asked.]

Q. *Let's focus on January of 1996. What were the non-Microsoft browsers that, in your view, were competing with Internet Explorer in January of 1996?*

A. Well, users could choose from a number of browsers, including the original Mosaic browser, the Netscape Navigator, and I don't know what version they had out at the time. The AOL browser. And some others that were in the market.

The Mosaic browser mention in the last answer was really considered a part of the Netscape Navigator, so this last answer was really no more complete than the one given much earlier. Boies could have stopped when he got the partial admission in response to the fifth time he asked the question (see previous example) and been no worse off regarding the substance of Gates' answers. When a witness does not answer the question, decide how important it is that you get the exact answer you want since you will have to expend time and energy pursuing the answer you want.

Another lesson is that if a witness does not answer a simple question, you may not get the admission you want, but the jury will discredit the witness for failing to answer simple questions which the jury expects a witness to do. Gates' continuing efforts to duck questions, redirect questions by pretending not to understand the question, and his failure to understand words such as "concerned" and "non-Microsoft browsers" give Boies all the ammunition he would ever need to prove Gates was disingenuous.

The above excerpt was played at the trial, and it had just the effect Boies was looking for. Microsoft was so worried about how Gates came across that it hired an expert to try and explain to the media why he was not more forthcoming. In essence, the hired expert declared that depositions are often messy and that Gates did not want Boies to put words in his mouth.

6.5 WITNESS PRETENDS TO FORGET

Sometimes witnesses, either through coaching or through their own devices, display sanctionable conduct. Below, the witness—who happened to be an attorney—feigns amnesia when asked about what was discussed during the break.

Q. *During the last recess that we had that we just reconvened from, did you consult with your attorney concerning this deposition?*
A. I don't understand the question.

Q. *We just had a recess.*
A. I understand that.

Q. *Do you understand that? During that recess period, did you take that time to consult with your attorney regarding this deposition?*
A. I don't know what you mean by the word consult.

Q. *Did you speak with your attorney regarding this deposition?*
A. I don't think so. I don't know.

Q. *Do you know how-did you write anything to your attorney during that recess?*
A. Write anything?

Q. *Correct.*
A. No.

Q. *Did you speak with your attorney during that recess?*
A. I had words with my attorney. We exchanged a conversation.

Q. *Did any of the comments in that conversation or those conversations refer to any aspect of this deposition?*
A. I can't recall.[4]

The *Dobson* deposition got so out of hand that every side, including the witness, was punished. If a situation ever occurs like the one above where you are taking a deposition and the witness pretends to forget, ask the question in a couple of different ways to build a record of the witness' refusal to answer simple questions. If that does not work, follow the four steps that Boies used earlier in this chapter. If the witness still does not answer, go

---

[4] *Redwood v. Dobson*, 476 F.3d 462, 468-69 (7th Cir. 2007).

on to your other questions. As discussed above, a disingenuous answer is all you need to succeed. But if you feel that is not enough in a particular circumstance, file a motion to compel seeking the court's help to order the witness to answer the questions.

If you are defending a deposition and your witness feigns amnesia or doesn't answer simple questions, you need to take a break and instruct your witness to answer the questions—unless the questions invade the attorney-client privilege. While the questions above invade the attorney-client privilege, that privilege may well be waived if the attorney was indeed improperly coaching his witness during the break.

6.6 PROTECTIVE ORDERS

Chapter Four discussed the circumstances when a defending attorney can suspend a deposition and seek the court's help when the questioning becomes harassing. But, there are also times when seeking the court's assistance by both sides *prior* to the deposition makes sense. If the examining attorney anticipates that his questions (i.e. the finances of the witness) may result in an instruction not to answer from opposing counsel, prior approval from the court to inquire into the subject matter should be obtained. The motion made under Rule 26(b)(1) can be very simple with an explanation of the anticipated problem and why questioning should be allowed. Likewise, the defending attorney should seek a protective order if he anticipates inappropriate questions. Such a motion is made under Rule 26(c) and can prevent questions that may cause embarrassment, harassment, disclosure of trade secrets, disclosure of confidential information and more.

6.7 DEFENDING LAWYER PRETENDS NOT TO UNDERSTAND QUESTION

Sometimes it is the lawyer who pretends not to understand the question.

Q1. How many employees do you supervise?
[Defending attorney] Objection, vague, the witness does not know if you mean employees she directly or indirectly supervises or whether the employees are full or part time.

Even though this is an obvious attempt by the attorney to coach his witness, the witness may not always agree with the objection. Why not? If you have developed a rapport with the witness, she may realize that the quickest way to end

> Sometimes a lawyer will object that a question is vague or confusing—even though it isn't—to signal his witness to pay close attention to the question.

the deposition is to answer the questions you ask. She may also want to signal to her attorney that his repeated objections are annoying her. Before rephrasing your question, simply ask the witness if she understands the question. You may be surprised at the answer you get.

Q2. Do you understand the question?
A. Yes. I supervise six employees.

6.8 ASSERTING THE ATTORNEY-CLIENT PRIVILEGE

The attorney-client privilege is the source of many confrontations. While communications between a lawyer and his client are protected, that protection can be lost in certain situations if the communications are made in the presence of others who are not on the lawyer's staff. Let's look at how it was handled in the Simpson case. Goldman's attorney was trying to determine if there were any video recordings of O.J. talking about the murders. He knew there was at least one: a promotional video that was going to be released where O.J. explained his innocence. However, there was also evidence that O.J. may have been videotaped in a mock cross-examination in preparation for possible testimony for the criminal trial.

Example: (Simpson Deposition)

Q. *[Petrocelli]. Now, is that the only time that you have been recorded discussing the facts and circumstances surrounding Ron and Nicole's deaths?*
   [Baker] Don't answer that question unless you exclude anything that was done vis-à-vis your attorneys. . . .

[Petrocelli] I would like to know if he is excluding anything.
[Baker] He is going to exclude everything that was done with and through and by his attorneys.

[Petrocelli] But all I am saying, Mr. Baker, so that we know whether or not there is a relevant contact with an attorney where we might want to attack the assertion of the attorney-client privilege, we have to know the basic foundational facts. That's all I'm saying.
[Baker] I understand what you're saying, and I'm not assenting to that, and we are not going to allow you to inquire as to what he did with his attorneys, whether he was taped, videotaped or anything else.

[Petrocelli] Well, I am going to inquire into that, and I haven't asked so far about any communications. I have simply asked for the mere existence of such recordings, if they do exist.
[Baker] And I am going to instruct him not to answer that, and you can certify it, and we can argue that point with the court.

Petrocelli has the right to explore—without asking specific questions about communications—whether the privilege has been waived because third parties were present. That is why Petrocelli said that he had the right to know the basic foundational facts. Baker was wrong not to agree with Petrocelli which put Petrocelli in a bind. Given how hard this deposition had been to arrange, the last thing Petrocelli should have done was suspend the deposition and file a motion with the court. Instead, Petrocelli pressed on to other topics. After the deposition, he could decide if it was worth the effort to get his questions answered by seeking help from the court.

6.9 GUESSING

Most jurisdictions do not prohibit an attorney from asking a witness to guess. But asking a witness to guess rarely helps. For example, if a witness says she does not know something and then you ask her to guess, what good is the answer? *Webster's Dictionary* defines "guess" as follows: "to form an opinion of from little or no evidence."[5] At trial, a witness can only testify about facts she knows. Nonetheless, if you are the examining attorney, it is worth exploring why a witness does not know the answer to an important question. Those follow-up questions can lead to helpful information.

The problem defending attorneys confront is when their witness is asked a straightforward question and instead of saying "I don't know," the witness guesses but doesn't state that in her answer. Then, the guess becomes a sworn fact in the case.

6.10 EIGHT STEPS TO RESOLVING CONFLICT WITH OPPOSING COUNSEL

It is fair to say that depositions can easily become confrontational. Tension starts with the witness who does not want to be there. This tension also manifests itself in the attorney defending the witness whose job it has been to prepare this witness for the dreaded event and to do what he can within the rules to protect the witness during the deposition.

Couple this tension with the fact that the deposing attorney assumes that the information he really needs from the witness won't be obtained because opposing counsel has coached the witness to be evasive. Finally, there is no judge to referee. So, battle lines have been drawn before the deposition ever begins. The final ingredient to this combustible mixture is that people often don't perform well under pressure. They become tense, anxious and impatient.

Given this atmosphere, you first need to be careful not to jump to the wrong conclusion that opposing counsel is being deceitful. It may be that

---

[5] *Webster's Ninth New College Dictionary* at 541 (1985).

opposing counsel is simply ineffective in asking appropriate questions or making correct objections.

> The key to dealing successfully with opposing counsel is making the correct judgment call as to whether his behavior is an innocent mistake or deceitful conduct.

For example, many attorneys taking depositions are plainly unprepared. Their exhibits are a mess, their questions unorganized. Although you have objected, "asked and answered," the attorney may return to the same question throughout the deposition because he has not listened to previous answers. He may be asking irrelevant questions not in an attempt to harass the witness but because he does not know what he should ask.

One misconception about depositions is that they are often ugly affairs. The truth is that the vast majority of depositions go fairly smoothly. You could go years and never bring or face a motion regarding inappropriate conduct. The reason is that attorneys realize that it takes a tremendous amount of time to file a motion with the court and get a hearing and once a hearing is obtained, judges are usually not very sympathetic. The judge usually tells the parties to work it out, or he splits the baby. So, in the back of most attorneys' minds is the realization that it is better to work things out with opposing counsel.

Nonetheless, even in a typical deposition, it is very easy to lose your patience and even briefly your temper. Opposing counsel may be the most pleasant person in the world, but it can be difficult to remain calm after spending all day with someone whose goal is to weaken your case and strengthen his. In other situations, it is only natural to get exasperated with questioning that is going nowhere or takes two, three, or even four times as long as it should.

Whether you find yourself in a big or small confrontation, keep in mind these two famous quotes. There is nothing known about Tony Petito other than the fact that he said, "In most instances, all an argument proves is that two people are present." You are never going to "win" an argument by getting mad at opposing counsel. By arguing you have only proven one thing: you have risen to opposing counsel's bait and lost your concentration.

If you are not persuaded by the unknown Petito, perhaps Buddha's wise words will ring true: "Holding onto anger is like grasping a hot coal with the intent of throwing it at someone else; you are the one who gets burned." The reason you get burned at a deposition is that your anger distracts you from the task at hand. In short, when you are angry you are thinking about the past and not concentrating on what you need to do next.

Whether the confrontation is big or small, follow the steps below. These steps will work even if opposing counsel's conduct is a calculated gamble to violate the Rules and take advantage of you. As a last resort, you can suspend the deposition and seek sanctions by filing a motion with deposition excerpts attached.[6] The party against whom the court rules may have to pay the costs the other side incurred in filing or defending the motion.[7]

1. **Ignore Opposing Counsel.** Although you should always be on your guard, it is best to assume the other attorney has good motives and simply ignore his bad deposition skills. What you see as coaching the witness may be a lawyer's sincere attempt to clarify your question so the witness can understand it. Likewise, if opposing counsel is taking the deposition, his repetitive questions may be symptoms of an unorganized deposition and not malicious intent on the lawyer's part.

   Having said that, once you determine the attorney is violating the Rules, still ignore his behavior unless it affects the substance of the deposition. Getting a court to rule in your favor when counsel behaves badly may take more time than it is worth. But, don't be afraid to go through steps two through eight if necessary.

2. **Calmly Build a Record with Several Objections**. If opposing counsel continues to act inappropriately, calmly make your objections. Unless it is a critical moment in the deposition, you will have a much better chance to prevail on a dispute if the court has several examples of opposing counsel's inappropriate conduct.

3. **Confer with Opposing Counsel Off the Record**. If the problem persists even after your objections, ask the court reporter to go off the record. The reason to do this is that opposing counsel is more likely to respond if you complain informally. Don't put opposing counsel on the defensive, but explain why you are objecting to his behavior and see if you both can reach an understanding about how to proceed.

   For example, you might need to explain that you think that the same question has been asked so many times that it has

---

[6] See e.g. Rule 30(d)(2) and Rule 37.
[7] Rule 37(a)(5).

become harassing. Such an explanation given off the record is more likely to change opposing counsel's behavior than an on the record attack where you state, "counsel, objection for the third time, asked and answered. You are harassing this witness, and you need to move on." The problem with such an attack is that no one likes to be lectured by others, especially attorneys. Moreover, Rule 37(a)(5)(A)(i) requires you to try to resolve the dispute in good faith with opposing counsel in order to get costs awarded to you for opposing counsel's behavior.

4. **Respectfully Listen.** It is also important to listen to opposing counsel. Politely ask him why he is acting the way he is. Maybe there is a good explanation. Even if there is not, everyone likes to feel that he is being heard. Listening to his concerns will go a long way toward reaching a mutual understanding.

5. **Use Humor if Possible.** If you can find a way to lighten the tense atmosphere, try it. Do not follow the advice of *Successful First Depositions*. In that book, the authors suggest you say to the intimidating attorney: "I see you have lost your composure. Let's resume the deposition in another fifteen minutes, so you can take the time to regain control of yourself and proceed in a civil manner."[8] Such a condescending lecture fuels the flames of the fire.

6. **Final Warning on the Record.** If the off the record discussion fails, you need to wait for the next opportunity to object. Make it clear on the record that if opposing counsel continues with his behavior, you will terminate the deposition until you can get relief from the court.

7. **Seek Court's Help.** If this has been a difficult deposition to arrange and the issue is clear, consider calling the court's chambers to see if the judge or magistrate is available to resolve the dispute. However, counsel's behavior can usually only be revealed by examining the transcript after it has been prepared by the court reporter. But if the problem is clear, such as when a defending attorney instructs his witness not to answer without

---

[8] Bradley Clary, Sharon Paulsen, and Michael Vanselow, *Successful First Depositions* at 132 (West Group 2001).

any basis for the objection, such a problem can easily be resolved by the court over the phone. If the problem is cumulative and more difficult to pinpoint, it would make sense to wait until the transcript has been prepared so that the court will have several examples to support a ruling in your favor.

In addition, know whether or not your judge will handle disputes during a deposition by phone before you start the deposition. Also, have the phone number ready. Finding a judge's number by calling information or someone at your office can quickly add to your frustrations.

8. **Video the Deposition.** A video is the best way to show a judge the sanctionable conduct of opposing counsel. A bland transcript often does not do justice to opposing counsel's behavior. Seeing unprofessional conduct in living color will make it easy for a judge to rule in your favor. Second, it is a great preemptive strike that almost guarantees opposing counsel will behave professionally. Most attorneys will tone down their combativeness if they realize their actions are being recorded. Likewise, seasoned lawyers know that a deposition that is only being transcribed by a court reporter will not reveal an attorney who raises his voice or the length of time he confers with a client. Depending on the court reporter, the transcript may not even reflect that the attorney has conferred with the witness.

6.11 THREE STEPS TO REMEMBER IF YOU CAN'T REMEMBER EIGHT

The first time you are in the heat of battle, you probably won't remember the eight steps above. If that is the case, remember these three: ignore opposing counsel, stay calm, and decide beforehand to video the deposition if you anticipate a problem. If you ignore opposing counsel's antics and don't lose your temper, your problems will almost always get resolved. Also, no one likes to be caught behaving badly on camera. With the video running, you are very likely to prevent bad behavior from ever occurring.

6.12 HARASSING QUESTIONS

When there is attorney misconduct, the real difficulty is determining whether to continue with the deposition after you have made your objections. What would you do in the following situation if you were the defending attorney?

Example: Attorney Misconduct (Scenario One)

This is the plaintiff's deposition of the defendant's expert witness.

[Plaintiff's attorney raises his voice] Q1. *Doctor, your opinion has been bought and paid for by the defendant, hasn't it?!*

A.   No, I only gave an opinion based on the facts.

Q2. *Indeed, your explanation is made up out of thin air isn't it?*

A.   Let me explain.

Q3. *No, I'd rather you answer my question! [plaintiff attorney raises his voice]* [Defense Attorney] Objection. This is harassing the witness. He is trying to answer the questions as best he can and has asked for an opportunity to answer the question. I think that is reasonable.

[Plaintiff's Attorney] Counsel, this is my deposition, and I am going to ask the questions I want until I get the answer I am entitled to.

If you were the defending attorney, would you terminate the deposition, call the judge to protect your witness from these questions or let the deposition proceed? The answer depends on your calculation of the judge's assessment of this conduct. If the judge were unavailable, you need to determine the inconvenience involved for you and the witness to resume the deposition at a later date in order to give you time to file a motion with the judge. With an expert's busy schedule, it probably won't be easy to reset this deposition. It may be best to suffer through opposing counsel's behavior and finish. Your considerations would be different if the witness were your client.

In the next case, the defense counsel was taking the deposition of the plaintiff's expert doctor. The following series of exchanges took place. Unlike the previous example, the conduct below was more abusive and more frequent. Such consistent behavior certainly requires you to suspend the deposition and seek relief from the court.

Example: Attorney Misconduct (Scenario Two)

1.   *[Defense counsel to plaintiff's expert witness] You're going to get three strikes and you're out today . . . .No games today.*

2.   *[Defense counsel to plaintiff's counsel] Don't lecture me . . . . Don't even think about it . . . . Don't even dream about it.*

3.   *[Defense counsel is frustrated with witness' answer and scolds her] Say "no" then.*

   [Plaintiff's counsel] She did.

   [Defense counsel] She said the long-winded version, which she loves to do, and which got her into trouble before.

4. *[Defense counsel to witness] Just answer the question. Let's start anew for once. I'm tired of your old answers which don't answer the questions.*

5. *[Plaintiff's counsel to defense counsel], Keep your voice down.*

   [Defense counsel] Quiet. I'm asking the questions, I resent the interruption.

6. *[Defense counsel to witness] I appreciate the legal objection, Dr. Ziem [expert witness], it seems like you know more than you've pretended to know all along about your legal knowledge. . . .I'm curious, are you going to instruct yourself not to answer certain questions today?*

7. *[Defense counsel responding to witness who said she did not understand question] Should I be surprised?* [9]

6.13 PERSONAL ATTACKS ON THE WITNESS

While the above example involved argumentative questions and personal attacks on a professional witness (i.e. an expert) who may be used to such abuse, don't be surprised if an attorney crosses the line with witnesses who are not experts. The following example took place at a deposition in a malicious prosecution case.

Q. Mr. Gerstein, have you ever engaged in homosexual conduct?
[Defending counsel] Objection, relevance. I believe it violates Rule 30, and I'm instructing him not to answer the question.

Q. Mr. Gerstein, are you involved in any type of homosexual clique with any other defendants in this action?
[Defending counsel] Same objection. Same instruction.[10]

If opposing counsel continues to ask this type of question, firmly ask him to stop. Such a conversation may be better made off the record where a calmer discussion can take place between you and the attorney. If no agreement can be reached, you should instruct the witness—on the record—not to answer because the question is being asked in "bad faith" and is intended to "unreasonably annoy" or "embarrass" the witness. Then, tell opposing counsel that you are suspending the deposition so that you can file a motion with the court to approve your decision. Your authority for taking such action is Rule 30(d)(3).

> You don't need to know the exact rule number in the heat of the moment. What is important is to know your rights and remedies.

---

[9] *Freeman v. Schointuck*, 192 F.R.D. 187, 190-191 (D. MD 2000).
[10] *Redwood v. Dobson*, 476 F.3d 462, 468-69 (7th Cir. 2007).

6.14 CONFERRING WITH WITNESS

This section addresses one of the more hot button issues for attorneys on both sides of the table: conferring with the witness while a question is pending and conferring with the witness during a break. Let's first look at the issue of conferring with a witness after a question has been asked. Decide what you would do if you were the defense attorney who is deposing the plaintiff, and plaintiff's counsel confers with his client after you have asked a question.

> [Defense counsel] Q. Certainly ask me to clarify any question that you don't understand. . . .
> [Plaintiff's counsel] Mr. Hall [plaintiff], at any time if you want to stop and talk to me, all you have to do is indicate that to me.
> [Defense counsel] Q. This witness is here to give testimony, to be answering my questions, and not to have conferences with counsel in order to aid him in developing his responses to my questions.
>
> [Defense counsel] Q. Do you have any documents relating to the issue of . . . .
> A. I would like to confer with my attorney about the word "document."
>
> Q. Let me ask you a question about this particular document.
> [Plaintiff's Attorney] I've got to review it with my client.
> [Defense Attorney] I object to you trying to review documents with your client when I am questioning him about them.

The example comes from a well-known case, *Hall v. Clifton*,[11] which highlighted the problem of witness conferences. The defense attorney wants to take the plaintiff's testimony without interruption. The plaintiff's attorney feels obligated to provide advice to his client during his deposition. So who is right? In most jurisdictions, unless you are discussing whether the question invades the attorney-client privilege, conferring with your witness about the question or about a document referred to in the question before he answers is prohibited.

In finding that the plaintiff and his attorney had acted improperly, *Hall* held that "[t]here is no proper need for the witness's own lawyer to act as an intermediary, interpreting questions, deciding which questions the witness should answer, and helping the witness to formulate answers."[12] The court explained that depositions should be conducted under the same rules as at trial and that during a trial, "a witness and his or her lawyer are not permitted to confer at their pleasure during the witness's testimony."[13] Similarly, another court declared, "It is too late once the ball has been snapped for the

---

[11] *Hall v. Clifton*, 150 F.R.D. 525, 526 (E.D. PA 1993).
[12] *Id.* at 528.
[13] *Id.* at 528.

coach to send in a different play."[14]

Also, some federal courts have adopted local rules that specifically prohibit "interrupting examination for an off-the-record conference between counsel and the witness, except for the purpose of determining whether to assert a privilege. . . ."[15] Even without *Hall's* guidance, it stands to reason that if the federal rule prohibits you from making an objection which suggests an answer (see next section), you should not be able to privately confer with your witness after a question to suggest an answer.

A second issue is whether you can talk to your client about his testimony during a break in the deposition. Although *Hall* declared that you cannot, other courts and commentators have refused to extend Hall's prohibition regarding conferences during the deposition to those during breaks. *Hall* reasoned as follows: "[o]nce the deposition has begun, the preparation period is over . . . . Private conferences are barred during the deposition, and the fortuitous occurrences of a coffee break, lunch break, or evening recess is no reason to change the rules."[16] *Hall* further held if there are any conferences during breaks, the examining attorney may ask what was discussed.[17]

In contrast, other courts have reasoned that such a prohibition on conferences during recesses undercuts the duty of an attorney to represent his client effectively. For example, one court held that it "would not preclude an attorney, during a recess that he or she did not request, from making sure that his or her client did not misunderstand or misinterpret questions or documents, or attempt to help rehabilitate the client by fulfilling an attorney's ethical duty to prepare a witness."[18] That ethical duty also includes correcting false or misleading testimony.[19]

Even in jurisdictions that don't allow you to discuss the substance of a witness' testimony, you may still be able to give tips regarding performance. One commentator instructs that such a prohibition would not prevent "some limited 'wood-shedding' . . . . Indeed, little harm would be caused by allowing an attorney to remind the witness to listen to the question, to give verbal answers instead of head bobs, or to stop twisting in the chair."[20]

Unfortunately, "given the paucity of cases on this 'short break' issue in depositions and civil trials, and the conflict among the few authorities that do exist, no clear rule currently exists in most jurisdictions."[21] Check to see

---

[14] *Eggleston v. Chicago Journeyman Plumbers*, 657 F.2d 890, 902 (7th Cir. 1981).
[15] D.Colo. Local Rule 30.3(A)(2).
[16] *Hall*, 150 F.R.D. at 529.
[17] *Id.* at 532.
[18] *In re Stratosphere*, 182 F.R.D. 614, 621 (D. Nev. 1998); see also *State v. King*, 520 S.E.2d 875, 881 (W. Va. 1999).
[19] Model Rules of Professional Conduct R. 3.3 (2006). Although the rule requires an attorney to take remedial measures, the rule does not require the attorney to correct the mistake at the deposition.
[20] *The Law and Ethics of Civil Depositions*, 57 MDLR at 340.
[21] Id. at 339.

what the custom is in your jurisdiction.

There is no clear guidance for the issue of conferences during breaks because the coaching issue rarely comes up. The reason is that there may well be a "tacit understanding among civil trial lawyers that they will not look too deeply into each other's witness preparation. The practical literature makes clear that preparation activities are ordinarily left untouched by discovery."[22] Nonetheless, be aware that during breaks, more than a few attorneys are talking to their witnesses about the substance of their testimony whether they are allowed to or not.

Practice Tip

To prevent coaching during breaks (whether allowed or not), limit the breaks as best you can to about one every hour and a half.

6.15 SPEAKING OBJECTIONS

Rule 30(c)(2) states that objections "must be stated concisely in a nonargumentative and nonsuggestive manner. A person may instruct a deponent not to answer only when necessary to preserve a privilege, to enforce a limitation ordered by the court, or to present a motion [to terminate deposition]." The rule prohibits attorneys from coaching witnesses by giving a long objection. You should only say, "objection form" or "objection [reason stated in a few words such as 'lacks foundation']."

In the following example, the plaintiff claimed the defendant committed legal malpractice by preventing the plaintiff from establishing a legal relationship with his child where there was a dispute over custody.

[Defense Attorney] Q. Why don't you do your best to tell me what you say he did wrong?
[Plaintiff's Attorney] I think that's a very broad, broad question . . . .He had no connection, he had no contact directly with Chuck Douglas except for one hearing.

Q. Can you tell me anything that you say Mr. Douglas did wrong that caused you to sue him?
[Plaintiff's Attorney] Well he read the deposition of Carlene Keniston. . . .There might be other things. There might be things like lying in lawsuits, like misrepresenting facts to the court.

[Defense Attorney] You're not supposed to suggest an answer, it's specifically prohibited by the Federal Rules of Civil Procedure.[23]

---

[22] See *Witness Preparation*, 68 Tex. L. Rev. at n. 12.
[23] *McDonough v. Keniston*, 188 F.R.D. 22, 24-25 (D. N.H. 1998).

The plaintiff's attorney improperly suggests to his witness that he had no direct contact with Chuck Douglas, and one reason for the lawsuit is that he read Carlene Keniston's deposition. He then suggests a litany of other reasons why he filed the lawsuit. All of these suggestions amounted to improper coaching. You might let opposing counsel get away with coaching one answer if it is not too important. But when there is conduct as egregious as the above example, your only choice is to seek sanctions. Unfortunately, it is too late to get an uncoached answer from the witness. However, by seeking sanctions, you will have put the court on notice of counsel's unprofessional conduct which helps to prevent similar conduct in the future.

Example: Improper Speaking Objections and Coaching

The following five examples from another case show extreme examples of coaching and violations of the rules on speaking objections.

1. *Q. What employee policies were in effect for the New York offices in 1998?*
   [Defending counsel] You want him to tell you every policy that was in effect off the top of his head?

   Q. So you don't know what policies were in effect for Zondo, Inc.'s New York employees in 1998, is that your testimony?
   [Defending counsel] He didn't say that he didn't know any of them. He said that he didn't commit—

   [Deposing counsel] If you would not coach my witness; I would like his answers as best he can to my questions.
   [Defending counsel] Okay. I object to the characterization that I was trying to coach my client. . . . I'm still trying to clarify your question. You ask a question, you get an answer, then you ask a question as if that prior question had never been asked and answered. Try to listen to the witness's answers and it will help . . . .

2. *Q. From your recollection, what employee policies were in effect at Zondo Inc.'s New York offices in 1998?*
   [Defending counsel] . . . . Are you asking the witness to tell you every policy he recalls on whatever subject?
   [Deposing counsel] Yes.
   [Defending counsel] Okay. Tell him what you recall and take as long as you need.

3. *Q. Is there some reason why you're not familiar-assuming that these documents are, in fact, issued to my client by your company; is there some reason why you would not be familiar with the format and appearance of such documents?*

A. I am familiar with the format and appearance of this document—of these documents.

Q. *So they're familiar to you then?*

[Defending counsel] Oh, how many more times are you going to ask him if he's familiar? Direct the witness not to answer. This is abusive . . . . You're not going to get any more answers on this nonsense, because you can't take an answer for granted.

4. Q. *When did you learn that Ms. Morales was pregnant?*

A. I don't recall.

[Defending counsel] Can we note that it's 5 o'clock and we're finally getting to a question that's relevant to the claim pending in the case?

5. Q. *During the time that you had these dinner meetings with Ms. Morales, would you describe or characterize your relationship with her as a cordial one?*

[Defending counsel] You mean did he have to drag her to dinner by her hair?

A. Yes.

[Defending counsel] That wasn't a yes to my question, it was a yes to his, right?[24]

6.16 PERSONAL ATTACKS ON OPPOSING COUNSEL

These attacks cover a wide range of conduct from simply annoying to sanctionable. Sometimes opposing counsel will just try to get under your skin: "how many times are you going to cover this," "get to the point, my client has a plane to catch," or "how much longer are you going to take?" Other times, opposing counsel may intentionally look bored out of his mind or sigh loudly to signal his displeasure to you. Such bad behavior only affects the deposition if you let it—and you shouldn't.

Other behavior is so bad, that anyone would rightly be upset. Still, it is better—if you can—to remain calm and continue with the deposition *as long as you are getting the facts you need from the witness*. The following example shows how heated a deposition may get. Obviously, there is no place for such conduct in a deposition. The deposition was taken in connection with a suit for injunctive relief related to a company's merger. Joe Jamail, the well-known Texas attorney, was representing the witness who was a director on the board for Paramount Co.

---

[24] *Morales v. Zondo, Inc.*, 204 F.R.D. 50, 55-57 (S.D. NY 2001).

A. I vaguely recall Mr. Oresman's letter . . . .I think I did read it, probably.

Q. *Do you have any idea why Mr. Oresman was calling that material to your attention?*

[Joe Jamail] Don't answer that. How would he know what was going on in Mr. Oresman's mind? Don't answer it. Go on to your next question.

[*Deposing counsel*] *No. Joe, Joe—*

[Jamail] Don't "Joe" me, asshole. You can ask some questions, but get off of that. I'm tired of you. You could gag a maggot off a meat wagon. Now, we've helped you every way we can.

[*Deposing counsel*] *Let's just take it easy.*

[Jamail] No, we're not going to take it easy. Get done with this.

[*Deposing counsel*] *We will go on to the next question.*

[Jamail] Do it now.

[*Deposing counsel*] *We will go on to the next question. We're not trying to excite anyone.*

[Jamail] Come on. Quit talking. Ask the question. Nobody wants to socialize with you.

[*Deposing counsel*] *I'm not trying to socialize. We'll go on to another question. We're continuing the deposition.*

[Jamail] Well, go on and shut up.

[*Deposing counsel*] *Are you finished?*

[Jamail] I may be and you may be. Now, you want to sit here and talk to me, fine. This deposition is going to be over with. You don't know what you're doing. Obviously someone wrote out a long outline of stuff for you to ask. You have no concept of what you're doing. Now, I've tolerated you for three hours. If you've got another question, get on with it. This is going to stop one hour from now, period. Go.

[*Deposing counsel*] *I don't need this kind of abuse.*

[*Deposing counsel*] *All right. To try to move forward, Mr. Liedtke [the deponent] I'll show you what's been marked as Liedtke 14 and it is a covering letter . . . .*

[Jamail] You fee makers think you can come here and sit in somebody's office, get your meter running, get your full day's fee by asking stupid questions. Let's go with it. [25]

Notice how the deposing attorney remains unruffled. He is determined to get the information from the witness despite all the efforts of Jamail to disrupt his concentration by making personal attacks. However, he would have done even better by *ignoring* Jamail even more. His comments "are you finished?" and "I don't need this kind of abuse" are understandable, but only engage Jamail and distract the attorney from his task to get information from the witness.

Practice Tip

Don't personally attack opposing counsel even when insulted. Ignore him instead. That will make him even angrier and less effective. Stay poised.

6.17 ATTORNEY OBJECTS TOO MUCH

Sometimes opposing counsel will object simply to interrupt your train of thought or to alert her client to pay attention to a particular question. If this happens frequently, the best way to stop such a tactic is to ask her to state the reasons for her objection each time. Since your questions are not objectionable, she will be very hard pressed to come up with good reasons. Also, since she knows the court reporter is recording her reasons, she won't want to look like a fool.

6.18 SUMMARY OF INAPPROPRIATE ATTORNEY BEHAVIOR

In *Calzaturficio v. Fabiano Shoe Co.,*[26] there is a good summary of the behaviors that are prohibited in a deposition. The defending lawyer asserted the "asked and answered" objection eighty-one times, engaged in lengthy colloquies on the record, and made personal attacks against opposing counsel. He conferred with his client during questioning and left the room with the witness while a question was pending. Moreover, he instructed his client not to finish answers and not to answer some questions.[27]

In addition, although the defending attorney claimed he was speaking just to help clarify the question, the court found that he was improperly interpreting questions for the witness. In fact, the court found that all of the defending attorney's conduct was improper and pointed out that "a deposition is meant to be a question-and-answer conversation between the deposing lawyer and

---

[25] *Morales,* 204 F.R.D. at 56-57.
[26] 201 F.R.D. 33 (D. Mass. 2001).
[27] *Id.* at 39.

the witness."[28] Another case involved an attorney who made objections to questions that were asked on 64 pages of a 102 page deposition.[29]

In dealing with unruly opposing counsel, one court diagnosed the problem perfectly. "It is precisely when animosity runs high that playing by the rules is vital. Rules of legal procedure are designed to defuse, or at least channel into set forms, the heated feelings that accompany much litigation. Because depositions take place in law offices rather than courtrooms, adherence to professional standards is vital, for the judge has no direct means of control."[30]

What would you do in the following situations where defense counsel makes attacks on you and your witness?

1. *[Defense counsel] She [referring to the witness] always has to hedge, doesn't she, Mr. Erwin [plaintiff's counsel]. You[referring to the witness] always have to cover yourself; nothing's ever a straight answer.*

2. [Witness] They're all related to reactive airway disease and how it's produced.

   [Defense counsel] Sure they are.

   [Plaintiff's counsel] We don't need sarcastic comments.

   [Defense counsel] I'm not being sarcastic. I'm totally believing everything your witness says, and I'm taking everything she says on face value, unchallenged. You know, I'm the naïve attorney you've always dreamed of.

3. *[Defense counsel] I'll check up on you, Dr. Ziem, see if you're telling the truth. That is the point of this exercise.*

4. *[Defense counsel to plaintiff's counsel after he objected to one of defense counsel's questions] You don't like the compound part of it, is that the problem, Mr. Erwin [plaintiff's counsel], too difficult for you?*

5. *[Defense counsel to plaintiff's counsel] Yes, you are nervous, Mr. Erwin, because this case is rapidly diminishing.*

6. [Witness] I'm trying to be scientific.

   [Defense counsel] And evasive, which you get an A plus in.

7. *[Defense counsel to plaintiff's counsel] And you've been right now how often in this litigation . . . . How often have you been right in this litigation in your viewpoints?[31]*

Let's take a brief look at the attitude you should have. When dealing with counsel that is obstructing the deposition, never rise to the bait—as tempting

---

[28] *Id.* at 40.
[29] See *Damaj*, 164 F.R.D. at 560.
[30] *Redwood*, 476 F.3d at 469-70.
[31] *Freeman v. Schointuck*, 192 F.R.D. 187, 187-192 (D. MD 2000).

as that might be. There are two reasons for this. First, if it becomes necessary to seek the court's help as it was in the example above from *Freeman*, you want all the attention on opposing counsel. You do not want the court to have to consider that your conduct, as well as opposing counsel's conduct, is sanctionable. You will have a better chance of prevailing the more obvious it is that you were courteous despite opposing counsel's failure to be.

Another reason to keep your cool is that opposing counsel may be deliberately behaving badly in order to get you angry so that you will become distracted. For example, the more emotional you become, the more likely you are to miss an important objection. If you become angry, you also send a bad signal to your witness who will be taking his cues from you on how to behave. This does not mean you just sit there and take it. Follow the steps to resolve conflicts mentioned earlier.

Practice Tip

Kill opposing counsel with kindness. Moreover, if you treat opposing counsel well, it is more likely that he will reciprocate even if he is a jerk. Nevertheless, never compromise your fundamental principles.

6.19 INSTRUCTING A WITNESS NOT TO ANSWER

Rule 30(d) permits an attorney to instruct a witness not to answer "only when necessary to preserve a privilege, to enforce a limitation on evidence directed by the court, or to present a motion under paragraph (3)." Below, the attorney incorrectly gives the instruction without any basis for doing so.

[Defending counsel] I'm going to direct him not to answer that.
[Deposing counsel] On what basis?

[Defending counsel] That's too broad of a question.
[Deposing counsel] You have no right to instruct him on that basis.

[Defending counsel] It's the form of the question . . . . I think it is just harassing him. I direct him not to answer.
[Defending counsel] Objection; asked and answered. I direct you not to answer.
[Deposing counsel] You've got to be kidding me.[32]

---

[32] *McDonough v. Keniston*, 188 F.R.D. 22, 25 (D. N.H. 1998).

6.20 IMPROPER OBJECTIONS

Below is a list of some common improper objections. The timing of the objection (i.e. during an unimportant or critical question) and its frequency will determine how many steps you need to take to resolve the problem with opposing counsel (see Eight Steps discussed above).

1. Counsel, that is an improper question because it is vague. I don't understand what you mean by the word _____ [i.e. meeting].
2. Only answer if you know the answer.
3. The witness may answer, but I am instructing him not to guess.
4. That question has been asked and answered three times. Each time the witness has said _____ [i.e. the light was red].
5. Objection relevance. I don't know why you are asking the witness about "x" when the only thing that matters in this case is "y."
6. Counsel, please get on with your questioning, we only have so much time left.
7. How much longer are we going to be here [said antagonistically]?
8. Where are you headed with these questions?
9. I'm instructing the witness not to volunteer and only to answer the question that has been asked.
10. I want to make a statement for the record. The witness is confused by the numerous documents you are showing him. He has no knowledge who wrote document number 1 because . . . .

Objections one through eight can often be handled by simply ignoring counsel. You will find that if you ignore him, his own witness will start to ignore the objections also, since he knows that the sooner he answers the questions, the sooner the deposition will be over. Objections nine and ten are hard to ignore. One of your main goals is to get the witness to volunteer information, and counsel's objection that cautions the witness against this interferes with your ability to get facts from the deposition. Number ten involves blatant coaching.

⚎ CHECKLIST

Under Rules, Communication with Expert Protected Unless It Relates to:

1. Expert's compensation
2. Facts or data the attorney provided and were considered by expert
3. Assumptions the attorney provided that expert relied on

When Witness Pretends Not to Understand a Commonly Used Word (i.e. concerned)

1. Ask the witness what he does not understand about the word.
2. Ask if witness is familiar with that word as it is used in the English language.
3. Ask the witness if he is familiar with the meaning of that word.
4. Ask witness your original question beginning with the phrase, "Using the word '(i.e. concerned)' consistent with the normal meaning it has in the English language, what . . . . .?"

Common Problems and Solutions

1. When witness is backed into corner, he'll never confess but you have still won because the jury won't believe his excuse.
2. If witness hedges his answer with, "I'll I can remember now," ask if there is anything that could refresh his memory. If witness answers, "No," he will look foolish at trial when he all of a sudden remembers important facts.
3. If witness pretends not to answer question, make your question as simple as possible and ask witness what he doesn't understand about it.
4. Lawyers sometimes pretend not to understand question in order to coach witness by explaining why the question is "confusing." Be ready to object if this happens.
5. If lawyer asserts the attorney-client privilege objection, you have the right to ask questions about the basis for the objection. (i.e. was anyone else present).
6. Some attorneys are incompetent and some are deceitful. Know the difference.

Dealing with Annoying Counsel

1. Ignore his behavior. Your goal is to collect information. Do not lose your temper.
2. Build a record with several objections if behavior gets out of hand.
3. Confer with counsel off the record if your objections don't change behavior.
4. Respectfully listen to opposing counsel's explanation.
5. Use humor to relieve tensions if possible.
6. Make final warning on the record.
7. Seek court's help.
8. Best advice, video any deposition where you expect bad behavior.

Three Sure-fire Rules to Handle Opposing Counsel

If you can't remember the eight rules above, simply do the following:

1. Be firm.
2. Stay calm.
3. Video the deposition.

Improper Objections

Be familiar with the most common improper objections.

1. Counsel, that is an improper question because it is vague. I don't understand what you mean by the word [i.e. meeting].
2. Only answer if you know.
3. The witness may answer, but I am instructing him not to guess.
4. I'm instructing the witness not to volunteer and only to answer the question that has been asked.

CHAPTER SEVEN

Using Depositions at Trial

No pleasure is comparable to the standing upon the vantage-ground of truth.

—*Francis Bacon*

P erhaps the most fun a trial lawyer can have is using a deposition to prove that the other side's witness is lying at trial. As Francis Bacon said, you have the power of truth on your side, and seeing the witness squirm while you confront him with the deposition provides a lot of pleasure. But before we look at this technique on cross-examination, let's first learn how to use depositions to your advantage with your own witnesses.

7.1 HOW TO SUMMARIZE

A deposition is essential to winning at trial. However, for the deposition to be useful for direct or cross, you must first summarize its important points and index them so that they will be easy to find. Given the time constraints prior to trial, it may be very tempting to delegate this task to another lawyer or paralegal. Such a decision is a big mistake. How can anyone but you know what is truly important about the case? If you do not do the work yourself, you will get burned at trial when you are unable to cross-examine on a point in the deposition because your assistant failed to recognize its significance.

One way attorneys *try* to have their cake and eat it too is to have someone summarize *everything* in the deposition. But you have gained nothing other than a second copy—although somewhat shorter—of the deposition. By forcing yourself to summarize the deposition, you discipline yourself to decide what the important facts are in the case, since there is not enough time for you to summarize everything. Determining what the key facts are in a deposition will lead you to see how other witnesses have discussed those facts. Soon you will analyze the three or four important topics each witness talks about. Those topics will become your case's themes at trial.

You might feel that you are leaving out important details by limiting yourself to three or four topics for each deposition. However, a jury decides a case based on what it remembers, not on the information presented. It is better to present the jury with three coherent themes supported by facts which it will remember, rather than to overload it with ten themes, none of which it will remember.

Below is an abbreviated summary for direct in a simple car wreck. If you are on the fence regarding whether something said is important or if you just don't know where to fit it in, put it at the end of your outline under the heading "miscellaneous." There are many ways to summarize a deposition. The worst way is to do it chronologically from page one to the end. The reason is that the questioner invariably jumps around from topic A-D to topics E-H and then back again. The deposition needs to be summarized by topics; otherwise you just create a copy of the original deposition but in a different format. Below is a typical topic outline. The summary is cited by a page number which is in parentheses. There is no need to put the line number, since that just takes more time, and you will have underlined or bracketed the important information in the deposition itself so that finding the particular line on the page in the deposition will be easy. For brevity's sake, substitute 'w" for the witness' name.

Example:

I. Background
—W. grew up in Chicago. . .captain of football team (7).
II. Discusses Accident (Topic One)
—W. arrived at the corner of Main and Elm streets etc. (13)
III. Discusses Emergency Room Visit (Topic Two)
—W. had back and shoulder pain and went to the emergency room etc. (29)
IV. Pain and Suffering (Topic Three)
—W. can no longer throw the football with his son. (48). He cannot stand for more than fifteen minutes at a time. (45).
V. Miscellaneous
—W. has been arrested—but not convicted—for writing bad checks. (77)

These summaries provide the basis for your opening statement and your outlines for direct.

7.2 DIRECT EXAMINATION OUTLINE

After you have summarized the deposition, use the summary to help you create an outline for direct examination. There are four sources of information which will provide the basis of your outline: 1) the deposition transcript, 2) witness interviews, 3) witness statements, and 4) documents authored by the witness. When you are making your outline, a good practice is not to write the question you are going to ask, but rather the answer you expect the witness to give. This technique will force you to focus on the answer you expect the witness to give and free you from trying to remember the precise words for each question.

Beside each answer, cite its source. If it is a deposition, list the page number (the line is not necessary). The reason to cite the page is that if your witness forgets the answer, you can quickly use the deposition to refresh the witness' memory.

For your outline regarding damages at section four above, then, your direct examination outline should look like the *second* example below. The first example follows the conventional way which has the *questions* you intend to ask. The second example has the *answers* you expect to get.

Example: Conventional Way To Write Outline

Damages
- —How much were your hospital bills?
- —Please explain what the bills were for.
- —Tell the jury about the pain you are in.
- —How does it affect you?

Example: Better Way To Write Outline

Damages
- —Medical bills total $50,300 (95)
     - —two surgeries account for about $50,000 (75)
- —Constant pain when standing (97)
- —Depressed a lot after accident, but getting better (99)
- —Unemployed since accident (101)
- —Made efforts to get job (103)
     - —applied online at Monster.com (105)
     - —met with recruiter (105)

7.3 REFRESHING RECOLLECTION

There will come a point in many trials where your witness will forget something important. For example, if your client is a plaintiff in an employment discrimination lawsuit,

> If something can go wrong, it will, especially on direct.

you will inevitably ask him about the meeting when his supervisor fired him. It may be that he does not remember everything that the boss said. If so, you can refresh his recollection—or memory—by using his deposition (the witness remembered the fact at the deposition because it occurred closer in time to the event than the trial). Federal Rule of Evidence 612 provides that a witness can use a writing to refresh his memory.

There is a simple acronym, DARTS, that will help you remember the steps to follow in order to refresh a witness' memory. How do you remember the acronym? See if this helps. You will agree that if a witness forgets an important part of his testimony, it is pretty frustrating. It is particularly frustrating given all the time and effort you have put in to preparing the witness for trial. How mad are you? Picture yourself throwing *darts* at the witness' head.

Example: Using DARTS to Refresh Recollection

Q. What did your boss tell you when he fired you?

A. He told me that my work product had become sloppy. He also said something else but I can't remember. [The witness forgets to mention that the boss also said he had been coming to work late].

Step 1: Determine if it is possible to refresh witness' memory without directly asking the witness.

Q. Do you remember being asked about this incident in your deposition? Yes.

Do not ask the witness, "Is there anything that would help you remember?" If you do, you could be at a dead end if the witness says, "No." Why? Because once the witness has said nothing will help him remember, the court won't permit you to refresh his memory, since he has already precluded that option.

Q. Would your deposition help you remember? [This will suggest to your witness that the deposition has the answer.]

A. Yes.

Step 2: Ask witness to read document silently.

Take the deposition up to the witness stand and show the exact page where the information is contained. Point to the relevant lines on the page and instruct the witness to read the page silently to himself. Stay up at the witness stand while the witness reads the relevant part silently.

Step 3: Retrieve the document.

After the witness has read the page, retrieve the document and return to the place where you were questioning the witness. This is important because many attorneys forget to retrieve the document, and then the witness continues his testimony by improperly reading from the document.

The key to being able to refresh a witness' memory with a document or deposition is that the witness must be able to testify from memory after being shown the document (see next step).

Step 4: Test to see if memory is refreshed.
Q. Does your deposition refresh your memory as to what your boss told you?
A. Yes.

Obviously, if the witness does not pass this test you cannot go to step five, and you might literally want to throw darts at your witness.

Step 5: Same question is asked as at beginning.
The final step is to ask exactly the same question that you did at the start when the witness testified that he could no longer remember.

Q. What did your boss tell you when he fired you?
A. He told me that my work product had become sloppy and that I had been coming to work late.

The Acronym DARTS helps you remember the five steps to refreshing a witness' recollection.

1. **D**etermine if it is possible to refresh witness' memory without directly asking witness.
2. **A**sk witness to read document silently.
3. **R**etrieve the document.
4. **T**est to see if memory is refreshed.
5. **S**ame question is asked as at the beginning.

7.4 CROSS-EXAMINATION OUTLINE

Now that we have seen how to construct a direct examination outline, let's look at how to build a cross-examination outline. From your deposition summary, pick three topics you think are important and will be successful. Remember, not all topics have to prove the witness is either wrong or lying. The witness could have agreed with facts in the deposition that will support your case and that is always fertile ground for cross-examination.

Once you have picked three topics, create a topic outline as you did for direct examination. For the same reasons above, write the answers you expect to get and not the questions you will ask. Reference each answer with a page *and* line number.

While in a direct outline you don't need to reference line numbers, you must do it for your cross outline. The reason you don't need the line numbers for direct is there is much less likelihood you will need to quickly refer to the exact line because you and your witness will have gone over the testimony many times. In addition, the pace of direct affords you more time to locate the line if you need to. By not putting the line number in your outline, you save time in preparing it. If you are worried your witness is going to forget a key point, you might want to reference the line number to raise your comfort level.

> Use a highlighter to mark any lines in the depo. that you might need on cross.

But in the heat of the moment on cross, you can't afford to waste one second trying to find the line on the page where the impeachment is. To help you find the page in a hurry, use Post-its or adhesive flags to mark the page. Also, always set out in your outline where the witness admits in the deposition that the oath is the same as that given at trial, and the witness agrees that he will let you know if he doesn't understand a question. (You may quickly need to find this during impeachment.)

Finally, your question on cross-examination has to mirror precisely the substance of the deposition testimony so that if you need to impeach the witness with his deposition, there is no room for him to wiggle away.

Example: Imprecise Questioning on Cross

*Q. Sir, you testified on direct that the light was green when you **went into the intersection.** Isn't it a fact that the light was red?*
A. No.

Q. Do you recall giving a deposition in this case?
A. Yes.

*Q. Isn't it a fact you were asked at the deposition,"Question: What was the color of the light when you **approached the intersection?** Answer, red."*
A. That is right. When I approached the intersection, the light was red but it turned green **before** I went into the intersection.

Here, the word "approached" in the deposition question dooms the impeachment. You need to listen carefully to the witness' answer at trial. Obviously, this is not an answer you would impeach the witness with.

Example: Precise Questioning on Cross

*Q. Sir, you testified on direct that the light was green **when you approached the intersection,** but the truth is that the traffic light was red.*
A. No.

Q. Do you recall giving a deposition in this case . . . .?

*Q. Isn't it a fact you were asked in your deposition, "Question: What was the color of the traffic light **when you approached the intersection?** Answer, red."*

Example: Precise Questioning on Cross Cont'd (Simpson Civil Trial)

In this example, Simpson was asked about a domestic violence incident with his wife Nicole in 1989. During the incident, Nicole had called 911, and the police had taken photos of her depicting a bruised and battered face. At trial, Petrocelli asked O.J. the following questions. Notice how Petrocelli achieves a successful impeachment because the deposition testimony—in substance—is the *exact opposite* of the trial testimony.

Q. And you hit her that day, didn't you, sir?
A. No.

Q. Did your hand make contact with her face at all to cause injuries on her face? Yes or no?
A. **I don't know.**

Q. Didn't you testify---you remember testifying in a deposition, sir?
A. Yes.

Q. Remember I took your deposition over a number of days and Mr. Kelly, Mr. Brewer also asked you questions?
A. Yes.

Q. Let me read from that deposition. By the way, you understand and you understood then, you were under oath and subject to the same penalty of perjury, just as you are today?
A. Yes.

Q. Page 1032, Mr. Baker, line 21.
"Question: You were in such a rage that you don't remember what you did; is that right?
Answer: **I remember exactly what I did.**"

Now tell this jury exactly how you caused all those injuries on Nicole's face.

The impeachment succeeds because the deposition testimony is precisely contrary—not just a little bit or almost—to the trial testimony. This is the key to having a successful impeachment.

7.5 IMPEACHMENT

There are six common mistakes that attorneys make when using a deposition to impeach. First, as pointed out in the previous section, attorneys try to impeach a witness with a prior statement in a deposition that is not precisely contradictory.

Second, attorneys try to impeach the witness with multiple inconsistencies instead of just one at a time. Look what happened in the Timothy McVeigh trial. Instead of taking one inconsistency at a time (i.e. FBI), the attorney lumps them all together.

Example: Impeaching with Too Many Facts
(*U.S. v. McVeigh*)

Q. *Ms. Fortier, would you agree with me that you either made false statements to agents of the Federal Bureau of Investigation; your parents, your mother and father; and your mother and father-in-law and your best friends in late April and May of 1995, or you're making false statements to this jury of strangers yesterday?*

[Opposing counsel] I object, Your Honor.

[The court] Sustained.

Third, attorneys impeach witnesses with inconsistencies that are either minor or are not found in the deposition. An impeachment is an effort to show that the witness is lying. If you impeach the witness on a minor point, what have you proven? It is likely that you have shown to the jury that the witness is not lying but is merely mistaken.

Your credibility will be lessened in the jury's eyes because the witness will have won the impeachment battle, and you will look petty. Moreover, the next time you try to impeach the witness on an important point, your success will be diminished because of your prior failure.

Fourth, attorneys do not make it clear to the jury that the witness has been untruthful at trial by testifying inconsistently but instead will attempt to refresh the witness' memory with his deposition (of course, if the witness makes an innocent mistake, refreshing his memory is appropriate). Often, attorneys when confronted with a significant inconsistent statement will not follow the steps discussed below (the ABC's) but will instead say, "Didn't you say in your deposition . . . ?" When the question is phrased in that manner, it lessens the impact of the impeachment and gives the impression to the jury that the witness has made an innocent mistake.

Fifth, attorneys mistakenly let the witness read the inconsistent statement in the deposition transcript. The attorney should always maintain control of the transcript. That way, you can emphasize what needs to be emphasized in the deposition when reading it aloud and prevent the witness from minimizing what was said in the deposition by either reading the transcript ineffectively or adding commentary after reading it.

The sixth mistake—which will be discussed further below—is that after successfully impeaching the witness with his deposition, the attorney asks the witness to contrast or compare the answer given in the deposition with the answer given at trial. The problem with this is that the witness always has a good answer.

Common Mistakes Made During Impeachment

1. The inconsistent statement is really not *precisely* inconsistent with trial testimony.
2. The inconsistent statement has too many facts.
3. The inconsistent statement is not important.
4. Attorney mistakenly refreshes the witness' recollection.
5. Attorney allows witness to read the depo. transcript.
6. Attorney asks witness to explain why the depo. statement is inconsistent.

Let's first look at the conventional way to impeach a witness, and then look at a better way. By looking at the standard way, we will see what it lacks and why the improved way is better. The standard way is known as the three c's: commit, credit, and confront. In other words, you commit the witness to what was said on direct, you then credit the authority of the deposition that you are impeaching with, and then you confront the witness with the inconsistent statement in the deposition.

The first step, commit, locks the witness into the answer given on direct. If, for some reason, the witness backs off the answer, then you have won the battle quickly, and there is no need to impeach.

Step One (Commit):

Q. You testified on direct that when you drove into the intersection the traffic light was green?
A. Yes.

Here, the attorney has locked the witness into his answer—or confirmed his testimony on direct—and can now impeach with a deposition answer that is different.

Step Two (Credit):

Q. Do you recall giving a deposition in this case?
A. Yes.

Q. We took it at your attorney's office?
A. Yes.

Q. Your attorney was present?
A. Yes.

Q. You were under oath?
A. Yes.

Q. You swore to tell the whole truth and nothing but the truth?
A. Yes.

Q. It was the same oath as the one you were given at trial today?
A. Yes.

Q. You were also given the opportunity to make changes to the deposition?
A. Yes.

Q. You didn't make any changes, did you?
A. No.

The attorney shows the jury that this prior statement has a lot of weight. For example, the statement was given under the same oath as if he were at trial, and the witness had his attorney present. The jury can infer that this is a formal proceeding and that the witness had benefit of having an attorney to protect his interests if necessary. However, one problem with the traditional impeachment technique is that during this long crediting process, the jury does not know how the witness testified differently in the deposition—the light could have been yellow or red—nor does it know the significance of the inconsistent statement in the deposition.

Step Three (Confront):
Q. [**After asking the court's permission to approach the witness, the attorney takes the deposition to the witness stand.**] *I am showing you page 33 line 14 of your deposition, and I would like you to read along silently with me. Isn't it true that you were asked the following question and gave the following answer: "Question. What color was the traffic light when you drove into the intersection. Answer. Red."*
A. Yes.

Q. Did I read that correctly?
A. Yes.

Now, the witness has been confronted with the deposition. Whatever you do, stop at the third "c"; don't add a fourth. Many attorneys make the grave mistake of continuing to a fourth "c" known as contrast. The naïve attorney thinks that since he has clobbered the witness with the impeachment, he can now get the witness to confess that he lied to the jury on direct examination. Although this confession never happens, it does not stop attorneys from trying. Here is how it plays out.

Step Four (Contrast):
The attorney asks one of the three following questions.

Q1. So, the truth is what you said in the deposition, that the light was red?

Q2. So, now, why don't you tell us why you lied to the jury when you said the light was green?

Q3. So, which is it? Was the light green or red?

All three of these questions spell disaster because they allow the witness to explain the discrepancy between the answers. Your goal with impeachment is not to get the witness to confess that he is a liar, but to prove that he is. The reason for this limited goal is that a witness is never going to admit on the stand that he is a liar.

Having examined the three "c's" (the standard way to impeach), let's look at a better way. One problem with the standard way is that attorneys have trouble remembering what each "c" stands for or their order. Many times attorneys will credit, confront and contrast. Remember, contrast is the one step you never want to take. Other times, attorneys will credit (step two), commit (step one), and then confront (step three). That is, they do the steps out of order by crediting the deposition first before committing the witness to what was said on direct. This is improper impeachment because, under the rules, you cannot impeach a witness unless you can show an inconsistency, and you cannot do that without confirming what the witness says first. Finally, many attorneys don't understand what "credit" means.

A better way to remember the steps, and a more memorable manner in which to conduct impeachment is to follow the ABC's. First, you "accuse" the witness of lying at trial; second, you "build up" the trustworthiness of the deposition; and third, you "confront" the witness with the deposition. One advantage of ABC is that there is only one "c" and you won't confuse what it stands for. Second, the phrase "build up the trustworthiness" makes more sense than the word "credit."

Other than the ease of remembering the steps, there are two main reasons why the "ABC" steps are better. First, when you accuse the witness of lying, it forces you only to pick a battle which is important. There is no way you are going to accuse the witness of lying about something trivial because you would look foolish in front of the jury.

Second, when you accuse the witness of lying, you make it very clear immediately to the jury why you are going through the impeachment process. Under the traditional method, where there is no accusation, the jury does not know what the attorney is trying to do when he is crediting the deposition.

Let's look at an example.

Step One: Accuse

Q1. You are telling this jury that the light was green when you drove into the intersection? [Your tone of voice should convey disbelief, and the pitch should get higher at the end of the sentence.]

A. Yes.

Q2. The truth is that the light was red? [You should have an authoritative tone of voice. There should be no doubt in the jury's mind that you disbelieve the witness and that you are about to prove it.]

A. No.

From this example, it is clear that the jury knows from the question asked and your tone of voice exactly what the anticipated inconsistency is. When you impeach a witness, it is a big moment in a trial, and the jury needs to be aware of it. The "commit" step from the traditional method leaves out Q2. Perhaps the traditional method leaves it out for fear that the witness will anticipate where the attorney is going. Or, perhaps it is left out because the attorney wants to build up a climax for the jury by keeping the inconsistency something of a mystery.

Either way, accusing the witness is better. Even though the witness knows where the attorney is headed, the witness can't do anything about it. Even if he had all day, he could not save himself. Why not? He is already locked into the deposition answer he has given. Since you are not going to ask him why he gave two different answers, the only thing he can answer is "yes, that is what I said."

The other two steps, build up and confront, are the same as credit and confront in the earlier example, so they won't be repeated here.

The ABC's of Impeachment
1. **A**ccuse the witness of lying at trial.
2. **B**uild up the trustworthiness of the deposition.
3. **C**onfront the witness with the deposition.

Finally, be prepared for the witness who will argue with you after the "confront" step by saying something such as "but what I meant to say in the deposition was that the light was red and then turned green as I drove into the intersection." A good attorney will hope the witness makes such a mistake. Why? Now you get the chance to hammer the point home again to the jury. Simply repeat your question. "My question was: Isn't it true you were asked the following question and answer . . . ." Now, the jury gets to hear the damaging inconsistency twice.

Before moving on to the next topic, it is worth briefly noting that depositions can be used not only when there is an inconsistent statement in the deposition, but also when there is an inconsistent omission in the deposition. A prior inconsistent omission occurs when a witness adds facts at trial that should have reasonably been stated in the deposition. The impeachment is effective because it shows the witness is not being truthful due to the embellishment at trial.

Example: Prior Inconsistent Omission
(Lawsuit Alleging Civil Rights Violations)

Step One: Accuse the Witness

Q. *You are telling this jury that when the officer stopped your car, he made you get out of your car and lie face down on the ground?*
A. Yes.

Q. *The truth is that he never made you lie face down on the ground?*
A. No.

Q. *Do you recall giving your deposition in this case?*

Step Two: Build Up the Prior Statement

This step is omitted from the example for brevity's sake.

Step Three: Confront

Q. *Let me direct your attention to page 21 line 5. Isn't it a fact you were asked the following question and gave the following answer: "Question. Tell me what happened when the officer came to your car. Answer. He asked me to get out of the car, and then he searched me."*
A. Yes.

Q. *Did I read that correctly?*
A. Yes.

Q. *Nowhere in this answer did you claim that you had been forced to lie face down on the ground, did you?*
A. No.

Q. *In fact, nowhere in this entire deposition did you ever make such a claim, did you?*
A. No.

7.6 IMPEACHING WITH A VIDEO DEPOSITION

Using a video to impeach is much more powerful than a transcript. Obviously, the jury gets to both see and hear the inconsistent statement. Not only will the jury remember the impeachment better, but the witness will be more scared for the remainder of your cross after having seen her dishonesty being caught on video. Prior to trial, you must pick only the very best parts to use for impeachment. For a typical witness, this would be three or four video clips at most (one for each of your themes). In contrast, if you had twenty video clips you would be spending an inordinate amount of time trying to edit the deposition prior to trial.

> Make sure that the impeaching video can be quickly shown to the jury. You don't want to accuse the witness of lying and then fumble around trying to prove your point.

Moreover, once in the courtroom, your assistant needs to quickly find the video clip you need. Having fewer to choose from will make the process easier, quicker, and less stressful. After direct examination is over, tell your assistant to get ready for a particular clip or clips so that when the time comes, the video will be ready to play as soon as you give the signal. The steps for impeachment are the same except that instead of reading the transcript to the witness, you play the video for the witness and the jury.

7.7 REHABILITATE WITNESS ON REDIRECT

When your witness is impeached with her deposition, you have the opportunity to rehabilitate her on redirect examination. You will need to rehabilitate your witness when opposing counsel has impeached your witness by taking the "inconsistent" statement from the deposition out of context. In such a situation, your job is to rehabilitate your witness on redirect by giving her the opportunity to explain the impeaching statement in the context of the entire deposition.

Practice Tip

Be fair when you impeach. If you are not, opposing counsel can rehabilitate the witness on redirect and show the jury that you took the witness' words out of context from the deposition.

Example: Rehabilitating Witness

Q. Do you recall Mr. Meyer [opposing counsel] implying that you were distracted because you had been talking on your cell phone at the time of the accident in the intersection?

A. Yes.

*Q. Let me show you **all** of page 55 from your deposition which Mr. Meyer did **not** show you and read along silently as I read lines 8-12. Isn't it true that you answered, "I* *was talking on my cell phone while I was driving but ended the conversation a couple of minutes before I drove through the intersection.”*

Be on the lookout when your witness is impeached. It is often not done precisely, giving you a wonderful opportunity to show that opposing counsel was not being fair to your witness on an important point. When this happens, you will get the benefit of having the witness give the damaging testimony on direct and then again on redirect examination when you show that your witness has testified consistently in the past.

7.8 PROVING UP IMPEACHMENT

Although this happens so rarely it is debatable whether it is worth mentioning, there may come a time when the witness denies the deposition's accuracy. That is, the witness says something bizarre like, “Well, you read the deposition correctly, but that is not what I said.” In such a situation, you would ask the witness why he did not make the corrections when reviewing the deposition. The witness will probably answer, “I did not have time to review it.”

To remedy this problem, when it is your turn to put on witnesses at trial, you will need to call the court reporter who took the deposition and have her testify that the transcript is accurate. Have the court reporter compare the disputed transcript with the tape recording (court reporters often tape as well as transcribe depositions) made at the time of the deposition. Nonetheless, this is another good reason to video depositions if your budget allows. A witness can never deny that he did not say what the transcript says or that he did not understand the question with the video proving otherwise.

7.9 UNAVAILABLE WITNESS

This is a critically important issue that you need to pay attention to. Rule 32 provides that a party may use a deposition at trial if the witness is unavailable. A witness, whether a party or not, is unavailable if the court finds that the witness is dead, that the witness is more than 100 miles from the trial (unless the witness' absence was procured by the party offering the deposition), that the witness cannot attend because of “age, illness, infirmity, or imprisonment,” or that there are exceptional circumstances.

This rule often catches attorneys off-guard because they just assume witnesses will show up at trial. So, if opposing counsel seeks to use a deposition as a substitute for live testimony, your only hope is to subpoena the witness under Rule 45. Under that rule, you may subpoena the witness to trial if he lives within the state.[1]

---

[1] See *Mohamed v. Mazda Corp.*, 90 F.Supp.2d 757,778 (E.D. Tex. 2000) (“One of the purposes of this revision [to Rule 45] was to enable the court to compel a witness found within the state in which the court sits to attend trial.”)

In any event, if you can't subpoena the witness, you are out of luck. Consequently, that brilliant cross-examination with all the questions which you did not ask at the deposition can't be used at trial. Instead, you will have to suffer not only that defeat but the prospect that you won't be able to put *any* questions before the jury since you did not ask them at the deposition. As a result, opposing counsel will be able to get in the good questions and responses that he asked at the deposition, and you are left with nothing.

The only way to avoid such a predicament is to think about this possibility during the deposition. If the witness is more than 100 miles away from the courthouse (and particularly if the witness is in another state), you need to assume that the witness will not testify live at trial but by deposition. Given that scenario, you should ask questions at the deposition to protect yourself at trial.

Even if the witness lives within 100 miles, circumstances can change between the time of the deposition and the long wait for trial. Witnesses can move away, become ill, or die. Those possibilities need to weigh into your considerations whether you should ask certain questions at a deposition.

7.10 HOW TO USE A DEPOSITION FOR AN UNAVAILABLE WITNESS

Under Rule 26(a)(3)(A)(ii), the court requires that a party make pretrial disclosures of the witnesses who are expected to testify by deposition at trial. Under Rule 26(a)(3)(B), these disclosures must be made at least 30 days before trial. Within 14 days of the disclosure, the opposing party may submit grounds for objections to the deposition being designated. Often, the court will add to these requirements that the proposing party designate the line and page number of the deposition excerpts being offered and that the opposing party submit reasons for its objections. A sample follows.

Example: Pre-trial Disclosure of Deposition Excerpts

The plaintiff expects to call the following witness by deposition:

1. Doctor Adam Kidney

Page: Line

3: 5 through 9: 29

45:7 through 48:3

82:12 through 95:7.

The opposing attorney can then submit objections to the court regarding admissibility.

Example: Objections to Deposition Excerpts

The defendant objects to the following parts of Dr. Kidney's deposition:

3:5 through 3:10: hearsay (Rule 801)

82:12 through 84:15: hearsay (Rule 801)

Once the court has ruled on the proposed deposition excerpts, the attorney must decide how to present the excerpts at trial. Using a deposition instead of a live witness should be a last resort. There are many reasons for not using a deposition, even if you could. For example, a jury is going to give more weight to a live witness' testimony than the bland "testimony" of a transcript. Indeed, a jury pays more attention to a witness' non-verbal communication than to what the witness actually says. The jury desperately wants to know if the witness' body language and tone of voice convey truthfulness or not. It goes without saying that a jury is more inclined to believe a witness it likes. Unfortunately, a transcript robs the jury of this vital information.

> In contrast, one reason to have a witness testify by deposition transcript is if he comes across in person as unlikeable or untruthful.

Even if the deposition is videoed, there are reasons why a live witness is better. Testimony in a courtroom is often dull. The testimony in a video deposition is even duller. Your questioning at a deposition is naturally going to be less focused and less prepared than at trial. In addition, the video makes any witness less charismatic than he would be if seen live.

Your best chance for having the jury credit the testimony in a deposition is if you already have the jury on your side based on your opening statement and the evidence that has been presented at trial. If the jury is leaning your way, it will give you the benefit of the doubt that the witness in the deposition is telling the truth.

Once attorneys decide to present testimony through a deposition transcript, they usually present the testimony in such a boring manner that it does no good at all. The worst way to present the testimony is for the attorney to read both the questions and answers. This method is only successful if the excerpt is very short (i.e. less than a minute). The better way is for an assistant to take the stand. Then, the attorney reads the questions and the assistant reads the answers. Amazingly, many attorneys do not take the time to even edit the deposition. Thus, the jury is forced to hear the entire deposition read. It will not take long for the jury to lose interest and stop paying attention to what is being said.

Do everything you can, therefore, to make sure the assistant commun-icates the information clearly. The assistant should know the deposition well. This is not the time to have the "witness" fumble with pronunciation or convey the wrong meaning through improper intonation. Moreover, it is important for the assistant to speak in a conversational manner so that it is easy for the jury to listen to the testimony. The assistant should emphasize the important parts without appearing to have rehearsed it too much. You don't want opposing counsel to object or the jury to think that it is watching a play. It is a difficult balancing act for the assistant to achieve and is another reason why reading depositions into evidence at trial is a bad idea.

Example: Using a Deposition at Trial

Defense counsel: Your honor, the defense would like to call Danielle Lightbourn to the stand by deposition. With the court's permission, I would like my assistant Caroline McElroy to take the stand and read the answers to the questions I ask from the deposition.

Judge: That's fine.

Defense counsel: We will start at page 15 line 3. "Ms. Lightbourn, where were you standing when the accident occurred?

Assistant: "I was standing outside the CVS Pharmacy . . . ."

There is no need subsequently to refer to the page and line numbers you are reading from. You have already designated those portions in your pretrial disclosures to opposing counsel. The only reason you would reference the page and line numbers is if you were going to deviate from those pretrial disclosures that have already been approved by reading fewer excerpts.

> Whether it is a transcript or a video that is presented at trial, neither goes into the jury room for deliberations. Just like live testimony, you have one chance to get it right.

Many of the same principles apply to video depositions. Attorneys do not take the time to edit them because they think it doesn't matter. Attorneys are wedded to the mistaken belief that jurors base their decision on the information presented at trial. The truth is that jurors base their decision not on the information presented but on what they remember. If they are forced to watch a long and boring deposition, they not only won't remember much of it, but their anger at having to watch it will be directed at you.

7.11 ADMISSION OF OPPOSING PARTY

Even if the witness is available, you may present the deposition at trial without calling the witness in order to put into evidence admissions made by the opposing party. See Rule 32(a)(3). For example, in a car wreck case, it may be important for the plaintiff to establish that the defendant was within the scope of employment when he had the wreck as opposed to being on a trip for pleasure. A deposition excerpt of the defendant's designated corporate representative could be read to show that the employee was on a sales call when he had the accident. By offering the deposition excerpt, the plaintiff could efficiently prove his point without having to call a witness that might open up irrelevant matters.

7.12 THE TRIAL DEPOSITION

Sometimes it is necessary to take the deposition of a witness because both parties realize that a witness will be unavailable for trial. This can happen during discovery if the witness appears ill or lives far away and is not expected to come to the trial. However, it also often happens after discovery is finished, and the trial date has been set. It is then that both sides realize the need for a trial deposition. It may be that both sides have witnesses who will be unavailable (such as experts) or both sides will benefit from having the witness testify by deposition. If the deadline for discovery has passed, the attorneys will agree to take the deposition if it is allowed by the court's local rule or practice. If not already allowed by their rules, courts usually grant such agreed requests.

Here are some of the differences from a discovery deposition. First, the deposition will start with a direct examination and then a cross-examination. The reason is that a trial deposition occurs generally when the sponsoring party needs the witness.

Second, since the trial date is often looming, there will be less time to edit the deposition. Whether you are conducting a direct or cross, be well prepared so that a good portion of your questions are coherent and can be used without editing. You need to assume that there may be no time to edit the video; your questions, then, need to be concise and clear, just like at trial. Third, since the jury won't be able to judge the witness' credibility, it is best to go into a little more detail on the witness' background than you would normally do at trial so that the jury gets a better feel for the witness.

Fourth, if your witness is the one being deposed, he needs to be prepared as if he were at trial. If the deposition is being videoed, the video won't be kind to a witness who looks unprepared, fumbles, and pauses a lot. On the other hand, if there is no video, take your time between questions and topics so that you develop coherent questioning (the transcript won't reveal the pauses between questions).

☷CHECKLIST

Deposition Summaries

1. Don't let assistant prepare summary; do it yourself to ensure important points aren't left out.
2. Organize by topic, not chronologically.
3. Limit summary to three or four most important points. That is all you need for trial.

Creating Outlines for Direct

1. Outline is created from witness interviews, witness statements, and deposition.
2. When creating outlines for direct at trial, write answer you expect, not the question you will ask. This will help you focus on the information you expect to get from witness.
3. Reference answers you expect in outline with page numbers in deposition.

Creating Outlines for Cross

1. From deposition summary, pick three topics you can successfully cross on.
2. Write answers you expect, not questions you are going to ask.
3. Unlike direct outline, reference answers with page *and* line number.
4. Highlight in depo. transcript the testimony you expect you will need to use for impeachment.

Refreshing Recollection

Remember the acronym **DARTS**.

1. **D**etermine if it is possible to refresh witness' memory without directly asking the witness.
2. **A**sk witness to read document silently,
3. **R**etrieve the document from the witness.
4. **T**est to see if the witness' memory is refreshed.
5. **S**ame question is asked again.

Six Common Mistakes Made During Impeachment

1. The inconsistent statement in the depo. is really not *precisely* inconsistent with trial testimony.
2. The inconsistent statement in the depo. has multiple facts.
3. The inconsistent statement made at trial is minor.
4. Attorney allows witness to read depo. transcript.

5. Attorney mistakenly refreshes the witness' recollection.

6. Attorney asks witness to explain why the depo. statement is inconsistent.

Three Easy Steps to Impeach Witness

Remember the **ABC**'s

1. **A**ccuse the witness of lying at trial. That is, make it clear to the jury that the witness has made an incorrect statement at trial and that you have a truthful statement to confront him with.

2. **B**uild up the trustworthiness of the deposition (i.e. under oath, chance to review, etc.).

3. **C**onfront the witness with the deposition.

Proving Up Impeachment

If witness denies accuracy of deposition, call the court reporter as a rebuttal witness to verify transcript.

Witness Unavailable for Trial

Only use a deposition at trial instead of a live witness as a last resort. If you must use a deposition, edit it ruthlessly. Jurors become bored very quickly with depositions.

The Trial Deposition

A trial deposition is taken shortly before trial when both sides know a witness will be unavailable. At the deposition, be organized and well-prepared. You may not have time to edit the deposition prior to trial, so everything you do may be seen by the jury.

CHAPTER EIGHT

Analysis of President Clinton's Deposition

> Oh what a tangled web we weave, when first we practice to deceive.
>
> —*Sir Walter Scott*

L et's look at how the skills we've learned work in Clinton's deposition. In *Jones v. Clinton*, the plaintiff, Paula Jones, filed a sexual harassment lawsuit claiming that while Clinton was governor of Arkansas, he sexually assaulted her. She complained she lived in fear of retaliation by Clinton for her refusal to consent to his sexual advances.

To help understand the deposition, let's take a closer look at the allegations. Jones was a state employee with the Arkansas Industrial Development Commission (AIDC). On May 8, 1991, she helped run a management conference at the Excelsior Hotel in Little Rock, where Governor Clinton was giving a speech. A member of Clinton's security team, Danny Ferguson, spoke with Jones and told her that the governor would like to meet her in his hotel room. Thinking such a meeting might help her advance in her job, she accepted the invitation and went to Clinton's room. After some small talk in which Clinton mentioned that Jones' supervisor, Dave Harrington, was his good friend, Clinton unexpectedly grabbed her hand and pulled her toward him.

Jones pulled away. She claimed that Clinton made some other sexual advances and finally dropped his pants and asked her to kiss his erect penis. Jones said that she was "not that kind of girl." As she left the room, Clinton stopped her momentarily and sternly said, "You're a smart girl, let's keep this between ourselves."

Jones continued to work for the state. Her duties included delivering documents to the Governor's Office. On a subsequent trip to the Governor's office, Clinton accosted her when he put his arm around her, held her tightly, and asked his bodyguard, "Don't we make a beautiful couple, Beauty and the Beast?" Another incident occurred when she was at the governor's office, and Ferguson came up to her and said that he had told Clinton how good she looked since she had come back from maternity leave.

Jones claimed that she was in constant fear that Clinton would retaliate against her because she had refused to have sex with him at the Excelsior Hotel. This fear prevented her from enjoying her job. Her supervisors also treated her rudely, which was something that had not occurred before her encounter with Clinton at the hotel. Her supervisors also refused to give her meaningful work, moved her work location, and failed to give her flowers on Secretary's Day in 1992 when others received them.

During discovery, the court allowed Jones to inquire about other instances when Clinton allegedly had harassed women while he was governor or president.[1] One such incident involved Kathleen Willey. Kathleen Willey and her husband were well-known Democratic fund-raisers in Virginia. She worked as a volunteer in the White House social office when Clinton was president. On Nov. 29, 1993, she met with Clinton in order to get help acquiring a full-time job, needed because of her husband's financial difficulty. According to Willey, Clinton groped her in a hallway near the Oval Office. By coincidence, while they were meeting, Willey's husband committed suicide. The attorney representing Paula Jones was James Fisher. Robert Bennett represented Clinton.

Below are excerpts from the deposition divided by subject matter. We will examine Clinton's answers regarding Kathleen Willey, a sexual harassment policy, Monica Lewinsky, Jane Does (other unnamed victims), and Gennifer Flowers.

Example: Clinton Answers Questions Regarding Kathleen Willey

Q1. Mr. President, did Kathleen Willey ever give you permission to touch her breasts?
A. No, I never asked, and I never did.

Q2. Did she ever give you permission to kiss her on the lips?
A. No.

Here, Clinton is asked questions about permission "to touch her breasts" and "kiss her on the lips" that assume the prohibited acts occurred. They are like the well known trick question, "When did you stop beating your wife?"

---

[1] For the deposition, sexual relations was defined as follows: "a person engages in sexual relations when the person knowingly engages in or causes 1) contact with the genitalia, anus, groin, breast, inner thigh, or buttocks of any person with an intent to arouse or gratify the sexual desire of any person; 2) contact between any part of the person's body or an object and the genitals or anus of another person; or 3) contact between the genitals or anus of the person and any part of another person's body. "Contact" means intentional touching, either directly or through clothing."

In Clinton's first answer (but not the second), he handles the question well by dispelling the impression left by the question and offers an explanation instead of giving an overly simplistic answer.

If a question's wording and its answer would give the wrong impression, then the witness should explain his answer. For example, if Clinton had answered Question one (Q1), "No," one reasonable inference is that Clinton touched her breasts without her permission. If Clinton had answered that way, it would have been important for his attorney to correct the potentially bad inference by asking specifically at the end of the deposition, "Have you ever touched her breasts?"

> Teach your witness to explain his answers if the question assumes the witness has done something wrong.

Q1. *Did Kathleen Willey ever give you permission to take her hand and place it on your genitals?*
A. No, she didn't.

Q2. *Do you recall, sir, that you met with Kathleen Willey at or near the time of her husband's death?*
A. The meeting I recall occurred before her husband's death. She had requested, my recollection is that she requested several times to come in to see me. She wanted to come in and see me, and kept asking to do that. **[Clinton volunteers information.]**

Mr. Bennett [Clinton's lawyer]: Mr. President, just answer his questions, please, sir.
A. And my—she did come in to see me.

Here, Clinton's lawyer tries to correct a repeated mistake that Clinton makes. Unlike the first example where Clinton adds information to prevent the answer from giving the wrong impression, in this second example, Clinton simply volunteers information which helps the examiner by filling in gaps without his having to ask for it. The second question (Q2), asking when he met with Willey, requires a simple one word answer, "Yes."

Q1. *What did you have to drink?*
A. I don't remember.

Q2 *Was it alcoholic?*
A. Oh, no, no, I don't serve alcohol there in the office of the White House.

Q3. *Not ever?*
A. Never.

Whenever a witness answers "I don't remember" or gives you some variation, (i.e. "I don't recall"), make sure to follow up with a question that forces the witness to approximate in a more general way than the preceding question which may have been too specific. This technique is useful in getting more information.

Here, the attorney doesn't move on after Clinton says he does not remember the specific drink he had but makes him give a more general answer—it wasn't alcoholic and "I don't serve alcohol there." In this case, it is doubly effective because Clinton not only answers the question but volunteers the information that he doesn't serve alcohol in the White House. By volunteering that he "never" serves alcohol there, Clinton could be exposing himself to being caught in a lie if Fisher (Jones' attorney) ever developed proof to the contrary.

Q. Do you know why she would tell a story like that if it weren't true?
A. No, sir, I don't. I don't know. She'd been through a lot, and apparently, the financial difficulties were even greater than she thought they were at the time she talked to me. Her husband killed himself, she's been through a terrible time. I have—I can't say. All I can tell you is, in the first place, when she came to see me she was clearly upset. I did to her what I have done to scores and scores of men and women who have worked for me or been my friends over the years. I embraced her, I put my arms around her, I may have even kissed her on the forehead. There was nothing sexual about it. I was trying to help her calm down and trying to reassure her. She was in a difficult condition. But I have no idea why she said what she did, or whether she now believes that actually happened. She's been through a terrible, terrible time in her life, and I have nothing else to say. I don't want to speculate about it.

> The question,"Is the accuser lying?", usually provokes a strong reaction in the witness that will let you gauge his credibility.

This credibility question ("Do you know why she would tell a story like that if it weren't true?") is a variation of the standard question, "Is the accuser lying?" Look at the non-verbal communication as well as the answer itself. Here, the answer reveals clearly that Clinton is having trouble explaining why Willey would make up this story. As the lawyer asking the question, you need to assess how a juror would perceive the witness' testimony versus that of the accuser. Who is more credible? Asking the question the way Fisher did is a lot more effective than simply asking, "Did you sexually assault Ms. Willey?" It forces the witness to give an explanation why the accuser would lie.

Example: Clinton Answers Questions Regarding Sexual Harassment Policy

Q. *Is this a copy of a sexual harassment policy that you signed when you were the governor of the state of Arkansas?*

A. It is. I signed it in 1987, and I'm fairly sure that I was, we were the first or one of the very first states to actually have a clearly defined sexual harassment policy.

Mr. Fisher: Objection, nonresponsive beginning with the words, 'I'm fairly sure.'

Fisher makes a good and necessary objection. Remember objections to a question's form or non-responsive answers are waived unless made at the deposition. If Fisher does not object "non-responsive" and needs to use the deposition at trial because Clinton might be unavailable to testify, the self-serving statement about Arkansas being a leader in sexual harassment policies would be admitted even though it is non-responsive to the simple question, "Is this a copy?"

Example: Clinton Answers Questions Regarding Monica Lewinsky

Monica Lewinsky, age twenty-one, came to work as a White House intern in July 1995 and was assigned to the West Wing later that year. In November 1995, Lewinsky had direct contact with Clinton, and on one of those occasions, he asked if he could kiss her, and she agreed. Later that night, they had the first of approximately ten sexual encounters over the next year and a half. After eight encounters, Clinton tried to end the relationship, and Lewinsky was reassigned to a position outside the White House at the Department of Defense. Nonetheless, two more encounters ensued in early 1997.

The sexual encounters (usually Lewinsky performed oral sex or Clinton fondled her) took place at the Oval Office on weekends when only a few people (i.e. Clinton's secretary, Bettie Currie) were in the building. When the affair was finally over, Lewinsky sought employment in the private sector. Clinton asked his longtime confidant, Vernon Jordan, to meet with Lewinsky to talk about job possibilities in the fall of 1997.

Q. *Is it true that when she worked at the White House she met with you several times?*

A. **I don't know about several times.** There was a period when the, when the Republican Congress shut the government down that the whole White House was being run by interns, and she was assigned to work back in the chief of staff's office, and we were all working there, and so I saw her on two or three occasions then, and then when she worked at the White House, I think there was one or two other times when she brought some documents to me.

Whether the topic was Lewinsky or other alleged indiscretions, Clinton repeatedly said, "I don't recall," "I don't know," "I'm not sure," "it's possible," and "I can't remember." Saying such things regarding Lewinsky became implausible when other witnesses corroborated Lewinsky's version.

Q. *Well, you also saw her at a number of social functions at the White House didn't you?*

A. **Could you be specific? I'm not sure.** I mean when we had, when we had like big staff things for, if I had a, like in the summertime, if I had a birthday party and the whole White House staff came, then she must have been there. If we had a Christmas party . . . .

Practice Tip

"I'm not sure" is only a good answer for your witness if it is the truth.

Clinton's propensity to volunteer information undermines all the witness prep his lawyer had done. He should have just stopped after his first sentence, "Could you be specific?" That is exactly what a lawyer instructs his witness to do: if you don't understand the question, ask for clarification. But instead of stopping there, Clinton not only goes on to talk about birthday and Christmas parties but goes on for twice as long (not reprinted above) about other possibilities. Also, notice that Clinton continues to pretend to have a bad memory by saying, "I'm not sure."

Q. *Did it ever happen that you and she went down the hallway from the Oval Office to the private kitchen?*

Mr. Bennett: Your honor, excuse me, Mr. President, I need some guidance from the Court at this point. I'm going to object to the innuendo. I'm afraid, as I say, that this will leak. . . .Counsel is fully aware that Ms. Jane Doe 6 [Lewinsky] has filed, has an affidavit which they are in possession of saying that there is absolutely no sex of any kind in any manner, shape or form, with President Clinton, and yet listening to the innuendo in the questions—

Judge Wright: No, just a minute, let me make my ruling. I do not know whether counsel is basing this question on any affidavit, but I will direct Mr. Bennett not to comment on other evidence that might be pertinent and could be arguably coaching the witness at this juncture. . . .[2]

The rules prohibit speaking objections that suggest the answer to your witness. Although Bennett appears to be genuinely concerned about a leak

---

[2] Given the unusual nature of a president being deposed, the presiding judge in the case was present at this deposition to make any necessary rulings.

and about the innuendo, the Judge takes no chances that Bennett might be using this as an excuse to coach Clinton and remind him about the affidavit stating there was no sex.

The reason that Bennett does not appear to be coaching Clinton on this point is that it is unlikely Clinton would forget what was contained in Lewinsky's affidavit. On the other hand, it is possible that Bennett wanted to remind his client that he could freely deny having sex, given the affidavit from Lewinsky that would support such a denial. Either way, the example proves that even the appearance of coaching during a deposition is strictly prohibited.

This exchange would haunt Clinton. The House would later vote to impeach Clinton for allowing his attorney to make misleading statements to Judge Webber, who was presiding at the deposition. The House voted to impeach Clinton even though he told the grand jurors that he was not listening to his lawyer when the statement was made and that even if he had been listening, his lawyer's statement was technically true. This passage and others will be discussed in more detail in Chapter Nine.

Q. *At any time were you and Monica Lewinsky alone together in the Oval Office?*
A. **I don't recall**, but as I said, when she worked at the legislative affairs office, they always had somebody there on the weekends. I typically worked some on the weekends. Sometimes they'd bring me things on the weekends. She - it seems to me she brought things to me once or twice on the weekends. In that case, whatever time she would be in there, drop it off, exchange a few words and go, she was there. I don't have any specific recollections of what the issues were, what was going on, but when the Congress is there, we're working all the time, and typically I would do some work on one of the days of the weekends in the afternoon.

Q. *So I understand, your testimony is that* **it was possible, then, that you were alone with her, but you have no specific recollection of that ever happening?**
A. **Yes, that's correct.** It's possible that she, in, while she was working there, brought something to me and that at the time she brought it to me, she was the only person there. That's possible.

On the video, Clinton paused five seconds before beginning his answer, "I don't recall." Later, the grand jury looked into whether Clinton committed perjury when evidence surfaced—including Lewinsky's infamous blue dress with semen stains—that he had indeed met with Lewinsky alone in the Oval Office. Yet, in any event, the House voted 229-205 not to send this alleged perjury crime to the Senate for impeachment proceedings.

Q. *What in particular was given to Monica?*
A. **I don't remember.** I got a whole bag full of things that I bought at The Black Dog. I went there, they gave me some things, and I went and purchased a lot

at their store, and when I came back I gave a, a big block of it to Betty, and I don't know what she did with it all or who got what.

This is another example where Clinton claims not to remember in the deposition when evidence would later show that at the time of the deposition he was asking his secretary to go to Lewinsky's house to collect the gifts he had given her.

Q1. Recently you took a trip that included a visit to Bosnia, correct?
A. That's correct.

Q2. While you were on that trip, did you talk to Monica Lewinsky?
A. I don't believe she was on that trip.

Q3. Did you talk to her on the telephone?
A. No.

Q4. While you were on that trip, did you ask anyone to talk to her?
A. I don't believe so, no.

Fisher asks good follow-up questions (see discussion of inverted pyramid in Chapter Two) so that he can be sure Clinton claims he did not communicate with Lewinsky in any way. Notice how Clinton does not answer Q2 directly. Fisher won't know if Clinton is sidestepping the answer to the question unless he follows up with Q3 and Q4. Fisher does one better by further narrowing the possibilities by asking if Clinton caused anyone to talk to her in Q4.

Q1. Did you have an extramarital sexual affair with Monica Lewinsky?
A. No.

Q2. If she told someone that she had a sexual affair with you beginning in November of 1995, would that be a lie?
A. It's certainly not the truth. It would not be the truth.

Q3. I think I used the term 'sexual affair.' And so the record is completely clear, have you ever had sexual relations with Monica Lewinsky, as that term is defined in Deposition Exhibit 1, as modified by the Court.
A. I have never had sexual relations with Monica Lewinsky. I've never had an affair with her.

Practice Tip

If a term or phrase is important, define it for the witness or have the witness define it. For example, "Did you have sexual relations as defined in exhibit one?"

Notice two things. First, Fisher asks a credibility question (Q2) regarding whether Clinton thinks Lewinsky is lying. This is the same question he asked (see above) regarding Kathleen Willey's claim. Clinton does not answer the question with a simple "yes". Having to repeat his answer twice shows his defensiveness.

The second lesson is that Fisher wants to make sure he has not let Clinton off the hook. He realizes that Clinton may have a different idea of what a sexual affair is and that he could truthfully answer that question "no." What might be an affair to one person might be something else to another, depending on how one defines "sexual affair." So, he follows up with a very precise question that gets to the lawsuit's core: Did he have sexual relations— as defined by exhibit one—with Lewinsky.

Q. *My question, though, is focused on the time before the conversation occurred, and the question is whether you did anything to cause the conversation [between Vernon Jordan and Lewinsky] to occur.*
A. I think in the mean—I'm not sure how you mean the question. I think the way you mean the question, the answer to that is no, I've already testified. . . .

Clinton's answer, "I think the way you mean the question," is just what a deposing attorney wants to hear and what a defending attorney dreads. Fisher gets helpful information without having to ask for it. On the other hand, Bennett is frustrated that Clinton tries to help Fisher by volunteering information. To the extent the witness volunteers information or tries to offer an interpretation of the attorney's question, the witness helps the deposing attorney reach his goal.

Q. *Did anyone other than your attorneys ever tell you that Monica Lewinsky had been served with a subpoena in this case?*
A. **I don't think so**.

Q. *Did you ever talk with Monica Lewinsky about the possibility that she might be asked to testify in this case?*
A. Bruce Lindsey, I think Bruce Lindsey told me that she was, I think maybe that's the first person who told me she was. I want to be as accurate as I can.

[Mr. Bennett]: Keep your voice up Mr. President.
[Clinton]: Okay.

A. But he may not have. I don't have a specific memory, but I talked with him about the case on more than one occasion, so he might have said that.

Again, Clinton's reliance on "I don't think so" would get him in trouble with the grand jury (see Chapter Nine). Vernon Jordan would later tell the grand jury that he had told Clinton just three weeks before Clinton's deposition that Lewinsky had contacted him about being subpoenaed in the Jones lawsuit. Although Clinton thinks it is safer to say, "I don't think so" than "No," they are both lies which harmed his credibility.

Q. Mr. President, have you ever paid any money to Monica Lewinsky?
A. No, sir.

Q. Have you ever caused money to be paid to her?
A. Absolutely not.

Q. Have you ever paid off any debt that she owed to some other person?
A. No, sir.

Q. Have you ever caused a debt that she owed to some other person to be repaid?
A. No, sir.

Fisher: That's all I have on that subject.
Judge Wright: All right, how much time—I'm suggesting we have lunch for, within the next half-hour and then come back here in half an hour.

Bennett: Would you like to break now—
Clinton: Mr. Fisher, is there something, let me just—you asked that with such conviction and I answered with such conviction, is there something you want to ask me about this? I don't, I don't even know what you're talking about, I don't think . . . .

This may be Clinton's worst case of volunteering. In previous examples, there was at least a question pending. Here, there is no question, the lawyer has declared, "That's all I have on the subject," and the Judge is suggesting a break for lunch. However, Clinton interrupts the Judge and his own lawyer to suggest Fisher ask him more questions about Lewinsky. No matter how much you prepare your witness, you can only do so much. In the end, your witness makes the choice whether to listen to your advice or not.

Example: Clinton Answers Questions Regarding Jane Does

The Jane Does in the deposition refer to other unnamed women who may have been sexually harassed by Clinton while he was governor or president. The following examples concern the different Jane Does.

Q. While you were governor, was there a store in Little Rock named Barbara Ann's?
A. Barbara Jean's.

Q. Barbara Jean's?
A. Yes.

Q. Do you recall—
A. Isn't that right? [asking his attorney]

Bennett: Barbara Jean's is correct.
Clinton: I think that's right.

Bennett: But you should not feel a moral obligation to correct his errors.
Q. Do you recall ever sending any of the state troopers who were on your security detail to Barbara Jean's to pick up a gift that you were going to give to a woman other than your wife or a relative?

Clinton not only volunteers information, but now he is correcting the deposing attorney. If Clinton had not corrected the attorney, Fisher would have gotten worthless answers because he would have asked about a non-existent store, Barbara Ann's.

Q. What was the purpose of these visits to Jane Doe 2's house when her husband was not there?
A. The fact that her husband was not there was incidental. She was a friend of mine, and I would go by and see her from time to time. I hadn't been visiting with her in a long time. Sometimes I saw him when she wasn't there. He was a friend of mine, too.

This is a loaded question that presumes something sinister because Clinton went to Jane Doe 2's house when she was alone. Clinton sees the trap, and appropriately qualifies his answer.

Q1. On the first of these two occasions [meeting with Jane Doe 1], what time of day did you meet?
A.   I don't remember.

Q2. Do you remember if it was dark outside?
A.   No.

It is important to ask precise questions. Although the more likely inference from the answer to Q2 is that Clinton does not remember if it was dark outside, the question is ambiguous enough to allow Clinton to argue later that he did remember and that "no," it was not dark outside. If this were an important point to explore, Fisher should have followed up with a question to confirm the answer: "So, you don't remember if it was dark or light outside?"

Example: Clinton Answers Questions Regarding Gennifer Flowers

Q. Do you recall going to Los Angeles, California with her?
A. No, sir. When was this? I don't recall.

Bennett: Don't assume that it happened.
A. I don't believe I ever took a trip outside of Arkansas with Gennifer Flowers.

Notice how Bennett's coaching affects the deposition. Initially, Clinton says that he does not recall if he went to California with Flowers. Then, after Bennett intervenes, he asserts that he never left Arkansas with her.

Q. And her [Judy Gaddy] husband was named Bill Gaddy, correct?
A. That's correct.

Q. He also held a state employment position, right?
A. Yes, he did.

Q. What was his position in 1991?
A. I don't know what his position was in 1991. He held more than one position when I was governor. If you think you know, and you tell me I'll be grateful . . . .

Q. Did you ever talk to Bill Gaddy about Gennifer Flowers getting a job?

It is important for the attorney taking the deposition to be respectful to the witness. The reason is that if the witness respects you, he is more likely to give forthcoming answers. Here, Clinton asks Fisher a simple question and Fisher, instead of answering the question, ignores it, and goes onto his next question.

Likewise, tell your witness in the preparation session to always show respect to opposing counsel. If your witness maintains his cool and does not let emotions cloud his demeanor, he will think more clearly and be able to protect himself in the deposition.

Example: Clinton Answers Questions from his Lawyer

Many attorneys decide correctly not to ask their witness questions at the end of the deposition. But there are two occasions when you might want to ask questions. First, if there is a chance the witness will be unavailable for trial. For example, a doctor may not be available for trial due to his schedule, and you will be severely hampered if he cannot attend and you are stuck with a deposition being used as a substitute for live testimony at trial that does not contain the questions and answers you need.

> The prevailing wisdom is that you don't want to open the door for more questions from opposing counsel by asking your witness questions that might raise new issues.

Second, there may be a need to clear up the record on important testimony. Here, Clinton's lawyer, Bill Bennett, wants to clear up the record because he is fearful that the deposition will be leaked to the public. So, he asks succinct questions to make his point.

Q. In paragraph eight of [Lewinsky's] affidavit, she says this: 'I have never had a sexual relationship with the president, he did not propose that we have a sexual relationship, he did not offer me employment or other benefits in exchange for a sexual relationship, he did not deny me employment or other benefits for rejecting a sexual relationship.' Is that a true and accurate statement as far as you know it?

A. That is absolutely true.

Below is another example that illustrates the proper scope of questions. Rule 26(b)(1) states that "parties may obtain discovery . . .that is relevant to any party's claim or defense. . . .Relevant information need not be admissible at the trial if the discovery appears reasonably calculated to lead to the discovery of admissible evidence." In a prior ruling, Judge Wright had limited discovery to women who worked under Clinton while he was governor or president. The plaintiff's attorney felt that he should be entitled to ask the following question because it might be relevant to their sexual harassment claims. Judge Wright correctly ruled that such a question would not lead to the discovery of admissible evidence at trial.

Judge Wright: We're going to stay on the record just so Mr. Fisher can make his record, because I'm not letting him ask certain questions.

Mr. Fisher: Number one, Please name every person with whom you had sexual relations when you were either governor of the state of Arkansas or president of the United States; Number two, Please name every person with whom you sought to have sexual relations when you were either governor of the state of Arkansas or president of the United States. If any names are given in response to either/or both of those questions, then obviously there would be follow-up questions to determine whether there are factors that make those incidents relevant.

Given that Judge Wright had already made her ruling prior to the deposition, it was unnecessary for Fisher to preserve the record by asking the two questions above. It was redundant but probably done to make a point in the realm of public opinion when the deposition became public.

CHAPTER NINE

Lessons from Clinton's Grand Jury Testimony

If you tell the truth, you don't have to remember anything.

—Mark Twain

In many ways, Clinton's grand jury testimony was much like a deposition where an attorney asks questions to get admissions and discover information. While the merits of having a grand jury investigate the charges against Clinton divided the country, let's set aside those opinions because there is a lot to learn for your next deposition from studying Clinton's testimony.

By way of background, the Office of Independent Counsel (OIC) had been investigating allegations that Clinton had committed impeachable offenses related to a land deal called Whitewater. However, the OIC expanded its scope when it learned that Monica Lewinsky had tried to influence the testimony of a witness (Linda Tripp) in the Paula Jones lawsuit[1] and had filed a false affidavit claiming that she had never had sexual relations with Clinton. After his deposition in the Jones lawsuit, Clinton spoke with his secretary, Bettie Currie. He attempted to influence her by suggesting that he had never been alone with Lewinsky or done anything inappropriate.

On August 17, 1998, Clinton faced a grand jury that was investigating whether he committed perjury in his deposition or obstructed justice in the Jones lawsuit. On December 19, 1998, the House of Representatives (controlled by the Republicans) voted to impeach Clinton and sent two articles of impeachment (the charges) to the Senate for a trial. The first article concerned whether Clinton provided perjured and misleading testimony to

---

[1] Paula Jones, a government worker, filed a sexual harassment lawsuit against Clinton claiming that while he was governor of Arkansas he retaliated against her at work when she refused his sexual advances in a hotel room.

the grand jury concerning: 1) the nature and details of his relationship with a subordinate employee (Lewinsky), 2) prior misleading statements in the Paula Jones deposition about his sexual encounters with Lewinsky, 3) prior misleading statements made by his attorney in the Jones deposition, and 4) his efforts to influence the testimony of other witnesses in the grand jury investigation.

As for the first and second allegations above, Lewinsky had told investigators and the grand jury that Clinton had fondled and kissed her breasts and touched her genitalia during ten encounters at the White House. She had also told many friends about this. Although Clinton admitted that Lewinsky performed oral sex on him, he denied any additional fondling.

The third allegation related to whether Clinton knew that his attorney had made misleading statements at the deposition when the attorney said that Lewinsky had submitted an affidavit saying that she had not had sex with Clinton. Although the attorney believed the affidavit was true, Clinton knew that it wasn't (he had not told his attorney about his sexual encounters with Lewinsky). The fourth claim concerned whether Clinton had told his secretary and aides that he had not had sex with Lewinsky so that they would repeat those denials to the grand jury and investigators.

The second impeachment article alleged that Clinton had violated his oath as president to take care that the laws of the United States be faithfully executed when he obstructed justice by: 1) encouraging Lewinsky to submit a false affidavit in the Jones lawsuit, 2) encouraging Lewinsky to give false testimony if she were called to testify in the Jones lawsuit, 3) supporting a scheme to conceal evidence that had been subpoenaed in the Jones lawsuit, 4) succeeding in getting a job for Lewinsky in order to prevent her truthful testimony in the Jones lawsuit, 5) allowing his attorney to make false statements to a judge at his deposition, 6) telling a false account about his deposition testimony to a witness in order to influence that witness' testimony, and 7) making several false statements to witnesses in the grand jury investigation in order to influence their testimony corruptly.

Some claims in the second article are self-explanatory or overlap the charges in the first article (like in the first, second, and fifth). But a few need further explanation. The third allegation relates to evidence that Betty Currie, Clinton's secretary, had visited Lewinsky's home and retrieved gifts that Clinton had given Lewinsky so that Lewinsky could claim that she did not have any gifts in her possession if subpoenaed by investigators.

The fourth allegation involved the claim that Clinton had asked his confidant, Vernon Jordan, to arrange for a job for Lewinsky in the private sector in exchange for her affidavit and testimony denying sex with Clinton.

The sixth count relates to an incident where Clinton spoke to Currie the day after his deposition with Lewinsky. He told her, "We were never alone . . . . You could see and hear everything . . . Monica came onto me and I never touched her, right?" Clinton knew that Currie would be asked to testify, and he wanted to make sure she was on board.

Other alleged lies were considered by the House but not submitted to the Senate for impeachment. One lie was Clinton's response to a question at his deposition that asked, "At any time were you alone with Lewinsky in the Oval Office?" Clinton paused for five seconds before answering, "I don't recall," despite Currie, Lewinsky, and several secret service agents testifying that he had been.

Also, the House did not submit the allegation that Clinton had lied about having sexual relations as it was defined in the Jones lawsuit. Another allegation that the House did not submit was Clinton's statement in the deposition that "I could have given her a gift, but I don't remember a specific gift." A few weeks before the deposition, Clinton had given Lewinsky several gifts, including a pair of sunglasses, a stuffed animal, and a Rockettes blanket.

Much like a jury's verdict, there is no way to know why the House voted to impeach on some allegations and not others. After a trial in the Senate, Clinton was acquitted largely along party lines: 55 to 45 for acquittal on the perjury count and 50 to 50 on the second article (which was still short of the two-thirds needed for conviction).

Now, let's narrow our focus to the tips we can learn for our next deposition. Almost all the excerpts below have a video clip which you can also study. Remember that non-verbal communication is often more important than verbal communication. There is a wealth of information to be gained from a witness' body language, and the same is no less true for Clinton. To view the video clips, go to **http://winningatdeposition.com/** and click on the tab at the top that is labeled Chapter Nine.

Example: Prosecutor Explains Oath to Clinton (Video Clip 1)

At the beginning, the prosecutor explains the oath to Clinton. Do you think he goes into too much detail?

Q1. Mr. President, you understand that your testimony here today is under oath?
A. I do.

Q2. And do you understand that because you have sworn to tell the truth, the whole truth, and nothing but the truth, that if you were to lie or intentionally mislead the grand jury, you could be prosecuted for perjury and or obstruction of justice?
A. I believe that's correct.

Q3. Is there anything that you—I've stated to you regarding your rights and responsibilities that you would like me to clarify or that you don't understand?

A.   No, sir.

Q4. Mr. President, I would like to read for you a portion of the Federal Rule of Evidence 603, which discusses the important function the oath has in our judicial system. It says that the purpose of the oath is one, 'calculated to awaken the witness' conscience and impress the witness' mind with the duty' to tell the truth. Could you please tell the grand jury what that oath means to you for today's testimony?

Before you read the answer, it should be easy to predict what Clinton—or anyone—is going to say.

A. I have sworn an oath to tell the grand jury the truth, and that's what I intend to do.

Time is precious, particularly here where the parties had agreed that there would be a strict four hour limit to the testimony. While it is understandable that an attorney might want to go into so much detail about the oath, since it is the backdrop for the grand jury investigation, it is unlikely a witness would answer any differently from Clinton. Watch how the prosecutor struggles to get Clinton to answer his questions.

Q5. You understand that it requires you to give the whole truth, that is, a complete answer to each question, sir?

A.   *I will answer each question as accurately and fully as I can.* **[Clinton does not answer with a "yes"]**

Q6. Now, you took the same oath to tell the truth, the whole truth, and nothing but the truth on January 17th, 1998 in a deposition in the Paula Jones litigation; is that correct, sir?

A.   I did take an oath then.

Q7. Did the oath you took on that occasion mean the same to you then as it does today?
A.   I believed then that I had to answer the questions truthfully, that is correct.

Q8. And it meant the same to you then as it does today? **[prosecutor repeats question]**

A.   Well, no one read me a definition then and we didn't go through this exercise then. I swore an oath to tell the truth, and I believed I was bound to be truthful and I tried to be.

Perhaps, a cleaner way to ask Q7 is, "Did you swear to tell the truth in your deposition?" Then you could ask, "Do you swear to tell the truth here today?" Clinton would look more than foolish if he answered anything but "yes."

There is still something more to learn from Clinton's indirect answers. He never answers "yes" when he should. When a witness does not answer a question, keep repeating the question until the witness does. If after a couple of tries the witness still does not answer directly, instruct the witness that the question calls for a "yes" or "no" answer. Nine times out of ten the witness will comply. If he doesn't, instruct the witness that you will seek a court order compelling him to answer the question.

> Less is more. A simple straightforward question is much more likely to force the witness to give you the answer you want than a long and complicated one.

Q9. *At the Paula Jones deposition, you were represented by Mr. Robert Bennett, your counsel, is that correct?*

A.   That is correct.

Q10. *He was authorized by you to be your representative there, your attorney, is that correct?*

A.   That is correct.

Q11. *Your counsel, Mr. Bennett, indicated at page 5 of the deposition lines 10 through 12, and I'm quoting, 'the President intends to give full and complete answers as Ms. Jones is entitled to have.' My question to you is, do you agree with your counsel that a plaintiff in a sexual harassment case is, to use his words, entitled to have the truth?*

A.   I believe that I was bound to give truthful answers, yes, sir.

Q12. *But the question is, sir, do you agree with your counsel that a plaintiff in a sexual harassment case is entitled to have the truth?*

A.   I believe when a witness is under oath in a civil case, or otherwise under oath, the witness should do everything possible to answer the questions truthfully.

Here, the prosecutor again repeats Q11 because it was not answered directly. If the question is so important, it needs to be repeated until the witness answers. The problem is that the prosecutor has a different interpretation from Bennett regarding Clinton's duty. Bennett implied that the President intended to give as complete answers as Ms. Jones is "entitled to have." Obviously, Clinton, or any witness, would have to answer truthfully to the questions asked, but no witness would be required to give the plaintiff the truth in a sexual harassment case if the proper questions were not asked. For example, if only a narrow question were asked, Clinton would not be obligated to give broad explanations that went beyond the narrow answer required.

Perhaps, the prosecutor is holding the president to a higher standard than the typical witness to tell the truth. Or, he believes Clinton lied by saying "I don't know" and "I don't remember" repeatedly when he did. Either way, if your question gives the witness a chance to explain his answer, he will.

Example: Clinton Gives Non-verbal Answer
(Video Clip 2)

This is just a quick excerpt to make sure you notice if your witness shakes his head instead of answering. When you look at the video, it seems like Clinton does not even hear the question because it seems as if he is lost in thought in another world.

Q. Did you tell her in the conversation about her being subpoenaed – she was upset about it, you acknowledge that?
(Witness nodded, indicating an affirmative response.)
Q. I'm sorry, you have to respond for the record. Yes or no? Do you agree that she was upset about being subpoenaed?
A. Oh, yes, sir, she was upset . . . .

In this example, the court reporter has put the non-verbal response, the head nod affirmatively, in the record. However, you should not rely on your court reporter to be so helpful. Consequently, the prosecutor correctly instructs the witness to answer the question verbally. Although not seen here for brevity's sake, the video clip shows that Clinton does not simply answer yes or no as instructed, but volunteers a ton of information and argues with the prosecutor. By doing so, Clinton looks defensive and loses credibility because he refuses to answer a simple question.

Example: Clinton Defines Being "Alone" with Monica
(Video Clip 3)

One issue the grand jury investigated was whether Clinton had lied in the Jones deposition when he had said that he had never been alone with Lewinsky. The day after that deposition, Clinton spoke with his secretary, Bettie Currie, and asked her a series of rhetorical questions about her knowledge of his meetings with Lewinsky.

Q. Let me ask you about the meeting you had with Betty Currie at the White House on Sunday, January 18 of this year, the day after your deposition. First of all, you didn't— Mrs. Currie, your secretary of six-some years, you never allowed her, did you, to watch whatever intimate activity you did with Ms. Lewinsky, did you?
A. No, sir, not to my knowledge.

Q. And as far as you know, she couldn't hear anything either, is that right?
A. There were a couple of times when Monica was there when I asked Betty to be places where she could hear, because Monica was upset and I—this was after there was—all the inappropriate contact had been terminated.

Q. No, I'm talking—

A. But—

Q. —about the times that you actually had the intimate contact.

A. She was—I believe that—well, first of all, on that one occasion in 1997, I do not know whether Betty was in the White House after the radio address in the Oval Office complex. I believe she probably was, but I'm not sure. But I'm certain that someone was there. I always, always someone was there. In 1996, I think most of the times that Ms. Lewinsky was there, there may not have been anybody around except maybe coming in and out, but not permanently so. I—that's correct. I never—I didn't try to involve Betty in that in any way.

Q. Well, not only did you not try to involve her, you specifically tried to exclude her and everyone else, isn't that right?

A. Well, yes. I've never—I mean, it's almost humorous, sir. I'd, I'd, I'd have to be an exhibitionist not to have tried to exclude everyone else.

Q. So, if Ms. Currie testified that you approached her on the 18th, or you spoke with her and you said, you[Currie] were always there when she [Monica] was there, she[Currie] wasn't was she? That is Mrs.Currie?

A. She was always there in the White House, and I was concerned—let me back up and say . . . .

Q. So, you wanted—

A. After that deposition.

Q. —to check her memory for what she remembered, and that is—

A. That's correct.

Q. —whether she remembered nothing, or whether she remembered an inappropriate intimate -

A. Oh, no, no, no, no.

Q. —relationship?

A. No. I didn't ask her about it in that way. I asked her about what the —what I was trying to determine was whether my recollection was right and that she was always in the **office complex** when Monica was there, and whether she thought she could hear any conversations we had, or did she hear any. And then I asked her specifically about a couple of times . . . .

Q. If Ms. Currie testified that these were not really questions to her, that they were more like statements, is that not true? [In video, prosecutor uses intonation to show disbelief in Clinton's answer]

A. Well, I can't testify as to what her perception was. I can tell you this. I was trying to get information in a hurry. I was downloading what I remembered. I think Ms. Currie would also testify that I explicitly told her, once I realized that you were involved in the Jones case—you, the Office of Independent Counsel—and that she might have to be called as a witness, that she should just go in there and tell the truth, tell what she knew, and be perfectly truthful.

So, I was not trying to get Betty Currie to say something that was untruthful. I was trying to get as much information as quickly as I could.

Q. *What information were you trying to get from [Currie] when you said, "I was never alone with her, right?"*
A. I don't remember exactly what I did say with her. That's what you say I said.

Q. *If Ms. Currie testified to that, if she says you told her, "I was never alone with her, right?*
A. Well, I was never alone with her—

Q. *Did you not say that, Mr. President?* **[Notice in video that prosecutor effectively uses intonation to show disbelief in Clinton's answers. This technique signals to the grand jurors that they should also not believe Clinton's answers]**
A. Mr. Bittman, just a minute. **"I was never alone with her, right," might be a question. And what I might have meant by that is, in the Oval Office complex.**

Q. *Well, you knew the answer to that, didn't you?*
A. We've been going for more than an hour. Would you mind if we took a break? I need to use the restroom.

(The proceedings were recessed)

Just because a witness says it's so, does not make it so.

Clinton's suggestion that when he had previously testified that he was never "alone" with Lewinsky meant only that he was never alone with her in the entire Oval Office *complex* (i.e. White House)—as opposed to just the Oval Office—does not fit with anyone's understanding of the meaning "alone."

Also, notice how the prosecutor uses Currie's testimony to undercut Clinton's explanation that he was just trying to get facts. The grand jurors were shown a stark contrast: Clinton claiming he was asking questions and Currie testifying that Clinton was making statements that he hoped she would agree to. The scale is tipped in Currie's favor when Clinton gives his implausible definition of "alone."

Example: Clinton Defines "Is" (Witness Gives Implausible Answer) (Video Clip 4)

Q1. *The statement of your attorney, Mr. Bennett, at the Paula Jones deposition, "Counsel is fully aware that Ms. Lewinsky has filed, has an affidavit which they are in possession of saying that there **is** absolutely no sex of any kind in any manner, shape or form, with President Clinton."*
That statement [was] made by your attorney in front of Judge Susan Webber Wright, correct?
A. That's correct.

Q2. That statement is a completely false statement. Whether or not Mr. Bennett knew of your relationship with Ms. Lewinsky, the statement that there was "no sex of any kind in any manner, shape or form, with President Clinton" was an utterly false statement. Is that correct?

A. It depends on what the meaning of the word "is" is. If the –if he—if "is" means is and never has been, that is not—that is one thing. If it means there is none, that was a completely true statement.

But as I have testified, and I'd like to testify again, this is—it is somewhat unusual for a client to be asked about his lawyer's statements, instead of the other way around. I was not paying a great deal of attention to this exchange. I was focusing on my own testimony.

Q3. You are the President of the United States and your attorney tells a United States District Court Judge that there is no sex of any kind, in any way, shape or form, whatsoever. And you feel no obligation to do anything about that at that deposition, Mr. President?

A. I have told you, Mr. Wisenberg, I will tell you for a third time. I am not even sure that when Mr. Bennett made that statement that I was concentrating on the exact words he used. Now, if someone had asked me on that day, are you having any kind of sexual relations with Ms. Lewinsky, that is, asked me a question in the present tense, I would have said no. And it would have been completely true.

This exchange was the most famous from the grand jury testimony. Clinton's tortured answer, "It depends on what the meaning of the word 'is' is," shows at what lengths Clinton would go to in order to split hairs to come up with a defense. Clinton is trying to say that since his relationship with Lewinsky had ended several months prior to the deposition, his attorney was making a true statement when he said in Q1 that "there *is* absolutely no sex of any kind." However, the Lewinsky affidavit declared clearly that there had not been any sex at any time between Lewinsky and the president. Any effort, then, by Clinton to define "is" does not hold up. Instead of giving this disingenuous answer, he should have just stuck with the more plausible defense that he was not concentrating on what his attorney was saying.

In Q3, the prosecutor uses powerful facts (i.e. "your attorney tells a *United States district judge*" rather than "your attorney said at the deposition") to frame the question so that the grand jurors can see how implausible Clinton's answer is.

Notice in the video clip that when Clinton answers Q2, even Clinton has to smile a little because he knows his answer is disingenuous. He smirks a little and looks to the right before launching into his circular answer.

Example: Clinton "Forgets" Who Told Him About Monica's Subpoena ("I Don't Think So" Is an Implausible Answer) (Video Clip 5)

Q1. *Mr. President, if Mr. Jordan has told us that he had a very disturbing conversation with Ms. Lewinsky that day [Dec. 19th, the day she got the subpoena], then went over to visit you at the White House, and that before he asked you the question about a sexual relationship, related that disturbing conversation to you, the conversation being that Ms. Lewinsky had a fixation on you and thought that perhaps the First Lady would leave you at the end of—that you would leave the First Lady at the end of your term and come be with Ms. Lewinsky, do you have any reason to doubt him that it was on that night that that conversation happened?*

A. All I can tell you, sir, is I, I certainly don't remember him saying that. Now, he could have said that because, as you know, a great many things happened in the ensuing two or three days. And I could have just forgotten it. But I don't remember him ever saying that.

Q2. *At any time?* [prosecutor uses great intonation to show disbelief (see video clip)]

A. No . . . .

Q3. *That is something that one would be likely to remember, don't you think, Mr. President?*

A. I think I would, and I'd be happy to share it with you if I did. I only had one encounter with Ms. Lewinsky, I seem to remember, which was somewhat maybe reminiscent of that. But not that, if you will, obsessive, if that's the way you want to use that word . . . .

Q4. *Mr. President, you swore under oath in the Jones case that you didn't think anyone other than your lawyers had ever told you that Monica Lewinsky had been subpoenaed. Here's the testimony sir.*

*Question: Did **anyone other than your attorneys** ever tell you that Monica Lewinsky had been served with a subpoena in this case? Answer:* **I don't think so.** [an implausible answer under the circumstances]

Q5. *Now, this deposition was taken just three and a half weeks after, by your own testimony [today before the grand jury], Vernon Jordan made a trip at night to the White House to tell you, among other things, that Monica Lewinsky had been subpoenaed and was upset about it. Why did you give that testimony under oath in the Jones case, sir?*

A. . . . . But this is an honest attempt here – if you read both these answers, it's obvious they were both answers to that question you quoted, to remember the first person, who was not Mr. Bennett, who told me. And I don't believe Vernon was the first person who told me. I believe Bruce Lindsey was.

Q6. *Let me read the question, because I want to talk about the first person issue. The question on line 25 of page 68 is, "Did **anyone other than your attorneys** ever tell you that Monica Lewinsky had been served with a subpoena in this case?" Answer, "I don't think so." **You would agree with me sir, that the question doesn't say*** *anything about who was the first person. It just says, did **anyone** tell you. Isn't that correct?*

A. **That's right.** And I said Bruce Lindsey, because I was trying to struggle with who—where I had heard this. And they were free to ask follow up questions, and they didn't.

Q7. *Mr. President, three and a half weeks before [the deposition], Mr. Jordan had made a special trip to the White House to tell you Ms. Lewinsky had been subpoenaed: she was distraught; she had a fixation over you. And you couldn't remember that, three and a half weeks later?*

A. Mr. Wisenberg, if—they had access to all this information from their conversations with Linda Trip, if that was the basis of it. They were free to ask me more questions. They may have been trying to trick me.

Notice how the prosecutor sets the stage in Q1 to make Clinton's answer sound implausible. He points out that Jordan informs Clinton that Lewinsky hopes to marry him after the first term. Who wouldn't remember such a conversation? When Clinton answers, "I don't remember," the prosecutor incredulously asks, "At any time?"

It is also not believable that anyone would forget the in-person meeting later that night when Jordan discussed how distraught Lewinsky was about being subpoenaed to testify. Clinton's answer

> The ability to lie is a liability.
> —author unknown

that he understood the deposition question to mean who was the *first* person to tell him about the subpoena is insincere. This excerpt is another good example that just because a witness says it's so, does not make it so.

Notice how in Q6, the prosecutor forces Clinton to admit that the question in the Jones deposition does not restrict the answer to who the *first* person was that told Clinton about the subpoena. The prosecutor is able to do this by asking a very simple question with only one fact in it. The simple question—as opposed to a complicated one—provides a stark contrast to Clinton's tortured answer. Consequently, when Clinton adds on to his initial answer and tries to explain that the attorneys were free to ask follow-up questions, he looks argumentative and evasive.

Example: Prosecutor Accuses Clinton of Perjury (Using a Question to Frame Issue) (Video Clip 6)

Q. *If Vernon Jordan has told us that you have an extraordinary memory, one of the greatest memories he's ever seen in a politician, would that be something you would care to dispute?*

A. No, I do have a good memory. At least, I have had a good memory in my life.

Q. *Do you understand that if you answered, "I don't think so", to the question, has anyone other than your attorneys told you that Monica Lewinsky has been served with a subpoena in this case, that if you answered, "I don't think so", but you really knew Vernon Jordan had been telling you all about it, you understand that that would be a false statement, presumably perjurious?*

A. Mr. Wisenberg, I have testified about this three times. Now, I will do it the fourth time. I am not going to answer your trick questions. . . .

The video clip shows how effective the prosecutor's voice is. He speaks clearly, slowly, and calmly. His tone of voice never waivers. From his tone, there can be no doubt in the grand jurors' minds that the prosecutor does not believe Clinton's "I don't think so" answers.

Also, the prosecutor was not trying to get Clinton to admit that he had committed perjury but asked the question to frame the issue for the grand jury. The prosecutor was also probably trying to gauge the believability of Clinton's response. Also, notice how he sets up Q2 by getting Clinton to acknowledge that his very good friend has testified that he has one of the best memories ever.

Clinton's emotional argumentative response that the question was a trick did not help his defense. A witness needs to be calm, especially when the lawyer is trying to get him emotional. Here, Clinton would have been better off calmly answering, "No, it was not perjurious because I answered the question the best I could at the time and was focused on who was the first person who told me about the subpoena."

Example: Clinton Explains Duty to Tell the Truth and "I Don't Think So" (Video Clip 7)

Q1. Well, you're not telling our grand jurors that because you think the case was a political case or a setup, Mr. President, that that would give you the right to commit perjury or

A. No, sir.

Q2. —not to tell the full truth?

A. In the face of their, the Jones lawyers the people that were questioning me, in the face of their illegal leaks, their constant, unrelenting illegal leaks in a lawsuit that I knew and, by the time this deposition and this discovery started, they knew was a bogus suit on the law and a bogus suit on the facts.

Q3. The question is –

A. In the face of that, I still had to behave lawfully. I wanted to be legal without being particularly helpful. I thought that was, that was what I was trying to do. And this is the first – you are the first person who ever suggested to me that, that I should have been doing their lawyers' work for them, when they were perfectly free to ask follow-up questions. . . .

On the video, you will see that Clinton gets very emotional and starts shaking his finger at the prosecutor when he answers Q2. As we saw in

Chapter Three, it is crucially important in preparing your witness that you make sure he vents all his emotions regarding the proceeding's unfairness before his testimony. The substance of Clinton's answer is good, but the emotion he brings to it suggests that he might feel that he has a license to lie given his perception that he was being attacked. Clinton's answer would have been much better if he had been relaxed and smiling like at the end of the answer to Q3.

This excerpt also reveals a witness' limited duty in a deposition to tell the truth: you have to answer truthfully, but you don't have to help the other side. However, it is unseemly when the President admits that he was withholding the truth because in his mind he was not asked the precise question necessary to reveal the truth. Indeed, Clinton later explains that he was justified in not helping—even though a higher moral standard might apply to a president—because of the political vendetta the Jones' attorneys were on. Notice in the video clip how angry Clinton is regarding the tactics used by Jones' lawyers. This is a great example how a transcript does not capture the emotion of a witness' words.

> There is no substitute for a video deposition to capture a witness' emotional response which can later be shown to undercut the witness' credibility.

Clinton's Explanation Cont'd (He Admits You Can't Answer "I Don't Know" If You Do Know)

Q4. *You didn't think you had a free shot to say, "I don't know," or "I don't recall," but when you really did know and you did recall, and it was just up to them, even if you weren't telling the truth, to do a follow-up and to catch you?*

A. No sir, I'm not saying that . . . . I've been pretty tough. So, let me say something sympathetic. All of you are intelligent people. You've worked hard on this. You've worked for a long time. You've gotten all the facts. You've seen a lot of evidence that I haven't seen. And it's, it's an embarrassing and personally painful thing, the truth about my relationship with Ms. Lewinsky. So, the natural assumption is that while all this was going on, I must have been focused on nothing but this; therefore, I must remember everything about it in the sequence and form in which it occurred. All I can tell you is, I was concerned about it. I was glad she saw a lawyer. I was glad she was doing an affidavit. But there were a lot of other things going on, and I don't necessarily remember it all. And I don't know if I can convince you of that.

But I tried to be honest with you about my mindset, about this deposition. And I'm just trying to explain that I don't have the memory that you assume that I should about some of these things.

The prosecutor points out the obvious to the grand jurors: the witness has no right to say, "I don't know" or "I don't recall" if he really does. While Clinton's answer regarding his focus and memory failures might make sense in other contexts, it does not make much sense given the devastating impact the affair's revelation might have had on his marriage and presidency.

If you were preparing Clinton for this testimony, you would have wanted to tell him to keep the sympathetic and very calm demeanor he displays in the answer to Q4. This is when Clinton is his most believable. Had the facts not been so bad for him, it is almost believable that he would not have been so focused on this as the prosecutor is and that he might indeed not be able to recall everything.

Example: Sexual Relations with Lewinsky (Objection to Form of Question) (No Video Clip)

The following questions relate to whether Clinton lied in the Jones deposition regarding having sex with Lewinsky. The definition of sex that governed the questions in that deposition was: "a person engages in 'sexual relations' when the person knowingly engages in or causes—(1) contact with the genitalia, anus, groin, breast, inner thigh, or buttocks of any person with an intent to arouse or gratify the sexual desire of any person. Contact means intentional touching, either directly or through clothing."

The following question follows some hypothetical scenarios the prosecutor was trying to get Clinton to comment on regarding sexual relations. By the time this next question was asked, the questions had become confusing.

> Q. Well if . . . a judge were to hold that you are incorrect and that definition (1) does include the hypo I've given to you – because we're talking in hypos, so that you don't—under your request here, if someone were to tell you or rule that you are wrong, that the insertion of an object into somebody else's genitalia with the intent to arouse or gratify the sexual desire of any person is within definition (1)
>
> [Mr. Kendall, Clinton's lawyer] Mr. Wisenberg, excuse me. I have not objected heretofore to any question you've asked. I must tell you, I cannot understand that question. I think it's improper. And if the witness can understand it, he may answer.
>
> Q. I'll be happy to rephrase it.

One of the two main objections (the other being non responsiveness to the question) to assert during a deposition is "objection, form." It is generally asserted when there is a compound question or when the question is confusing. Here, the question is obviously unclear, and the prosecutor immediately rephrases the question as soon as the objection is made.

Sexual Relations Cont'd
(Repeat Question for Clarity)

Q1.*Oral sex, in your view, is not covered [in the definition of sexual relations used in the Jones lawsuit], correct?*
A. If performed on the deponent.

Q2. *Is not covered, correct?*
A. That's my reading of this number (1).

The prosecutor repeats the question in case there could be any misunderstanding. However, an even better way to ask the question would be to use the witness' own words: "is it your testimony that if oral sex is *performed on the deponent,* then that act is not covered by the definition of sexual relations."

Example: Clinton Denies Affair to Aides
(Video Clip 8)

On January 21, 1998, reporters at the *Washington Post* wrote a front page story revealing that Independent Counsel Ken Starr had expanded his investigation to determine whether Clinton and Vernon Jordan had encouraged Lewinsky to lie to Paula Jones' lawyers about whether she had had an affair with him. The story said that Linda Tripp had provided audiotapes of several conversations where Lewinsky described in great detail a year and a half long affair and a recent conversation where she said that Clinton and Jordan had directed her to deny the affair in the Jones lawsuit. Clinton's staff was getting bombarded with questions about their knowledge of any affair or cover-up.

The grand jury was investigating whether Clinton obstructed justice when he told his staff, including John Podesta (deputy chief of staff), that he did not have sex with Lewinsky in the hope that they would spread this information to Ken Starr and the press. When asked, Podesta and others told investigators that Clinton was very specific in his denials of sex with Lewinsky. For example, he had told them that he "did not engage in any kind of sex, in any way, shape or form" with Lewinsky.

Below, Clinton argues that all he told Podesta and others was that he did not have sex with Lewinsky which was consistent with the definition of sexual relations in the Jones lawsuit (Remember that Clinton maintained that if oral sex were performed on the person being deposed (i.e. Clinton)—as opposed to vice versa—that such an act was not covered by the definition of sex in the Jones lawsuit). In order to maintain this defense, Clinton also testified that he never touched Lewinsky when she performed oral sex on him.[2]

Do you find Clinton's answer that he does not remember what he told Podesta believable?

Q1. *Do you recall meeting with [John Podesta] around January 23rd, 1998, a Friday a.m. in your study, two days after The Washington Post story, and* **extremely explicitly** *telling him that you didn't have, engage in any kind of sex, in any way, shape or form, with Monica Lewinsky, including oral sex?* [In the video, notice how the prosecutor emphasizes the words "extremely explicitly" to suggest that those were the words that Podesta used with investigators.]

A. . . . .The only thing I recall is that I met with certain people, and a few of them I said I didn't have sex with Monica Lewinsky, or I didn't have an affair with her or something like that. I had a very careful thing I said, and I tried not to say anything else.

Q2. *You don't remember denying any kind of sex in any way, shape or form, and including oral sex, correct?*

A. I remember that I issued a number of denials to people that I thought needed to hear them, but I tried to be careful and to be accurate, and I do not remember what I said to John Podesta.

Q3. *Surely, if you told him that, that would be a falsehood, correct?*

A. No, I didn't say that, sir. I didn't say that at all. That is not covered by the definition and I did not address it in my statement.

On the video, Clinton testily answers Q3. He continues to maintain that he was truthful in denying he had sex with Lewinsky due to the limited definition of sex used in the Jones lawsuit. However, the prosecutor is not trying to trick him here. If Clinton had told Podesta that he denied having "sex in any way, shape or form," that broad definition would trump the Jones' definition and would therefore be a lie.

---

[2] For purposes of the deposition, sexual relations was defined as follows: "a person engages in sexual relations when the person knowingly engages in or causes 1) contact with the genitalia, anus, groin, breast, inner thigh, or buttocks of any person with an intent to arouse or gratify the sexual desire of any person; 2) contact between any part of the person's body or an object and the genitals or anus of another person; or 3) contact between the genitals or anus of the person and any part of another person's body. "Contact" means intentional touching, either directly or through clothing."

Practice Tip

If you are summarizing another witness' testimony, emphasize the key words to show the witness that you are quoting word for word. This tactic will make it less likely that the deponent will deny that the statement was made. Clinton denies at his peril.

Example: A Badly Worded Question (Obstruction of Justice Regarding Lewinsky) (Video Clip 9)

The grand jury was also investigating whether Clinton attempted to get Lewinsky to lie about their relationship to the lawyers for Paula Jones.

Q1. Did you tell her [Lewinsky] anytime in December something to the effect: You know, you can always say that you were coming to see Betty [Clinton's secretary] or you were bringing me letters? Did you say that, or anything like that, In December '97 or January '98, to Monica Lewinsky?

A. Well, that's a very broad question. I do not recall saying anything like that **in connection with her testimony.** I could tell you what I do remember saying, if you want to know. But I don't – we might have talked about what to do in a non-legal context at some point in the past, but I have no specific memory of that conversation. I do remember what I said to her about the possible testimony.

*Q2. You would agree with me, if you did say something like that to her, to urge her to say that to the Jones people, that that would be part of an effort to mislead the Jones people, **no matter how evil they are and corrupt?***

A. I didn't say they were evil. I said what they were doing here was wrong, and it was.

There are two lessons here. First, notice how Clinton qualifies his answer by saying "in connection with her testimony." This qualification allows him to later say that he told her on other occasions that were *not in connection with her testimony* that she could always say that she was coming to see Betty. When you are trying to lock a witness down, in your next question, you should use the words the witness uses to qualify his answer, so the witness cannot escape. For example, in the next question (Q2), the prosecutor could have followed up, "You would agree with me, if you did say something like that to her *in connection with her testimony* that that would be part of an effort to mislead the Jones people."

Second, by asking a complicated question in Q2, that the statement was an effort to mislead *no matter how evil they are and corrupt*, the prosecutor gives the witness the chance to answer either part of the question when the prosecutor really only wants an answer to whether the statement was misleading. Clinton wisely challenges the second part and denies having ever said the Jones people were evil.

Example: Clinton Gives Implausible Answer (Lewinsky Affidavit) (No Video Clip)

A key to any good deposition is to realize that the witness is never going to admit that he is a liar or that he has done something wrong which will lose the case. Instead, your goal needs to be simply to get the witness to give implausible answers (answers that are not believable). The prosecutor does just that in the following exchange.

Q. *If Monica Lewinsky has stated that her affidavit [where she stated] that she didn't have a sexual relationship with you is, in fact, a lie, I take it you disagree with that?*
A. No, I told you before what I thought the issue was there. I think the issue is how do you define sexual relationship. And there was no definition imposed on her at the time she executed the affidavit. Therefore, she was free to give it any reasonable meaning.

Example: Refreshing Witness' Memory (Lewinsky Affidavit) (Video Clip 10)

Sometimes in a deposition, it is necessary to try and help a witness remember an event. In such a situation, you obviously can't be hostile toward the witness. Also, you must know your case inside and out so you can provide the witness the necessary information to see if he can remember. Here, the prosecutor is trying to ask questions regarding Clinton's conversation with Lewinsky before she signed her affidavit denying having sex with Clinton.

Q1. *Let me draw your attention to early January of this year, after Christmas, before your deposition. Do you remember talking to Betty Currie about Monica, who had just called her and said that she, Monica, needed to talk to you before she signed something?*
A. I'm not sure that I do remember that. But, go ahead.

Q2. **Let me see if I can jog your memory further.** *Monica talked to you in that phone conversation that told you that she had just met with her attorney that Mr. Jordan arranged with her, and the attorney said that if she is deposed that they were going to ask her how she got her job at the Pentagon. And Monica then asked you, what do you think I should say . . . .*
A. I don't believe—no. I don't remember her asking me that.

Q3. *Are you saying, Mr. President, that you did not then say to Ms. Lewinsky that you could always say that people in Legislative Affairs got you the job, or helped you get it?*
A. I have no recollection of that whatever.

*Q4. Are you saying you **didn't** say it?*

A.   No sir. I'm telling you, I want to say I don't recall—I don't have any memory of this as I sit here today. And I can tell you this, I never asked her to lie. I never did. And I don't have any recollection of the specific thing you are saying to me.

In Q4, the prosecutor employs a great strategy for a witness who claims not to remember. He pins down the witness further and asks, "Are you saying you *didn't* say it?" Although Clinton could still say he doesn't remember, it gives the prosecutor more ammunition when Clinton says "I never asked her to lie" despite Lewinsky saying that he did.

Example: Refreshing Witness' Memory (Lewinsky Gives Clinton a Christmas Present) (No Video Clip)

For Christmas, Lewinsky gave Clinton a book about the presidents. Unlike other times in the Jones deposition where Clinton answers, "I don't know" when it is later shown he did know, here, the prosecutor senses that the answer is genuine. It is a good example of refreshing a witness' memory so that the examiner can get the answer he needs. The reason the technique is successful here is that the prosecutor is not only listening to Clinton's answers but that he has the documents—in this case, the note—to help the witness remember.

Q. When you received the book, this gift from Monica, the Presidents of the United States, this book that you liked and you talked with Monica about, did it come with a note? Do you remember the note that it came with, Mr. President?

A. No, sir, I don't.

Q. Do you remember that in the note she wrote that, she expressed how much she missed you and how much she cared for you, and she later talked about this in this telephone conversation, and you said—and she apologized for putting such emotional, romantic things in this note, and you said, yeah, you shouldn't have written some of those things, you shouldn't put those things down on paper? Did you ever say anything like that to Ms. Lewinsky?

A. Oh, I believe I did say something like that to Ms. Lewinsky. . . .

Practice Tip

To get the information you need, be prepared to help a witness remember events by knowing key events and having important documents available for review.

Example: A Concise Question with One Fact
(Clinton Is Asked About Being Alone with Lewinsky)
(No Video Clip)

In depositions where you are trying to lock down a witness' answer, almost all your questions should have only one fact in them. The reason is that a simple question forces a witness to answer directly or risk being seen as evasive.

Here, the issue is Clinton's statement in the Jones deposition that he was never "alone" with Lewinsky.

> Have only one fact in your question so the answer will be exact, and the witness won't be able to avoid answering it.

Q. *Do you agree with me that the statement, "I was never alone with her," is incorrect? You were alone with Monica Lewinsky, weren't you?*

A. Well, again, it depends on how you define alone. Yea, we were alone from time to time, even during 1997, even when there was absolutely no improper contact occurring. Yes, that is accurate.

Clinton loses credibility at first when he fires back that it depends how you define the word "alone." He loses trust when he then further qualifies his answer by saying he was alone with her in 1997 when there was no improper contact. If a witness does not answer a straightforward question with a simple answer, the witness is much less likely to be believed.

Example: Clinton Denies Sexual Contact with Willey
(Judging a Witness' Credibility) (Video Clip 11)

Sometimes it is important simply to hear the witness deny the allegations. That way, prior to trial, you can evaluate how the witness will come across to the jury. Is he believable? Don't wait until trial to hear the denial for the first time. If so, the witness may turn out to be convincing to a jury, and then it will be too late for you to control the damage (either by settling the case or finding evidence to undercut the witness' testimony.) Below are very helpful questions, and the examiner has nothing to lose.

Q. *Mr. President, in fact, on [November 29, 1993] you did make sexual advances on Kathleen Willey, is that not correct?*
A. That's false.

Q. *You did grab her breast, as she said?*
A. I did not.

Q. You did place your hand on her groin area, as she said?
A. No, I didn't.

Q. And you placed her hand on your genitals, did you not?
A. I didn't do any of that, and the questions you're asking, I think, betray the bias of this operation that has troubled me for a long time. You know what evidence was released after the '60 Minutes broadcast that I think pretty well shattered Kathleen Willey's credibility. You know what people down in Richmond said about her. You know what she said about other people that wasn't true. I don't know if you've made all of this available to the grand jury or not. She was not telling the truth. She asked for the appointment with me. She asked for it repeatedly.

This is an excellent example of a witness defending himself. Notice in the video how calmly Clinton answers the last question. By not getting angry, Clinton appears sympathetic and is better able to make his case why Willey should not be believed.

_✥

Analysis of Actual Video Depositions

Seeing is believing.
—*American proverb*

Having examined transcripts from actual depositions, let's now analyze videos where seeing is truly believing. The videos can be found at the book's website **http://winningatdeposition.com/**. Once there, click on the tab "Chapter Ten" at the top of the home page to find the videos referenced below.

1. Witness Loses Cool (1 min.)

The man being deposed moved a tool shed from an area that was on a property line (the Keelers) to another area. The lawyer is asking him why he did it without getting prior approval from the homeowners' association to move the shed.

As you watch this video, ask yourself, how could you change the deposition's outcome? The answer is that once the deposition has started, there is nothing you can do. The witness is defensive and uses the "F" word because he feels he is backed into a corner. To change the outcome, the key is the witness preparation session. Let the witness know that he is going to be asked this question and that the opposing attorney's goal is to make him feel he has done something wrong. Practice the question until the witness can calmly say that he moved it without approval from the homeowners' association. The key is to let the witness vent about his predicament during the witness preparation session, not in the formal deposition with the cameras rolling.

2. The River Styx (30 sec.)

Here, the deponent challenges the lawyer and asks him if he wants to go down the river Styx together. While a lot of witnesses may feel boxed in and helpless by a lawyer's questions, it is fatal to your case if your witness shows those emotions.

This video is also another good example that once the cameras start rolling, there is very little an attorney can do to protect his client from saying damaging things or acting in a way that will guarantee that a jury will dislike him at trial. The key is effective witness preparation. If your witness is hot-tempered, let him vent in the witness prep session but also tell him that if there is one thing he has to do to make it a successful deposition, he has to be patient and not get mad. If this idea is reinforced to the witness, his competitive nature can be channeled into knowing that to win is not to challenge the lawyer but never to get mad no matter what is asked.

Finally, if you are taking a deposition, always video it if you can afford to do so. A picture tells the story of a thousand words.

3. Joe Jamail Deposition (3 min.)

This clip shows how quickly a deposition can get out of hand. Not one of the three lawyers does anything to defuse the situation. Instead, each lawyer escalates the argument by raising his voice and calling the other attorneys derogatory names such as "boy." Although Joe Jamail, the attorney taking the deposition, tries to maintain control initially by being firm and somewhat calm when the witness makes a derogatory remark toward him ("you have insipid diarrhea of the mouth"), he loses control of the deposition by calling opposing counsel "boy" and cussing at him. Once there is name-calling, it is hard to win any argument, much less defuse the situation.

After watching this heated argument for three minutes, it is likely you forgot—as the attorneys in the video most certainly did—what started the argument. It was simply a request by the lawyer who claimed to represent the witness that Joe Jamail and the witness not speak at the same time so that the court reporter could record the testimony clearly. Even if there were a question about whether the opposing attorney, "Ed," represented the witness, his objection was so minor that it should not have led to the argument that followed.

4. Mayor Donald Williamson's Deposition (9 min.)

What would you do when a witness answers "I don't know" to questions that he should obviously know? In this clip, Mayor Wilson does not remember how many—if any—lawsuits he has lost that have gone to trial or what crimes he has served prison time for. He continually answers, "I don't know . . . anything is possible. . .I don't recall."

At 3:40 in the video, the witness is asked if he has ever been arrested for a crime. The attorney asking the questions believes that the witness was arrested for bankruptcy fraud and served prison time for that crime. Notice throughout how the attorney maintains a calm demeanor. He readily cites a rule when challenged by opposing counsel to the relevancy of asking questions about crimes that occurred more than ten years ago. At 7:50, the witness finally admits to remembering that he was sentenced to prison but still maintains that he does not remember what the crime was that sent him there.

When faced with a witness who answers, "I don't know" to answers he should know, you win the battle simply by getting an implausible answer that the jury won't believe. Notice how effective it is to have a video of this deposition. Remember that 93% of communication is non-verbal. You can see the deception in the time it takes the witness to answer, his anger at the lawyer (7:09), and his facial expressions when he says, "I don't know."

When the witness angrily tells the lawyer not to ask him any more questions after he has said "I don't know," would you comply? Just because the witness tells you to back off does not mean you have to. Generally, when the witness is getting upset, you are winning the battle, and you should press forward. The only rule is that you can't harass the witness. Here, the attorney correctly does not repeat the question but asks it in a different way, such as "Do you have any recollection of the events that gave rise to the arrest? Was the conviction disturbing to you? And, Did you go into a courtroom?"

One would have attacked this witness better if written discovery had been sent out before the deposition seeking records of prior lawsuits and criminal judgments. If that had been the case, the lawyer could have confronted the witness with the documents and forced the witness to admit the truth.

5. Expert Can't Do Eighth Grade Math (9 min.)

The plaintiff is taking the deposition of the defendant's accident reconstructionist. The witness explains that an accident reconstructionist is someone who mathematically assesses traffic accidents and applies known formulas and laws of physics.

The heart of the questioning goes to the witness' determination that the distance on the diagram in the video translates to 68 feet in real life. Here, the witness is asked the distance from the stop line on the diagram to the point that the arc crosses the straight line in the diagram. He answers: "3 and 3/16 inches." The scale of the diagram is 1 inch = 20 feet.

He is then asked to show how he arrived at the 68 feet calculation. The witness says he can't because he does not know how to convert 20 feet to 3/16 of an inch without his formulas.

Here, the attorney is challenging the witness' alleged expertise. If the witness claims to be offering expert testimony, shouldn't he be able to explain the simple mathematical formula to arrive at his answer? To arrive at the answer, one needs to apply simple proportion formulas which are taught in eighth grade. It should be very easy for an expert to calculate who claims he can "mathematically assess traffic accidents."

Here is one thought about the attorney's tone. Although he has the right to be indignant, it is always better to stay calm. If you start getting angry at a witness, a jury may turn from finding the witness incompetent to feeling sorry for him because the attorney is being needlessly argumentative. The attorney does not cross the line completely, but gets too close to it. For example, at the four minute mark, the attorney gets too aggressive, and some sympathy builds for the witness. However, the attorney provides a good teaching example: ask the witness the same question until he gets an answer. Starting at 6 minutes and 50 seconds, he asks the witness if he can convert a fraction to a decimal. The witness continues to answer that he *won't* do it without his formula sheets. The attorney is persistent and does not stop his line of questioning until the witness admits that he *can't* do it without his formula sheets.

If you are curious, the formula is as follows:

1 inch/20 feet(the scale of the diagram)= 3 and 3/16 inches/x. The first step is to convert 3/16 inches to a decimal. That is the problem the witness mentions he does not know how to do in the beginning of the video. To convert a fraction to a decimal, divide 3 by 16. The answer is .1875. So now, the formula looks like this:

1/20 feet = 3.1875/x. The answer is 63.75, or 63 feet and 8 inches, not 68 feet as the witness testified.

6. Gates Deposition Part 1[1] (10 min.)

This is an edited clip of the Gates deposition. In the first part, the attorney for New York, Stephen Houck, asks Bill Gates some preliminary questions. Time is precious and Houck wastes it. It is unnecessary to ask Gates—or most witnesses for that matter—their previous job titles or the history of a company. Who cares when Microsoft was founded or what Gates' previous job titles were? Just get to the point; establish for the record in one question that Bill Gates is Microsoft's CEO.

The clip then skips to a later part in the deposition where Gates is being asked about the definition of operating system found in the Microsoft dictionary. It is a dictionary that Gates is not familiar with. Again, the attorney wastes time by asking Gates if he agrees with the dictionary's publicity statement that Microsoft is the world's most respected computer software company. There is no point in asking such a question. If the attorney were

---

[1] "Part" refers to the section of the clip referenced on YouTube.

trying to flatter the witness so that he might be friendlier, it clearly backfires because you can tell from Gates' body language that the question makes him uncomfortable.

Then, when Gates says the definition of "operating system" is incomplete because developments have occurred since the definition was written, the attorney mischaracterizes—either intentionally or unintentionally—the answer by then asking Gates to admit that the definition is incomplete (i.e. inaccurate). Gates rightly corrects the attorney and explains that it was not incomplete at the time it was written. However, Houck insists on trying to get Gates to admit that the definition is either "inaccurate" or "incomplete."

There are two lessons to learn. First, a well-prepared witness will correct an attorney's mischaracterization. Second, on the other side, you cannot gain the witness' respect—which will help you get information later—if you try and mischaracterize his answers.

Houck later asks if Gates agrees with the definition of "web browser" contained in the Microsoft dictionary. Gates never answers the question. When the witness does not answer the question, repeat it until he does. Otherwise, the witness has gained control, and you have not gotten the information you are entitled to.

The last five minutes show Houck repeatedly asking whether the definition of Internet Explorer is accurate. Who do you think wins the battle? Is Houck being too aggressive or is Gates being evasive? Whatever you conclude, imagine if you did not have the video. Remember that 93% of communication is non-verbal. In this clip, I think Gates is being sincere where in other clips his insincerity will be obvious.

7. Gates Discusses "Killer App." (10 min.)

The first minute overlaps with the last minute of the previous clip. The attorney for New York is trying to get Gates to admit that he knew that Internet Explorer would help Microsoft's sales because it was a "killer app." Notice how the video captures Gates' arrogance and combativeness in response to a simple question about a definition of "killer app" found in Microsoft's own dictionary. Factfinders at trial—in this case a judge—are always looking to see who is more credible, the lawyer asking the questions or the witness answering them. Here, Gates loses a lot of points for being confrontational instead of simply answering the question. Once the clip reaches 6 minutes and 10 seconds, there is no need to watch any further.

8. Gates Avoids Answering Questions (11 min.).

Let's focus on the first four minutes. Gates is asked about an e-mail from a Microsoft employee that says that "Windows distribution is our unique and valuable asset." For context, Marvel was a code name for a group at Microsoft that was looking how to attract users at sites. History would show that that group was unsuccessful.

This clip is a good example how a witness often will avoid answering questions at a deposition. The lesson to learn is that you need to repeat the question calmly until the witness answers. The attorney, Houck, knows that Gates is going to be evasive when he asks Gates if he sees the phrase "Windows distribution is our unique and valuable asset (0:34)." Gates spends much too long looking for it and then instead of simply answering, "yes," he says, "I see a sentence that has those words in it" (0:43). In a question that will need to be repeated, Houck asks, "Do you have an understanding as to what he meant?" (0:44). Failing to answer the question, Gates rambles on about the Marvel group's shortcomings.

Houck then admonishes Gates to answer the question when he refuses to answer (1:23). Gates gets testy and asks that the court reporter read back the question because he does not think it is the same question. When that is done, he has to admit that it is the same question, but he understood it differently the second time it was asked (2:27). Houck repeats the question for the third time, and Gates finally answers that the e-mail refers to the Marvel group's opinion that Windows distribution would be "helpful" and "an asset." The remaining seven minutes is more of the same.

9. Gates Deposition Part 15 (10 min.)

David Boies continues to ask Gates whether his comments to the media adversely affected Netscape's business. The quote attributed to Gates— but which he denied making—was "Our business model works even if all Internet software is free. . . .We are still selling operating systems. What does Netscape's business model look like if that happens? Not very good."

Just prior to the clip's beginning, Gates had sarcastically asked Boies if "adversely affected" meant "hurt feelings." So the tone has been set before the clip begins. Gates is going to weave and dodge any way he can. Here are the questions and answers immediately preceding the clip:

Q. *Do you think it [Gates' published comment] adversely affected Netscape's business prospects?*

A. I think the general work that we were doing to do strong Internet software had an effect on Netscape, but I don't think quotations like that had any direct effect.

Q. *Now, you're putting in the word "direct effect," and I know that you're a very precise person from the statement you've already made today. So, I'm going to ask you what you mean by the use of the word "direct" there that you put in the answer that was not in the question. What do you mean by "direct"?* *[video begins]*

Throughout the clip, Gates continually dodges Boies' questions. However, notice how Boies never lets up. In the first answer on the clip, Gates says that an analyst's comments might have an effect on Netscape. Boies, unflustered as always, simply ignores the non-answer, and repeats his question that he is asking not about analysts' comments but Gates' published comments (1:00). Observe how important it is to have a video deposition. Boies finishes his question at 1:32, and Gates waits 57 seconds before answering the question. He is clearly uncomfortable by the question and is desperately trying to avoid answering it. Boies does nothing to interrupt the awkward silence so that the full effect of Gates' avoidance in answering the question is captured on video.

Gates still does not answer the question but states that when other companies make comments on Microsoft, it does not affect Microsoft's business.

Notice at 4:22 that Boies summarizes Gates' previous answer. As he did throughout the deposition, Gates would ask for previous questions to be read back to him to disrupt the attorney asking the question. Boies teaches us how to handle such a tactic by his calm demeanor. In a polite way, he shames Gates into having to admit that his question was clear and there is no need to read the question back (4:44).

At 6:18, Gates again is being totally evasive. Even though the question is perfectly clear, he asks, "Who's doing the criticism in your hypothetical?" Boies remains calm and focused and asks his next question. Gates then responds, "I didn't say that. I said statements by competitors, whether critical or otherwise. . . .(7:08)" Boies simply adapts his next question to use Gates' word choice of "statements" instead of criticism.

At 8:10, William Neukom, an attorney representing Microsoft, objects (inaudible on video) that "if you read that one more time---that's seven times. Come on." Boies gives us a great teaching moment here. He is not offended by the objection, he doesn't snap back, he simply keeps going forward, responding politely to the attorney. The key to this whole exchange on the entire video clip is that Boies keeps asking Gates if he *believes* his published comments had an effect on Netscape, and Gates will only answer that he does not *know* of any effect. The remaining exchanges are continued on the next video clip.

10. Gates Deposition Part 16 (10 min.)

This clip begins where the previous clip ends. Gates waits 55 seconds before responding to Boies' question (1:10). No wonder Boies thinks Gates is hiding something. Why won't he answer the simple question? When Gates does not answer the question, Boies simply repeats his question, do you *believe*—whether or not he is aware of what effects it had—it adversely affected Netscape?

At 2:10, Boies asks Gates a question that was not answered in the previous clip. Although Boies is clearly referring to Gates' statement in the *Financial Times*—indeed for the last 12 minutes, that is all that Boies has been asking about—Gates pretends not to know what "like this" means when Boies refers to "statements [the *Financial Times*] like this. " While most attorneys might understandably blow a gasket at this point, Boies calmly asks Gates if he doesn't understand the word "like" or if he doesn't understand "what it means to be like something (2:20)." By remaining calm and in control, Boies makes Gates look foolish. He also shows Gates that evasive and disingenuous answers will not succeed.

At 4:52, the video skips ahead 5 minutes. The skipped portion was more of the same. In that portion, Gates' attorney objects to the last question as "hopelessly vague and ambiguous." Boies does not give in, but summarizes Gates' testimony and repeats his question about the *Financial Times* quote. When Gates does not answer the question, Boies asks the court reporter to re-read the question. In that portion, Gates finally gives a more direct answer when he says that "I think we can't run the experiment that held everything else the same, that is, the comments of analysts, the quality of the products, all those things going on, and didn't have that comment [the *Financial Times*] published, that their business prospects would have been the same. That's my *belief*, but we don't get to run that experiment."

Also on the skipped portion, Boies changes topics and asks Gates whether "one of the purposes of talking about giving away Internet software for free [was] to affect the way analysts looked at Netscape?"

Just prior to the video clip resuming, the following exchange takes place:

Q. Have you told people that Microsoft was going to give the browser away free and that indeed it would be forever free?

A. I said that it would be a feature of Windows and available to people who use Windows. In that sense, yes.

Q. Well, you may have said that. But what I'm now asking you about is whether you also said that Microsoft was going to give the browser away for free and that it would be forever free. Did you say that, sir?

A. When I was talking about Windows and the future of Windows, I did say that was one of the features that would come in Windows at no extra charge and that it wouldn't become an extra charge feature.

Q. You may very well have said that, and I accept that you said that. But my question to you, sir, is whether you said that Microsoft was going to give the browser away for free and it would be forever free. Did you say that, sir?

[Heiner] Objection, asked and answered.

I don't know why —what distinction you're drawing. [video clip resumes]

At 5:30, Boies asks Gates if he used the exact words "forever free" to describe that Microsoft would give away the Internet browser and never charge for it. Boies knows the answer must be "yes" because he has witnesses and documents to prove it. However, Gates claims that he does not remember saying it. Boies carefully follows up the denial by asking if he has ever used the words "forever free" in any context. Gates loses all credibility when he says that when he was a child, he said that he "wanted to be forever free (6:12)."

At this point there was a recess in the deposition. The clip resumes at a later point in the deposition. At 8:12 in the clip, Boies has asked Gates if it was part of Microsoft's intent to drive Netscape's revenues down to zero. Gates does not answer directly but instead says that it was Microsoft's intent to improve its own product. This battle continues in the next clip.

11. Bill Gates Deposition (Part 17) (10 min.)

This clip continues where part 16 ends. Boies is still trying to get Gates to answer whether "an intent to deprive Netscape of revenue played any role in any of the decisions that Microsoft made with respect to its browser or browsing technology." Gates dodges the question again. At 1 min. 25 sec., the video skips over some objections made at the deposition by Gates' lawyer who was complaining that Boies' question was "vague and ambiguous."

Although Boies continues to repeat the question, Gates does not answer it. He repeats that Microsoft was motivated to make its browser more popular and implies that depriving Netscape of revenue was not a consideration.

There are at least two lessons here. First, Gates should have been prepared in witness interviews to admit the obvious: that Microsoft intended to deprive Netscape of revenue. In any competition, that is generally the effect of a product that succeeds over a competitor. Second, notice that Boies spends a lot of time on this question. How important is the answer? The longer it takes to get an answer, the more energy you have wasted and taken away from other topics. Pick your battles carefully.

At 5:45, Boies asks that his original question be read back one more time. The usually unflappable Boies is showing some frustration. Gates says that he can't answer the question any better, and a short break is taken (6:45). At 6:45, the video skips because of the break. Boies moves to another topic. Boies realized that he got as good an answer as he was going to get and his time would be better spent elsewhere. There is no need to watch the remainder of the clip.

Clinton Grand Jury Testimony

These clips are analyzed in Chapter Nine. The video clips may be found at **http://winningatdeposition.com/**. Once at the website, click on the tab "Chapter Nine" at the top.

1. Prosecutor gets bogged down with oath.
2. Clinton gives non-verbal answer.
3. Clinton defines being "alone" with Monica.
4. Clinton defines "is."
5. Clinton forgets who told him about Monica's subpoena.
6. Prosecutor accuses Clinton of perjury.
7. Clinton explains duty to tell truth and "I don't think so."
8. Clinton denies affair to aides.
9. Question is badly worded.
10. A witness' memory is refreshed.
11. Clinton denies sexual contact with Willey.

Misc.

The following clips are posted on the website for further study (number one below) and entertainment (number two).

1. **David Boies Discusses Microsoft Trial at Harvard Law School Forum (48 min.).**

2. **Clinton Denies Having Sex with "That Woman" at Press Conference.**

Notes

APPENDIX

Summary of Trials Referenced in Book

The information below has been discussed throughout the book but is presented here for easy reference.

O.J. Simpson Criminal and Civil Trials

The Criminal Trial

Around 10:15 p.m. on June 12, 1994, O. J. Simpson's ex-wife, Nicole Brown, and her acquaintance, Ron Goldman, were stabbed to death outside of Nicole's condominium at 875 South Bundy ("Bundy") in Los Angeles, California.[1] The defendant at trial, O. J. Simpson, was a Heisman Trophy winner while at U.S.C., a Hall of Fame running back for the Buffalo Bills, and a well-known celebrity who had appeared in such movies as *The Naked Gun*.

When O. J. first met Nicole, he was a famous athlete and thirty years old; she was a waitress and eighteen years old. They married in 1985 (his second marriage) and had two children—a daughter, Sydney, and a son, Justin. On New Year's Day 1989, Nicole called 911 from their home because O.J. had beaten her. The couple was divorced in October 1992.

On the evening of the murders, Ron Goldman went to Nicole's condominium to return her mother's eyeglasses, which had been left at the restaurant where he had worked earlier that evening. Around 10:15 p.m., Nicole's neighbor heard a dog's "plaintive wail." Meanwhile, Allan Park, a limousine driver, arrived at O. J.'s home at 10:25 p.m. to drive O. J. to the airport for a trip to Chicago. Park, who had come early, did not see O. J.'s white Ford Bronco. At 10:40 p.m., he used the intercom to tell O. J. he had arrived, but no one answered. He repeatedly used the intercom for the next ten minutes; there was still no answer.

At approximately 10:55 p.m., Park saw an African American man wearing dark clothing enter O. J.'s house. O. J. answered for the first time around 11:00 p.m. At 11:15 p.m., O. J. left the house and was driven to the airport. Around midnight, a neighbor discovered Ron and Nicole's dead bodies.

At Bundy, there were bloody footprints leading away from the victims to the alley, with fresh drops of blood to the left of the footprints. (When O. J. was questioned by police the next day, he had a cut on a finger of his

---

1 Background based on trial transcripts, *The O. J. Simpson Murder Trial: A Headline Court Case*, by Michael J. Pellowski (Enslow 2001), and *The Run of His Life: The People v. O. J. Simpson*, by Jeffrey Toobin (Touchstone 1997).

left hand.) The footprints were made by Bruno Magli loafers, size twelve—O. J.'s size. The loafers were very uncommon and expensive. (O. J. was later to incriminate himself at the civil trial when he said in a deposition that he would never be caught wearing an "ugly ass" pair of Bruno Magli shoes. At that trial, he was confronted with a photo showing him wearing those shoes.) A knit cap was also found at the murder scene. Black hairs from the cap matched samples taken from O. J.; a hair fiber found on Goldman's shirt also matched O. J.'s; carpet fibers found in the cap matched the carpet of O. J.'s Bronco. Blood drops at the scene were consistent with O. J.'s blood and consistent with less than that of 0.5 percent of the world's population. A left-hand leather glove found at Bundy and a matching right-hand glove found by Detective Fuhrman at O. J.'s home were a rare and distinct style of glove known as Aris Lights.

O. J. was charged with two counts of murder, and the trial began on January 24, 1995. The not guilty verdict was returned on October 3, 1995, after deliberations of only four hours.

The Civil Trial

Shortly after the acquittal, Ron and Nicole's families filed a wrongful death lawsuit against O. J. in Santa Monica, California. The judge was Hiroshi Fujisaki. One significant difference from the criminal trial was that the judge did not allow the defense to argue that the police investigation was motivated by racial prejudice.

The jury returned a judgment of $8.5 million for compensatory damages for Ron Goldman's family (Nicole's family did not request compensatory damages so that her children would not have to testify against him) and $25 million for punitive damages to be split evenly between the Goldman and Brown families.

United States v. Microsoft

The Department of Justice and several states sued Microsoft for Antitrust violations for allegedly bundling its web browser Internet Explorer software with its Microsoft Windows operating system. The plaintiffs claimed that this bundling resulted in Microsoft's stifling competition since Windows users had free access to Internet Explorer as opposed to other browsers such as Netscape which had to be purchased at a store. Microsoft stated that the bundling of Microsoft Windows and Internet Explorer was the result of innovation that met consumers' needs.

The trial started on May 18, 1998, in Washington, D.C. A witness for the plaintiffs claimed that a Microsoft vice-president declared that it was

Microsoft's goal to extinguish Netscape (a rival browser) by giving away Internet Explorer with Windows. Judge Jackson issued his findings on November 5, 1999, which stated that Microsoft had a monopoly of the personal computer operating systems market and that Microsoft had smothered competition including Apple, Java, and Netscape.

After the appeal was decided, and the case was returned to the trial court for further proceedings, the case was settled in 2002. As part of the settlement, Microsoft agreed to share its programming interfaces with other companies so that other browsers and other products would be easily compatible with Windows, and it complied with certain rules to prevent practices that might stifle competition in the future.

Jones v. Clinton

In *Jones v. Clinton*, the plaintiff, Paula Jones, filed a sexual harassment lawsuit claiming that while Clinton was Arkansas' governor, he sexually assaulted her. She complained she lived in fear of retaliation by Clinton for her refusal to consent to his sexual advances.

Here are the details. Jones was a state employee with the Arkansas Industrial Development Commission (AIDC). On May 8, 1991, she helped run a management conference at the Excelsior Hotel in Little Rock where Governor Clinton was giving a speech. A member of Clinton's security team, Danny Ferguson, spoke with Jones and told her that the governor would like to meet her in his hotel room. Thinking such a meeting might help her advance in her job, she accepted the invitation and went to Clinton's room. After some small talk in which Clinton mentioned that Jones' supervisor, Dave Harrington, was his good friend, Clinton unexpectedly grabbed her hand and pulled her toward him.

Jones pulled away. She claimed that Clinton made some other sexual advances and finally dropped his pants and asked her to kiss his erect penis. Jones said that she was "not that kind of girl." As she left the room, Clinton stopped her momentarily and sternly said, "You're a smart girl, let's keep this between ourselves."

Jones continued to work for the state. One of her duties was to deliver documents to the Governor's office. On a subsequent trip, Clinton accosted her when he put his arm around her, held her tightly, and asked his body guard, "Don't we make a beautiful couple, Beauty and the Beast?" Another incident occurred when she was at the governor's office, and Ferguson came up to her and said that he had told Clinton how good she looked since she had come back from maternity leave.

Jones claimed that she was in constant fear that Clinton would retaliate against her because she had refused to have sex with him at the Excelsior Hotel. This fear prevented her from enjoying her job. She also was treated rudely by her supervisors which was something that had not occurred before her encounter with Clinton at the hotel. Her supervisors also refused to give her meaningful work, moved her work location, and failed to give her flowers on Secretary's Day in 1992 when others received flowers.

During discovery in *Jones v. Clinton*, the plaintiff was allowed to inquire about other instances when Clinton allegedly had harassed women while he was governor or president. [2] One such incident involved Kathleen Willey. Kathleen Willey and her husband were well-known Democratic fund-raisers in Virginia. She worked as a volunteer in the White House social office when Clinton was president. On Nov. 29, 1993, she met with Clinton in order to get help with a full-time job because of her husband's financial difficulty. According to Willey, Clinton groped her in a hallway near the Oval Office. By coincidence, while they were meeting, Willey's husband committed suicide. The attorney representing Paula Jones was James Fisher. Robert Bennett represented Clinton.

The court dismissed the lawsuit because Jones failed to prove any damages. But while the case was on appeal, Clinton paid Jones $850,000 to settle the case.

Clinton Impeachment Proceedings

The Office of Independent Counsel (OIC) had been investigating allegations that Clinton had committed impeachable offenses related to a land deal called Whitewater. However, the OIC expanded its scope when it learned that Monica Lewinsky had tried to influence the testimony of a witness (Linda Tripp) in the Paula Jones lawsuit[3] and had filed a false affidavit claiming that she had never had sexual relations with Clinton. After his deposition in the Jones lawsuit, Clinton spoke with his secretary, Bettie Currie. He attempted to influence her by suggesting that he had never been alone with Lewinsky or done anything inappropriate.

On August 17, 1998, Clinton faced a grand jury that was investigating whether he committed perjury in his deposition or obstructed justice in the Jones lawsuit. On December 19, 1998, the House of Representatives (controlled by Republicans) voted to impeach Clinton and send two articles of impeachment (the charges) to the Senate for a trial. The first article concerned

---

2 For purposes of the deposition, sexual relations was defined as follows: "a person engages in sexual relations when the person knowingly engages in or causes 1) contact with the genitalia, anus, groin, breast, inner thigh, or buttocks of any person with an intent to arouse or gratify the sexual desire of any person; 2) contact between any part of the person's body or an object and the genitals or anus of another person; or 3) contact between the genitals or anus of the person and any part of another person's body. "Contact" means intentional touching, either directly or through clothing."

3 Paula Jones, a government worker, filed a sexual harassment lawsuit against Clinton claiming that while he was governor of Arkansas he retaliated against her at work when she refused his sexual advances in a hotel room.

whether Clinton provided perjured and misleading testimony to the grand jury concerning: 1) the nature and details of his relationship with a subordinate employee (Lewinsky), 2) prior misleading statements in the Paula Jones deposition about his sexual encounters with Lewinsky, 3) prior misleading statements made by his attorney in the Jones deposition, and 4) his efforts to influence the testimony of other witnesses in the grand jury investigation.

As for the first and second allegations above, Lewinsky had told investigators and the grand jury that Clinton had fondled and kissed her breasts and touched her genitalia during ten encounters at the White House. She had also told many friends about this. Although Clinton admitted that Lewinsky performed oral sex on him, he denied any additional fondling.

The third allegation related to whether Clinton knew that his attorney made misleading statements at the deposition when the attorney said that Lewinsky had submitted an affidavit saying that she had not had sex with Clinton. Although the attorney believed the affidavit was true, Clinton knew that it wasn't (he had not told his attorney about his sexual encounter with Lewinsky). The fourth claim concerned whether Clinton had told his secretary and aides that he had not had sex with Lewinsky so that they would repeat those denials to the grand jury and investigators.

The second article alleged that Clinton had violated his oath as president to take care that the laws of the United States be faithfully executed when he obstructed justice by: 1) encouraging Lewinsky to submit a false affidavit in the Jones lawsuit, 2) encouraging Lewinsky to give false testimony if she were called to testify in the Jones lawsuit, 3) supporting a scheme to conceal evidence that had been subpoenaed in the Jones lawsuit, 4) succeeding in getting a job for Lewinsky in order to prevent her truthful testimony in the Jones lawsuit, 5) allowing his attorney to make false statements to a judge at his deposition, 6) telling a false account about his deposition testimony to a witness in order to influence that witness' testimony, and 7) making several false statements to witnesses in the grand jury investigation in order to influence their testimony corruptly.

Some of the claims in the second article are self-explanatory or overlap the charges in the first article. But a few need further explanation. The third allegation relates to evidence that Betty Currie, Clinton's secretary, had visited Lewinsky's home and retrieved gifts that Clinton had given Lewinsky so that Lewinsky could claim that she did not have any gifts in her possession if subpoenaed by investigators.

The fourth allegation involved the claim that Clinton had asked his confidant, Vernon Jordan, to arrange for a job for Lewinsky in the private sector in exchange for her affidavit and testimony denying sex with Clinton.

The sixth count relates to an incident where Clinton spoke to Currie the day after his deposition with Lewinsky. He told her, "We were never alone . . . . You could see and hear everything . . . Monica came onto me and I never touched her right?" Clinton knew that Currie would be asked to testify, and he wanted to make sure she was on board.

Other alleged lies were considered by the House but not submitted to the Senate for impeachment. One lie was Clinton's response to a question at his deposition that asked, "At any time were you alone with Lewinsky in the Oval Office?" Clinton paused for five seconds before answering, "I don't recall," despite Currie, Lewinsky, and several secret service agents testifying to the contrary.

Also, the House did not submit the allegation that Clinton had lied about having sexual relations as it was defined in the Jones lawsuit. Another allegation that the House did not submit was Clinton's statement in the deposition that "I could have given her a gift, but I don't remember a specific gift." A few weeks before the deposition, Clinton had given Lewinsky several gifts including sunglasses, a stuffed animal, and a Rockettes blanket.

Much like a jury's verdict, there is no way to know why the House voted to impeach on some allegations and not others, even though there appeared to be evidence to support them.

After a trial in the Senate, Clinton was acquitted largely along party lines. He was acquitted on article one by a vote of 55 for acquittal and 45 for conviction on the perjury count. He was also acquitted on the second article 50-50 which was still short of the two-thirds needed for conviction.

ACKNOWLEDGMENTS

There are too many people to name who have assisted me with this book. But a few cannot go without mention. Thanks to Brent Dobbs and Bill Kanasky Jr., Ph.D. at Courtroom Sciences Inc. for providing significant contributions to the chapter on witness preparation. Their unique skills and insights into witness preparation and jury persuasion have helped this book immensely.

Don Tittle, one of the finest trial lawyers in Texas, has been an inspiration and guiding force from the book's inception. He has constantly suggested ways to make the book more practical and provided much needed encouragement. Michael Kidney, who has been lead counsel on almost every type of complex litigation, has provided a wealth of ideas and advice. Many other outstanding attorneys such as Lee Brown, Robert Manley, Hardin Ramey and Bruce Alford have patiently reviewed key parts of the book and made significant improvements to the final version. Adam Slote has assisted with technical advice and a much needed sense of humor for the book's website.

Finally, every book needs a great editor, and there is no better one than Gloria Pennell.

ABOUT THE AUTHOR[1]

Shane Read is a nationally recognized expert who has helped thousands of attorneys throughout the USA and Europe transform their deposition, trial, and oral advocacy skills through his consultations, training programs, and keynote speeches.

He is the author of bestselling litigation textbooks such as *Turning Points at Trial* and *Winning at Deposition*. Two of his textbooks have won the Association of Continuing Legal Education's top honor for Professional Excellence. He is the only author to win this award twice. His textbooks have been adopted in law schools across the country and critically acclaimed by publications such as Bar Journals and Kirkus Reviews. In addition, his textbooks have been endorsed by judges, professors, a former U.S. Attorney General, a former U.S. Solicitor General, and past presidents of city, state and national trial lawyers' organizations such as IATL and ABOTA.

He has been an adjunct professor in trial advocacy since 1999 at Southern Methodist University's Dedman School of Law. He has also taught new and experienced lawyers throughout the United States, including training programs at national law firms, the National Institute of Trial Advocacy's headquarters, the Department of Justice's National Advocacy Center, and state bars around the country.

He is a graduate of Yale University and the University of Texas School of Law. He began his legal career in 1989 at Akin Gump in Dallas, before joining the U.S. Attorney's Office in Washington, D.C., from 1992 to 1998. Since 1998, he has worked at the U.S. Attorney's Office in Dallas in both the civil and criminal sections. He has tried over 100 trials to verdict over the past 30 years and has served as lead counsel for 22 oral arguments before appellate courts.

For more information go to www.shaneread.com.

---

[1]The views expressed in this book are solely those of the author and do not reflect the views of the Department of Justice.

STAY CONNECTED—
SUBMIT A REVIEW ON AMAZON.COM

Your praise of *Winning at Deposition* is very important to help other lawyers learn about this book. It only takes a minute to write a two or three sentence summary of what you learned from this book at the bottom of the book's product page on Amazon.com.

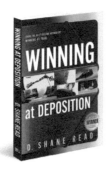

Customer Reviews

⭐⭐⭐⭐⭐ 38

4.8 out of 5 stars ▾

5 star	▓▓▓▓	87%
4 star	▓	10%
3 star		3%
2 star		0%
1 star		0%

Share your thoughts with other customers

Write a customer review

Made in United States
Troutdale, OR
06/30/2024

20902212R00151